Building a Corporate Culture of Security

Building a Corporate Culture of Security

Strategies For Strengthening Organizational Resiliency

John Sullivant CFC, CSC, CHS-IV, CPP, RAM-W
Diplomate, American Board of
Forensic Engineering & Technology
American College of Forensic
Examiners Institute

ELSEVIER

AMSTERDAM • BOSTON • HEIDELBERG • LONDON
NEW YORK • OXFORD • PARIS • SAN DIEGO
SAN FRANCISCO • SINGAPORE • SYDNEY • TOKYO
Butterworth-Heinemann is an imprint of Elsevier

Butterworth-Heinemann is an imprint of Elsevier
The Boulevard, Langford Lane, Kidlington, Oxford OX5 1GB, UK
50 Hampshire Street, 5th Floor, Cambridge, MA 02139, USA

Notices
Knowledge and best practice in this field are constantly changing. As new research and experience broaden our understanding, changes in research methods, professional practices, or medical treatment may become necessary.

Practitioners and researchers must always rely on their own experience and knowledge in evaluating and using any information, methods, compounds, or experiments described herein. In using such information or methods they should be mindful of their own safety and the safety of others, including parties for whom they have a professional responsibility.

To the fullest extent of the law, neither the Publisher nor the authors, contributors, or editors, assume any liability for any injury and/or damage to persons or property as a matter of products liability, negligence or otherwise, or from any use or operation of any methods, products, instructions, or ideas contained in the material herein.

ISBN: 978-0-12-802019-7

British Library Cataloguing in Publication Data
A catalogue record for this book is available from the British Library

Library of Congress Cataloging-in-Publication Data
A catalog record for this book is available from the Library of Congress

For information on all Butterworth-Heinemann publications
visit our website at http://store.elsevier.com/

www.elsevier.com • www.bookaid.org

Publisher: Candice G. Janco
Acquisition Editor: Tom Stover
Editorial Project Manager: Hilary Carr
Production Project Manager: Mohanapriyan Rajendran
Designer: Mark Rogers

Typeset by TNQ Books and Journals

Dedication

In loving memory to family who continues to energize me...

Peter (Serras) Sullivant

Stamatina (Serras) Sullivant

Jerry Sullivant

Nonda Sullivant

And to my beautiful grandchildren...

Maia and Jacobi who insist the better tomorrow is here

Contents

About the Author

John Sullivant has a strong record—five decades of problem solving and leadership—in executive security management, governance, consulting, and strategic planning in industry, government, and academia, both domestically and abroad. He is one of America's leading, trusted advisor, with the unique ability to help executives look at problems from a variety of sensible, constructive, ethical, and principled perspectives.

For more than fifty years John Sullivant has advised, coached, and counseled executives who run very large corporations and organizations, such as the Los Angeles Department of Water and Power, World Financial Center, and Raytheon and MasterFoods; the states of Texas, Louisiana, and New Hampshire; the National Nuclear Security Administration, the Department of Defense, and the Federal Aviation Administration. Experiences include work with the national intelligence community; national and international RDT&E centers; university medical centers and medical research laboratories; telecommunication; food and agriculture; manufacturing; banking and financing; entertainment; and civil aviation. He has held numerous positions of responsibility as a former chief executive, Vice President of two corporations, and senior program manager of several highly visible projects. Formerly, he held key leadership positions on national councils, committees, and advisory boards. The situations he helps to resolve often involve performance and compliance audits, inspections, and special investigations; revitalizing dysfunctional unit performance; discovering security technology deficiencies; defending against activist opposition, criminal actions, and terrorist threats; improving security emergency planning capabilities; and investigating grassroot causes of image, brand, and reputational threats.

His publications include "Strategies for Protecting the Telecommunications Sector", in *Wiley Handbook of Science and Technology for Homeland Security* (John Wiley & Sons, 2009); and *Strategies for Protecting National Critical Infrastructure Assets: A Focus on Problem-Solving* (John Wiley & Sons, 2007). He also has authored numerous position papers for various U.S. government agencies and published articles for *Security Magazine* and *Risk Mitigation Executive*.

A disabled veteran, a cultivated and educated board-certified professional, a successful business owner, an ombudsman, and a renowned author, John Sullivant is widely recognized as an authority in developing strategies to reduce risk exposure and is a trusted advisor for changing the security landscape. He is a certified forensic consultant (CFC), certified security consultant (CSC), certified in Homeland Security (CHS-IV), a certified protection professional (CPP), certified in risk assessment methodology for water utilities (RAM-W), and a distinguished diplomate of the

American Board of Forensic Engineering & Technology at the American College of Forensic Examiners Institute. He has addressed numerous industry and government forums, and lectured at the university level.

John Sullivant is a graduate of Southwest Texas University, received a bachelor of science in Occupational Education (Law Enforcement) with honors. He earned a master of science in Psychology (Counseling & Guidance) from Troy State University with high honors and academic fitness.

Foreword

John Sullivant, CFC, CSC, CHS-IV, CPP, RAM-W and Diplomate of the American Board of Forensic Engineering & Technology at the American College of Forensic Examiners Institute, has provided strategic advice, counsel, and leadership to industry, government and academia for more than five decades. He has advised and counseled the executives who run very large corporations and organizations, helping them face tough, touchy, sensitive corporate security issues. He served his country while in the U.S. Air Force for 25 years rising through the ranks to Chief Master Sergeant, and then later as a researcher, analyst, planner, teacher, trusted advisor and author in his own right in the private sector for more than 33 years. Mr. Sullivant is a former senior program manager and chief executive of his own company, serving in high-visibility, high-tension business environments. He has held numerous key leadership positions on national councils, committees, and advisory boards. He is well respected, widely recognized as an authority in his field, and a trusted strategic advisor for changing the security landscape.

I take great delight in introducing John Sullivant. He has one of the best security minds in the business and has the unique ability to view security problems and solutions in three dimensions. I have personally known John as a colleague and friend for many years. I had the distinct privilege of working under his leadership daily for more than 4 years. His vision to create strategic initiatives to increase performance, improve competency and enhance processes from conceptual development to operational production is, in my opinion, without equal.

Through the pages of this book, John brings to bear courage and keenness to unveil security issues, so many corporate executives hesitate to address and too many security professionals fail to adequately communicate to top management in the language they understand, while significant vulnerabilities linger within the infrastructure of corporations, only to surface at the most embarrassing moments.

I know of no other author or security professional able to display the objectivity and convey the sense of urgency and body of knowledge, necessary to produce a work of this magnitude. It is full of fresh stimulating ideas and practical strategies and advice that will change the way we think, talk, teach, and practice the science of security as well as the art of security management.

Well researched and well written, this book is one of the most important contributions to the security field and risk management literature, ever envisioned. It offers an insightful overview of the dynamic problems facing the security industry that only John dares to expose, and he places the issues squarely on the agenda of security directors and chief executives to tackle head-on. Hundreds of actual case histories give creditability to his exhaustive research of verifiable evidence that supports his findings. His writing is articulate and persuasive, and I take off my hat to him for a job well done. You will not be able to put the book down once you read this page. I am honored to be his colleague and friend.

James F. Broder, CPP, CFE, FACFE
Author, *Risk Analysis and the Security Survey*, fourth edition
Butterworth-Heinemann, Newton, MA 2012

Preface

An Idea Is Born

The seeds for this book were planted in November 2013, during a lunch I had with a colleague of mine, Jim Broder,[1] under the sunny skies of southern California. During lunch we discussed various topics, as we always do. Conversations with Jim are always meaningful and productive. Jim always finds the right moment in a conversation to ask, "When are you going to write your next book?" I always had an answer for him, but it never was acceptable.

A few days later, Brian Romer, a senior acquisitions editor at Butterworth-Heinemann, contacted me. I always suspected Jim put Brian up to making the call, but I never mentioned the matter to Jim—or Brian, for that matter. I submitted a proposal to Brian for review. Following a review by several anonymous reviewers to strengthen the material, I submitted a final proposal, which was entered into the publisher's system. Soon after the holidays, I had an offer from Butterworth-Heinemann. I called Jim for lunch and broke the news. Naturally, he looked surprised, congratulated me, treated me to lunch. When we departed he said, "Start writing today because you are doing another book after this one." The rest is history.

What Could Possibly Make This Book Unequivocally Different?

Few books enable you to not only rethink the way you make decisions but also improve your performance and competency in the process. *Building a Corporate Culture*

[1] James F. Broder, CFE, CPP, FACFE, is the author of *Risk Analysis and the Security Survey*, which is in its 4th edition (2012) and was translated and printed in Chinese for distribution in Asia in 2014. He has contributed to numerous other works: *Investigation of Substance Abuse in the Workplace*, *Security Management*, *The Encyclopedia of Security Management*, and the *Handbook of Loss Prevention and Crime Prevention*. Broder began his career as a special agent with the FBI and later joined the Foreign Service as a security advisor to the U.S. State Department. Initially employed as an instructor at the International Police Academy (Washington, D.C.), he subsequently served in Vietnam as an advisor to the South Vietnamese National Police Directorate, Counter Insurgency Division. Afterward, he worked as a special assistant to the chairman of the Special Investigations Subcommittee, U.S. House of Representatives, Washington, D.C. For many years Broder has been providing services as an independent security consultant. In 2005 I asked Jim to join me in a major security project, where we worked hand in hand for 4 years to improve the security resilience of a major U.S. utility. During this project we became staunch associates, creating a special bond of trust and confidence that continues to this day. I am honored to be dear friends.

of Security: Strategies for Strengthening Organizational Resilience is one of those books—a milestone in both the theory and practice of, which will shock the security industry by cutting through the fog of political correctness to expose circumstances and conditions that too many chief executives and too many security managers hesitate to talk about or want others to know exist.

Within the pages of this book, I unveil the true roots of real problems in real-world situations: a consolidated reporting and analysis of strategic security deficiencies, programmatic weaknesses, and human and technology inadequacies never before available under a single cover. This work will make you look inward, to yourself and your organization, to help you navigate the often treacherous waters swirling around security management.

It offers leaders powerful ways to tackle the obstacles they face. From industry to government practices, I expose the many fallacies that surround the issues while providing a wealth of rich, practical, and relevant insights and practical strategies. Persuasively argued, I deliver a playbook for anyone in a leadership position who must act responsibly. My diverse background, depth of experience, and hands-on battle skills in the trenches deliver advice and counsel that make the difference.

Building a Corporate Culture of Security stands out among competitive works because of its immense value to the readership. I take a striking look into the business relationships and practices of many security organizations to expose the uniqueness of their vulnerabilities: their source or origin, and how they tend to fester within the bowels of organizations before being discovered and acknowledged as major problems. I call for executive management and security professionals to take responsible, reasonable actions to address these issues.

In this book I bridge two worlds: *First*, I take on the ambitious goal of identifying gaps between what executives perceive or believe the effectiveness of their security programs to be, versus the reality of actually measuring the performance of these security programs. *Second*, I present a far-reaching road map for both the student and professional to review topics that have intimidated too many security managers at all levels when approaching executive management with issues that most likely have festered within the corporation because of previous executive management decisions or management's resistance to implement. I question why corporate security resilience takes a backseat on the boardroom agendas of many chief executives, and what we need to do to today to raise the topic higher on their list of executive priorities.

As far as I know, no other author has made available such an array of industry homegrown deficiencies, weaknesses, and inadequacies in any real depth in any other single publication. And few readers will find a publication that addresses the (human) side of security I expose here. For these reasons alone, this book is a must-read. I encourage you to read it and be inspired by it.

My goal in writing *Building a Corporate Culture of Security* is to share the valuable insight gained from the cumulative experience of assessing, auditing, and inspecting thousands of security organizations spanning more than half a century. I do not want to waste my time and energy—or yours, for that matter—assigning blame and pointing fingers; rather, I want to put my energy to use learning from the patterns and trends of others to fix problems. This experience, knowledge, and judgment gives creditability to the theme embedded throughout this book.

This comprehensive body of work takes you on a vigorous voyage of laser-focused strategies that work and resonate with executives. The laser reaches beyond the outer boundaries of traditional protocol and lays bare an uncomfortable truth: that most security organizations have strategies, policies, protocols, and practices that are muddled and indistinguishable, along with inexperience and weak executive and security management, including a lack of leadership.

I offer the reader a treasure trove of insight, personal experience, and knowledge, and the opportunity to use your skill sets wisely to build a new trust relationship for chartering a new professional course.

Building a Corporate Culture of Security offers promise in delivering a much-needed look into corporate security practices. It poses the question, "What are you going to do about…?" Your answer to this question is key, because whatever step you take, it will directly and indirectly affect your image, brand, and reputation, as well as the success of your career path.

Through the pages of this book you will gain insight into the many challenges chief executives, security directors, and other security professionals confront everyday— many of which you may not even be aware exist. It is packed with practical and useful tips that will open the eyes of C-suite executives and security professionals to security issues that too many organizations are hesitant to tackle:

- It presents a no-nonsense look at topics that too many corporate executives hesitate to address and too many security managers fail to adequately communicate to top management in terms that fit their business frame of reference and lexicon.
- It highlights a state of affairs that has intimidated too many security managers from approaching executive management with problems that most likely have festered within the "bowels" of the corporation, sometimes for years.
- It identifies sensitive problem areas and their root causes, addresses their business consequences, and offers practical solutions in the language executive management can understand.
- It emphasizes the importance of early detection, identification, and understanding of security and security-related problems, and the expertise and knowledge base necessary to fix problems early, at the source, while they are still manageable.
- It emphasizes the importance of security planning development and implementation as a holistic discipline without losing site of its purpose to protect assets, resources, and information in the support of business goals and objectives.
- It addresses complex challenges facing today's security professionals. From current and emerging issues to industry best practices, you will find a wealth of information that will help you become a better security professional and security leader.
- It addresses the difficulty in establishing and maintaining communications between C-suite executives and the security professional.
- It points the direction to strategies that can help executives solve the many critical issues on the table—provided that corporate leadership wants to commit earnestly to advancing corporate security in a constructive manner, without hesitation or pause.

Last, *Building a Corporate Culture of Security* gives insight to hidden systemic failures and places those issues directly in the center of the radar screen of C-suite executives, keeping them there throughout the entire book.

These egregious revelations are not easy for me to report, but their disclosure is important work because these deficiencies, weaknesses, and inadequacies unduly influence our business philosophy, our decision-making capability, and our relationships with others—particularly executive management—and we must do everything possible to improve our lot. James E. Lukaszewski (2008, pp. 17), a prominent trusted strategic adviser, mints no words when he says "fit it now, challenge it now, change it now, stop it now. Leaders learn that most strategies fail because of timidity, hesitation and indecision." I will talk about these attributes again and again throughout the book.

It is also disappointing to report that too many executives and too many security professionals are ill prepared and ill equipped to face the many challenges they confront. Let me put this statement in perspective.

Security professionals are mostly groomed from a young age and early in their career path. They obtain degrees in security management and other disciplines, regularly attend professional seminars and other training courses, and often learn on their own.

Conversely, there are no schools for becoming a chief executive officer (CEO) or other executive leader. They obtain degrees in business administration, finance, and other disciplines. But everyday for a CEO is a new learning experience. There is no instruction manual to read, no checklist to follow and complete. While the staff tries to protect the boss and get them to change his or her mind, that is a difficult task at best. Executives need advice from people who see the world from their perspective. A staff does not always respond in this manner; they are usually busy organizing or inventing work for themselves and protecting their turf. Giving the CEO advice may be contrary to their personal agenda, priorities, or, perhaps, their succession plans (Lukaszewski, 2008, pp. 3–20). I talk more about this situation in Chapter, How to Communicate with Executives and Governing Bodies. Notwithstanding the good intentions of the staff, no one is really qualified to train a CEO in the politics of being a leader. And if this did happen, such coaching would in all probability be biased—except for that from an outside, trusted strategic advisor.

I must rebuke any colleagues who lack strategic vision, wisdom, or the skill sets to carry out their awesome responsibilities, or who fail to hold themselves accountable for their shortcomings. This is unfortunate and unacceptable in today's turbulent business world. Conversely, I would be remiss if I did not recognize those colleagues, past and present, who have performed and continue to perform in a sustained exemplary fashion in all endeavors. Do not falter in your responsibility.

This Book Is as Important as You Want It to Be

Building a Corporate Culture of Security introduces proven security strategies that, when effectively embraced in a systematic manner, offer the potential to convert threats, hazards, risk exposure, vulnerabilities, and consequences of loss into actionable security strategies that will not only greatly improve security practices but also expressively enhance security awareness. I build security resilience in a common-sense fashion that is acceptable to executive management. The strategies I offer are practical, sensible, and proven to work in the real world, in all security organizations of all sizes.

This work is merely a stepping stone that uncovers flaws, ineffectiveness, inefficiencies, and poor management and leadership that must be overcome through strategic vision, determination, and exceptionalism. It moves past mere speculation and unfounded opinion to verifiable facts backed up by historical records, case histories and reliable human observations and judgments.

Anyone in a Responsible Leadership Position Can Benefit from Reading This Book

Books that focus on a narrow topic often appeal to only a narrow readership. Here, I make the exception and cover the entire spectrum of security activity. I write to attract the broadest of audiences and hold their interest with straight talk and laser-focused strategies. It is a must-read for:

- Anyone responsible and accountable for security risk management, security leadership, and corporate governance and compliance.
- Executive-level security decision makers responsible for planning, approving, establishing, and maintaining security programs and security operations.
- The serious security professional who thirsts for knowledge and solutions to enhance security resilience. This quest for knowledge serves as an excellent platform for those security professionals who simply implement the common body of knowledge without understanding why some programs work and others fail. This book is extremely valuable to this group because it not only fills the knowledge void; it also takes the gained learning experience to the next level: application.
- Security professionals responsible for developing, administering, and conducting educational and training programs. This group will find this book to be extremely useful in developing new training programs or upgrades existing course instruction.
- Information technology security professionals with key security responsibilities will benefit greatly from the cyber security information presented, as well as other topics.
- Security professionals who have the skill sets and experience to manage security organizations but possess less expertise and confidence in solving complex problems but have the determination to gain insight into new ideas.
- Security professionals who are steadfast in their ways, yet flexible to adapting new approaches and techniques.
- Security professionals who may not even know they can gain any wisdom from this work, unless perhaps a gentle nudge to open its cover is given by a friend.
- Inspectors general, governing authorities, and their investigative staffs, auditors, investigators, and consultants will gain a wealth of insight into the deficiencies, weaknesses, and inadequacies that plague security organizations.

I offer a thorough and fundamental education on the art and science of performing security management and exercising security leadership. It represents years' worth of practical experience knowing how CEOs think, what matters to them, what they expect to here from you, and in the way it needs to be heard. It is a great reference tool to keep at your desk to refer to when needed.

Features and Benefits

Building a Corporate Culture of Security

- is comprehensive and well organized. Fundamental concepts are dealt with first, followed by definition of problems and the identification of root causes; after which I delve into mitigation strategies
- is written in simple, direct language. A text reference designed with both students and professionals in mind, it presents specific information and methods for bringing security weakness and solutions forward to C-suite executives in a language they understand, enabling them to make sound, informed decisions
- is a useful textbook for university study and professional security management seminars
- provides a comprehensive understanding of the root causes of some of the most programmatic vulnerabilities that plague the security industry and how such root causes hinder moving security organizations forward
- contains a concentrated area of "hot topics" of significant importance to security practitioners, inspectors general, auditors, analysts, researchers, educators, attorneys, and C-suite executives
- emphasizes the importance of security planning, emergency preparedness planning, and problem development and implementation as a holistic discipline
- addresses the difficulty and importance in establishing and maintaining communications between the C-suite executive and the security professional, including the need and thirst for topics that security professionals often do not communicate in terms that fit the C-suite frame of reference.

Organization and Presentation Is Important to Understand the Big Picture

Many books feature figures, illustrations, and tables that do not clearly support the text, but this is not the case here. This work is comprehensive, well organized, thoroughly thought through, and exhaustively researched, with more than 220 footnotes. More than 30 figures, and tables are strategically placed throughout the text and appendices to selected chapters to strengthen the main ideas presented. Many of these graphics make excellent PowerPoint slides for briefing C-suite executives and staff management. More than 150 actual case histories examining self-induced failures that create obstacles and stifle individual initiative are interwoven throughout the narrative or set into appendices to specific chapters to refute the cynics and give faith to those who believe in a brighter tomorrow. The narrative includes more than 20 useful and meaningful security strategies that resonate with C-suite executives. Short conclusions at the end of each chapter capture the main ideas expressed in the section. Chapter takeaways introduce each discussion.

> Chapter 1, "Introduction" highlights the conditions, circumstances, and situations that repeatedly plague security organizations when performing their prime mission.
> Chapter 2, "Strategies That Create Your Life Line" describes a family of integrated security strategies that, when properly designed, developed, and deployed, improve productivity and

enhance security resilience. It provides systematic, pragmatic, and sensible processes for working at the highest levels and having maximum effect.

Chapter 3, "The Many Faces of Vulnerability Creep-in" describes the various forms of self-induced security deficiencies, programmatic weaknesses, and performance inadequacies that influence social behaviors and uniformed decision making.

Chapters 4, "The Evolving Threat Environment" and 5, "The Cyber Threat Landscape" survey the threat and hazard challenges facing corporations and agencies.

Chapter 6, "Establishing a Security Risk Management Program Is Crucial" describes strategies to forecast and manage challenges to reduce risk exposure. An appendix that resonates with CEOs contains a proven risk management framework and architecture platform that fits any size security organization.

Chapter 7, "Useful Metrics Give the Security Organization Standing" introduces useful and meaningful risk-based metrics that can be adapted for measuring any critical security activity. An appendix that resonates with CEOs offers a user-friendly metric framework and architecture platform strategy that resonates with chief executives.

Chapters 8, "A User-Friendly Security Assessment Model" and 11, "A User-Friendly Security Technology Model" address a family of proven strategies to help identify human, physical, and technology risk exposure; select mitigation strategies; increase competencies, performance, and productivity; and improve security resilience. Appendix A – Case Histories: Security Technology Deficiencies and Weaknesses.

Chapter 9, "Developing a Realistic and Useful Threat Estimate Profile" examines threats and hazards, vulnerabilities, and consequences; evaluates their effect on critical business operations and assets; and determines the impact of consequences and asset losses. It establishes a rank order of priorities to mitigate solutions, which helps to allocate resources and funds for those assets that need protection the most.

Chapter 10, "Establishing and Maintaining Inseparable Security Competencies" emphasizes how to measure and evaluate an organization's ability and capability to perform its prime security mission, identify and manage patterns of behavior, and recognize or forecast the results of various actions and decisions.

Chapter 12, "Preparing for Emergencies" highlights the systematic failures in effective security emergency planning that exist throughout the industry. Appendix A – Case Histories: Security Emergency Planning Fallacies.

Chapter 13, "A User-Friendly Protocol Development Model" presents the magnitude of ineffective protocol development that runs rampant throughout the industry, its affect on corporate risk exposure and liability, and how to measure and evaluate the effectiveness and efficiency of protocols. Appendix A – Case Histories: Protocols.

Chapter 14, "A Proven Organization and Management Assessment Model" describes a strategic integrated methodology to measure and evaluate the functional performance of an organization, including the effectiveness of the management and leadership elements. Appendix A - Case Histories: Management and Leadership

Chapter 15, "Building Competencies That Count: A Training Model" describes a proven, integrated strategy for a training needs analysis to help build competencies and proficiencies through the process of updating existing training programs or creating new ones.

Chapter 16, "How to Communicate with Executives and Governing Bodies" outlines the importance of speaking the language executives understand, and how to develop presentations and defend a business case that resonates with executives. It describes behaviors and attitudes of staff that may hold you back, making you less influential than you could be.

Chapter 17, "A Brighter Tomorrow: My Thoughts" ends the book with a discussion of predictable prospects for the future and anticipated challenges for the next-generation security leaders.

Running through every chapter in this book is the theme of management and leadership, performance effectiveness, competency, attitude, and knowledge of business operations other than the functional area of security activities. The shortcoming most quickly noticed by other operational managers is the failure of security professionals to gain any knowledge of corporate business or have serious interest in the actual work of the business. You need to learn what about the business matters and demonstrate by your actions and speech that you know what does matter.

Some of the topics presented here have been treated on an individual basis before by other authors, but never in the detail described in *Building a Corporate Culture of Security* and under a single cover. In this book, I tried not to duplicate these works (including my own previous writings) but to show a different and unique perspective to identified problems. I hope this work will help you profit from my experiences. A judgment on the extent to which I have succeeded remains the exclusive province of my readers. My critics will doubtlessly furnish me the necessary feedback to assist in revising and updating subsequence editions of this book.

John Sullivant, CFC, CSC, CHS-IV, CPP, RAM-W
Diplomate of the American Board of Forensic Engineering & Technology
American College of Forensic Examiners Institute

Acknowledgments

No book—or career, for that matter—can be successfully executed without the support of many colleagues, friends, and family: those serving as a sounding board and cheerleaders, sharing their insights and being inspirational, particularly in the toughest of times. I have been blessed to have these people by my side throughout my professional career, and family life. They are the silent heroes of this book. I thank them for their leadership, wise mentorship, and staunch support of my strategic vision of what should be rather than what is. I have served side by side with many others who inspired me through their individual careers and accomplishments. Both categories have influenced both my professional career and personal character, and throughout the years became the tapestry of all that I am and have accomplished. For those I know personally, I will always be grateful for their praise, criticism, and advice. The roll call goes far beyond the writing of this book; it spans five decades of friendship and association, working together with great professionals. For those I know only through the history of events, thanks for being a model for others, especially yours truly.

• M. F. Allington	• Richard H. Ellis	• Robert L. Mitchell
• James Baker	• Tommy Franks	• Oliver North
• Merton W. Baker	• Frederick P. Geier	• Robert A. Owen, Jr.
• Thomas D. Baldwin	• James W. Geist	• George S. Patton
• Benjamin N. Bellis	• Jack J. Gibson	• John W. Pauly
• James M. Bielinski	• Jack Gundrum	• Colin Powell
• Jack E. Bowerman	• Alexander Haig	• Elaine D. Rapanos
• Orval Brown	• John W. Hartman	• Gary W. Redecker
• Herbert R. Bull	• Gary R. Hichor	• Condoleezza Rice
• George W. Bush	• Raymond J. Huot	• Patrick M. Roddy
• George Campbell	• Jack Hurley	• Arthur B. Rupert
• Henry E. Carmine	• John F. Kennedy	• Norman Schwarzkopf
• Billy J. Carter	• Armin A. Krueger	• Bruce Seymour

• Gary Casali	• Albert J. Lilly	• Kalman D. Simon
• Larry Cassenti	• Jack E. Lockard	• William P. Smith
• Earnest A. Church	• Douglas MacArthur	• George B. Stackhouse III
• John J. Conley	• James Malloy	• John Sutton
• Philip J. Conley, Jr.	• Robert W. Maloy	• Ronald Thomas
• James A. Cook	• Melvin C. Manly	• Aubrey Tillman
• Steven C. Cote	• Robert C. Marcan	• Lowell H. Tillman
• Bobby R. Daniels	• John F. Marchi	• Lou Tyska
• Thomas Dexter	• Robert J. McClaurine	• John Wrona
• Joseph A. Duquette	• Wayne Messner	
• Dwight D. Eisenhower	• Bonnie Micheiman	

Clients and business associates have also been a valuable influence; they often shared their insights from the "trenches," I have always learned from their experiences, then translated the key ingredients into lessons that other leaders, associates, and peers need to hear. Their thoughts and viewpoints have been instrumental in guiding me in many different ways. I thank them for their efforts and enlightening debates.

Thanks to Butterworth-Heinemann for publishing this work and making me part of history. Thanks to Brian Romer and Tom Stover for believing in me, making this book happen, and introducing me to Hilary Carr, my editorial project manager. Her amazing chapter-by-chapter analysis, detailed review, and constructive comments give credit to the final book. Thanks to Hilary for her attentive coordination of the manuscript and to the Butterworth-Heinemann staff, whose editorial skills and constructive comments breathed life into the book. Thanks to Mohanapriyan Rajendran, my production manager, whose expert editorial skills and wisdom to offer penetrating commentary throughout the entire manuscript brought this book to life. Thank you for a job well done.

I thank the anonymous reviewers who provided useful suggestions not only to enhance the clarity of the original book outline but to go beyond in convincing me they had a better idea for some areas of the narrative than I first conceived. Their insight was invaluable, and I have embedded their individual footprints throughout the pages of this work. It is their product as much as it is mine.

I thank John Wiley & Sons for giving me permission to use some materials from my first book, *Strategies for Protecting National Critical Infrastructure Assets: A Focus on Problem-Solving*. And a very special thank to the University of Phoenix for permitting me to use of the results of their competency study.

I thank the students I have taught over the years—from Asia to Europe to Africa to the Middle East, and across America—for their intellectual insight and feedback.

The seminar sessions were extremely valuable in forming my vision for this and other works. You have taught me well.

I also thank my family for their continued support and encouragement. I wish to recognize Nika and Tina, who were always asking, "How's it going, Dad?" What a great cheerleading section. I really missed Nika's expert research and editing talents on this book. A growing family and two working parents made it difficult for her to help with the research, typing, and editing of draft copies. For this book, these tasks fell on my shoulders, so any errors and omissions are mine and mine alone. Many thanks to Toula, for checking in on me from time to time: making sure I was taking my medication, following my diet, and keeping my doctor appointments.

To Pamela Aughey who provided help on two crucial levels. As, my youngest: she has been my pal, friend, and confidant and my anchor of sanity throughout this entire project. Thanks for looking in on Dad all times of the day and night to check up on my temperament, optimism, and soundness of mind. As a professional project manager implementing Cloud applications, she would unleash her encyclopedic knowledge of web intelligence to validate "unfounded" URLs, locate the original source of information and breathed new life into the reference footnotes. Without her skills I would have been forced to delete valuable statical data. While I would occasionally show my frustration in trying to imitate her technique, she always sought pleasure in continuously teaching me new skill sets. Thank you so much for your wisdom, talent, and patience in teaching this old dog new tricks.

I want to give special thanks my dear friend and colleague, James F. Broder, and to my brother, George P. Sullivant. They have been a constant source of wisdom and inspiration, as well as strengthening my performance curve. I am grateful for their council and advice.

Last, I want to recognize you, the reader. If you are chipping away at preventing or solving some of the problems mentioned herein, then the value of the information I am sharing with you is priceless, and for that I am grateful.

John Sullivant

Introduction

1

When the goals of prevention, deterrence, protection, detection, assessment, response and recovery are not adequately addressed, or technology solutions sweep protocols, processes and people aside, the security organization will lack the capability to adequately perform its critical mission. When this occurs, the security organization has come face-to-face with the affects of vulnerability creep-in and must deal with the consequences: falling short of meeting performance expectations; a no confidence vote from business units that the security organization can support its business interests; and workforce physical and emotional stress.

John Sullivant

Top Takeaways

- Recognize some obstacles security professionals face when building security resilience and developing relationships
- Define the real meaning of "ability" and "capability" within the realm of security operations
- Identify some stumbling blocks that confront security professionals
- Describe the origin and theory of vulnerability creep-in
- Explain how vulnerability creep-in festers within an organization
- Identify factors causing vulnerability creep-in

Overview

Throughout the pages of this book, I tell my story of research and experience over fifty years of insightful advice to influence decision makers and their choices. There are two dimensions to my story. The first dimension has to do with business and professional values: integrity, honesty, and trust as an individual and competency as a professional. The second dimension has to deal with management and leadership: positive attitude, team building, empowerment, coaching and training others, and influencing decision makers to embrace new standards of achievement and social behavior that lead to appropriate security and organizational resilience.

Building Security Resilience and Developing Relationships

This book is packed with my personal experiences and research results that describe the frailty of security activity in both the private and public sectors, and the decision-making process that has shaped and continues to shape our security destiny. It focuses attention on our ability to achieve many security goals and objectives, our ability and capability to perform to expectations and standards, our craving to communicate effectively with chief executives and others, and our personal desire to improve our proficiency, competency, and productivity.

But What Do Ability, Capability, and Preparedness Really Mean?

Two prominent sources answer this question: Presidential Policy Directive (PPD) 21, "Critical Infrastructure Security and Resilience," and Homeland Security Presidential Directive (HSPD) 8, National Preparedness Guidelines.

PPD 21 describes resilience as the *ability* of an organization to resist, engage in, recover from, or successfully adapt to adversity or to a change in conditions. This includes preparing for, adapting to, withstanding, and recovering rapidly from disruptions, deliberate attacks, industrial mishaps and hazards, and weather-related calamities, and the return to an acceptable level of performance in an acceptable time after being affected by an event or incident.[1] Resilience is a concept that applies to individual assets, systems or networks of assets, and security activities and programs. Resiliency allows the asset, network, or system to fail gracefully rather than abruptly, or in such a way as to allow the consequences of failure to be minimized. Self-healing components, systems, and networks enhance resiliency.

HSPD-8 describes resilience as the *capability* of an organization to maintain its functions and structure in the face of internal and external change, and to degrade gracefully when it must. Under HSPD-8 guidance, "capability" means to accomplish the mission by performing one or more critical competencies under specified conditions and to a targeted level of performance standard or expectation. For security organizations, critical competencies include the ability and capability to deter, delay, prevent, protect, detect, assess, respond to, and recover from a security or security-related event. Chapter Establishing and Maintaining Inseparable Security Competencies relates to these capabilities. HSPD-8 further explains that capability may be delivered through any combination of properly planned, organized, equipped, and trained resources that can achieve the desired outcome. Capability also refers to features, operations, or policies that serve to benefit a protective environment and that may eliminate or reduce the need for particular protective measures without jeopardizing mission goals and objectives or performance outcome.[2]

---

[1] Presidential Policy Directive 21 (PPD 21): Critical Infrastructure Security and Resilience, The Whitehouse, Washington, DC, 2013.
[2] Homeland Security Presidential Directive 8 (HSPD-8): National Preparedness Guidelines, U.S. Department of Homeland Security, Washington, DC, 2011.

I often come across chief executive officers (CEOs) and security professionals who have no clue what "ability" and "capability" really mean. Sometimes it
seems that no matter how often we plead our case, or what actions we take, many
strong-minded executives just do not get the message. I talk more about this topic
in Chapter How to Communicate with Executives and Governing Bodies. For now,
it is important to know that this lack of basic knowledge is strikingly reflected in
corporate security and emergency preparedness planning, in the development of
policies and protocols, in training programs, and in demonstrated performance
outcomes that we have observed throughout our visits to all industry sectors.
There is more on these topics in Chapters Preparing for Emergencies, A User-
Friendly Protocol Development Model, and A Proven Organization and Management Assessment Model.

How Do We Relate Security Goals to Business?

As a security professional, you must have a clear understanding of the organization's
culture and management's knowledge base if you are to fully embrace the company's
strategic vision for pursuing business goals and objectives. This understanding is
essential if you expect to establish, implement, maintain, and effectively monitor the
effects of building security resilience (Sullivant, 2007, pp. 111).

Let us briefly examine the three categories of this strategy: an understanding of
the characterization of security requirements; the nurturing of business relationships
both internally between upper management and organizational divisions, and externally among stockholders and governing bodies; and community entities that have an
invested interest in the success of the company, its services, and security performance
expectations.

Key to characterization is the ability to clearly define:

- business services and security operations,
- business continuity and emergency operations,
- the rank order of assets that are critically important to the enterprise's mission, and
- the degree of service interruption the enterprise and the security organization can sustain
  should an event occur before an entity can collapse.

It is essential for those individuals who have a responsibility to meet the challenges
of achieving business and security goals and objectives to buy into this characterization,
and to have the unconditional support of C-suite executives.[3] I talk about these topics
in Chapters Strategies That Create Your Life Line, The Evolving Threat Environment,
The Cyber Threat Landscape, and Developing a Realistic and Useful Threat Estimate
Profile.

---

[3] The term "C-suite" refers to the most important and influential group of individuals within a corporation
who make high-stake decisions. C-suite is so named because the titles of top senior executives tend to start
with the letter C. For example, CEO, chief operating officer, and chief financial officer. Other designated
"chief officers" often vary within and between corporations and may be included in the C-suite group of
some corporations. The term "C-suite executives" is also referred to as "C-level executives."

Can We Speak Intelligently About the Threat Environment?

Concurrent with characterizing business services and security operations, you need to begin developing strategies for building security resilience. The key to this characterization is defining the possible threats, hazards, risks, and vulnerabilities that a corporation will face, including perceived and postulated threats and hazards, adversary modes of attack, threat capabilities, the likelihood of threats occurring, the potential consequences of losing assets, and solutions to these problems in terms that are meaningful and useful to executive management (Sullivant, 2007, pp. 133). Key to a comprehensive threat analysis is to determine the security organization's ability and capability to perform its critical operational mission: deter, delay (or deny), prevent, protect, detect, assess, respond to, and recover from acknowledged threats. No other mission is more important for a security organization—it could determine the survivability of the corporation. I discuss these capabilities in Chapters Strategies That Create Your Life Line, The Evolving Threat Environment, The Cyber Threat Landscape, Establishing a Security Risk Management Program Is Crucial, Useful Metrics Give the Security Organization Standing, A User-Friendly Security Assessment Model, Developing a Realistic and Useful Threat Estimate Profile, and Establishing and Maintaining Inseparable Security Competencies.

Watch Out for Stumbling Blocks

Let me briefly examine some significant conditions, circumstances, and situations that repeatedly plague the ability and capability of security organizations to perform as mandated or expected. First, if you are to gain acceptance and trust from executive management as a professional security expert, you must always—in all circumstances—demonstrate leadership value to the corporation. Second, you must not only understand the business and threat environments; you must also be able to achieve workable and practical solutions to security problems that mirror the corporate image, brand, and reputation that are acceptable to executive management. Last, to survive in today's business culture it takes resolve and strategic vision, which are really works in progress.

Experience and Knowledge Base of Senior Decision-Makers Can Cause Us to Trip

Wherever I go, chief executives proudly proclaim their security organizations are doing a good job protecting the company. These CEOs and those around them are always optimistic when describing their progress and accomplishments, and they often overrate performance, whether it is people, processes, technology, or production. Some CEOs take on too many outside commitments and become detached from the staff and operational managers, losing sight of true operational conditions.

One explanation for this limited knowledge rests with those individuals who surround chief executives and routinely brief them on security matters, although they know little, if anything, about security principles, operational philosophies and techniques, or compliance or regulatory mandates. Every staff person who supports an executive has a view that is biased by his or her staff function or agenda of expectations. They are busy protecting their turf, do not freely share information, and spend an inordinate amount of time organizing for their own possible succession. Another disadvantage staff briefers face is the tendency to unjustifiably "distance" the boss from bad news, giving many executives a misguided perception about the wellness of the corporate security organization. We know that the information CEOs get from their staff is sanitized, organized, homogenized, and often made as inoffensive and generalized as possible. Information that could lead to decisions counter to the stakes of the staff is often withheld completely (Lukaszewski, 2008, pp. 23–32).

Because of some staffers' zealous behavior, too many executives believe their respective corporate security programs are effective, when in reality analyses of numerous security organizations across America tell a different story. Wherever I observe this or similar conditions, I find the fundamental principles of security are often ignored, and time-honored security management principles, as well as standards of acceptable practice, are dissuaded (Broder, 2007, pp. ix). Moreover, there is a consensus among many of my colleagues that some executives do not fully understand or appreciate what the security profession is all about, or the importance of the security mission to the overall corporate profit margin (Broder, 2007, pp. 45). A recent national survey reported that 60 percent of upper management believes that security is stronger than it actually is, whereas only 22 percent of top executives are aware of their company's true security readiness. Our experience is that these locations are some of the worst seen to date. It is astounding that almost two-thirds of the nation's CEOs say they are in the dark about the true security status of their corporation. Certainly, this finding qualifies as an agenda item both in the executive suite and in the halls of the security organization.

Yet many staffers continue to feed the boss incomplete, misguided, or erroneous information, and then believe they can work with the security director to resolve issues that may arise during or after the briefing. When dealing with the senior staff, you may not exactly be in friendly territory. The most zealous staffers may try to make you irrelevant whenever possible to place themselves in a favorable position with executives. If you are the senior security professional of your organization, you and only you should be the spokesperson for the security organization. You must do whatever it takes to work hand in hand with staff members to discuss security issues and to encourage them to step aside when it comes to briefing executive management. Nothing can be more devastating to the image, brand, and reputation of the security organization than allowing a staffer to commit your organization and its capabilities without your approval under any circumstances. You must make it clear to the staffer that you do not give him or her permission to speak on your behalf. If they insist, you must place them on notice that they own the decision, including the aftermath of any consequences that may materialize. Fortunately, experienced executives have the insight to see through this mirage. Most executives I know frown upon anyone (staffer or division head) usurping the legitimate territory of another—especially when critical security decision-making is involved. And that is how it should be.

This is a dangerous game played among some members of the senior staff and executives. Do not play it. The stakes are too high. There are no winners here, and you may just become a causality without knowing it. That means it may be time to look elsewhere for a position where your knowledge and expertise are better appreciated.

Most CEOs do not like staffers briefing them unless it pertains to nonoperational issues. Many exclude them from operations-related meetings because their vision is limited to their staff experience. Most prefer to have operational managers brief them because they are in the trenches in the real world and in real time. CEOs sometimes bypass the staff because staffers (Lukaszewski, 2008, pp. 95–97):

- have the inclination to teach their function
- constantly seem to seek approval for their behaviors and confirmation of their value
- fail to demonstrate that they understand the business or the key issues the business faces
- speak a language the boss neither needs nor cares to learn
- focus on the unimportant
- constantly take up too much time, telling executives things they already know
- have oral skills that are unfocused and fail to provide information management can act on
- whine a lot to everyone

I focus on fallacies such as these throughout the pages of this book with actual case histories, which I have strategically placed within the main narrative or appendices to make a specific point.

What Do We Do with Misguided Executive Decision-Making?

A growing chorus of security consultants, including myself, have for years been advising chief executives and their security directors of the early telling signs that their security programs are on the brink of failure and in need of strengthening to keep pace with the changes in corporate business strategies, processes, and practices, as well as security technologies. For the most part, these warnings go unheeded, mainly because the staff believes they need to protect the boss from bad news.

As tough as I am on executives, I also have an obligation as a trusted strategic advisor to be objective and defend the worthy ones. The golden rule is that the boss is the boss for a reason. Unless what the boss is doing is immoral, illegal, unethical, completely stupid, or clearly financially irresponsible, the boss is the boss. He or she drives the bus and the bus belongs to him or her. They know where they have been and only they know where they are going. Where the boss takes the company and how the boss gets it there is clearly his or her decision to make. Enjoy the ride and contribute the best you can, or dust off your resume and hop on another bus line (Lukaszewski, 2008, pp. xxxix).

Executives react to pressures and the urgency of time. Often they just do not have the time to address the crux of the problem, as it should be studied. Against their better judgment, they find a quick "Band-Aid" to silence critics, governing bodies, and the media, hoping they can rebound with a long-term solution afterward. Unfortunately history tells us that competing demands always consume their valuable time and follow-up analysis to uncover the root causes of many problems to find a practicable and workable solution is seldom accomplished—yet another sign of vulnerability creep-in surfacing its head. Vulnerability creep-in is a topic I discuss in Chapter The Many Faces of Vulnerability Creep-in.

Experience of Security Professionals

The problem is further compounded because too many security managers have no clue they have a problem, and most do not want to know a problem exists (Broder, 2007, p. 45). Some of these professionals regard any suggestion to improve or enhance security as a criticism of their ability to manage and lead. Guess what? They are right, and they know it! How they can hide this ineptitude and incompetency from others in high positions of responsibility is a discussion for another time. These professionals significantly contribute—mostly unknowingly—to the many aspects of vulnerability creep-in. Without a doubt, colleagues who fall into this group are an embarrassment to the security profession.

Clueless security professionals need a wake-up call to always remember that a crisis is the product of poor strategic vision and planning and a lack of foresight, coordination, direction, and creative thinking (Tarlow, 2002, pp. 24). In other words, a problem is always a management problem before it becomes an operational problem. These "weak sisters" need to place their problems within a situational context in such a way that executives are able to determine what the risks are for a specific circumstance. Perhaps then these security professionals may achieve some redeeming value in the eyes of others. Three case histories highlight the result of such incompetency:

- More often than not, many of their security programs comprise several activities strung together in a rather haphazard fashion, with little or no coherence at the highest level.
- Often they are authoritative actors who give employees little or no opportunity to use their creative-thinking skills or buy into security improvements. There is no systematic approach to what they do.
- A poor security awareness program leading to employee complacency, poor attitudes and social behavior, and low competency levels.

Vulnerability Creep-in Just Showed Up—It Wasn't Here Before

Perhaps the greatest challenge I have confronted is those conditions, circumstances, and situations that create the social cancer that eats away at security resilience: vulnerability creep-in (Sullivant, 2007, pp. 162–164).

I can make a strong case that vulnerability creep-in is the product of many years of buildup that, with time and opportunity, spreads throughout all facets of an organization—mostly this occurs unintentionally, unknowingly, and is undetectable. I also contend that the theory of vulnerability creep-in puts forth the notion that the cumulative effects of conditions, circumstances, and situations created by management's actions or inactions affecting security matters directly influence the security organization's ability and capability to perform its critical mission. I further argue that the phenomenon of vulnerability creep-in stems from:

- lack of willpower to pursue practical strategies to correct a problem
- refusal or inability to acknowledge that a problem exists
- fallible decision-making, near-reckless planning, and mostly negligent management
- indecision, poor planning, or the poor execution of security activities
- inexperience, lack of knowledge, and disengagement from the problem-solving process
- arrogance, apathy, complacency, indifference, ineptness, insensitivity, and ignorance
- individuals charged with security decision-making failing to:
  - fully grasp the essential principles of security
  - recognize the benefits of security dependencies and independencies
  - recognize the benefits of operational program and technology integration
  - recognize false pretense and incomplete or inadequate research and information
  - recognize the difficulty of obstacles that influence security decision-making
  - recognize the benefits from lessons learned
  - develop a realistic threat profile, asset inventory, and consequences of loss impact
  - develop clear security emergency plans and exacting practices
  - shun political correctness based on false promises
  - demonstrate the wisdom and courage to make midcourse corrections
- management putting its head in the sand and ignoring security issues

All of the above are the cornerstone of predicable failure and should be evident to management.

Experience tells us that many of these conditions exist because of previous executive decisions vetoing recommendations to improve or enhance security, including some staff management resistance to embracing change. Vulnerability creep-in is the gateway through which security weaknesses are manifested. Just like the disease it is, it will eventually drain the energy, strength, and determination out of your people, taking its toll as frustration, disillusionment, and finally "burn out." I describe Vulnerability creep-in as a tsunami wave that never stops and obliterates everything in its wake. Singly and collectively, vulnerability creep-in has the potential to degrade an organization's ability and capability to implement strategic security planning initiatives. Jointly, these actions—if allowed to develop—puncture the very fiber of the corporate risk management framework and architecture, and will eventually lead to the weakening of security resilience whenever reasonable and prudent security measures are not implemented in an orderly, reasonably, prudent, and timely manner. As a security professional, it is your obligation to push back this malignant growth. For some, this may be a horrific challenge of epidemic portions.

Conclusion

In wrapping up this chapter, I must defend my colleagues and the security profession. It is in some instances extremely difficult for the typical security practitioner to understand and envision the scope, depth, and significance of many of the issues I examine in this book. In fact, the many faces of vulnerability creep-in have eluded even the most seasoned security professionals at one time or another.

Few security professionals possess the insight to uncover systemic conditions from afar. One approach is to use a security consultant with broad experience and expertise in problem solving. These professionals can recognize the telling signs of these repetitive phenomena, which in my view touch the boundaries of negligent management in its greatest form, although of course unknowingly.

Vulnerability creep-in takes a very long time—sometimes years—to mature into an identifiable problem, making it remarkably difficult for an otherwise conscientious enterprise staff and security professionals to recognize the havoc it can create and its subsequent consequence on security resilience. The embryos of this cancer remain in the dark shadows of the organization, hatching undetectably until something happens that prompts the staff or outside parties to start looking for answers. Sadly, when it comes to taking responsibility for security failures, shortcomings, and other related mistakes, some executives are quick to defend corporate actions and slow to admit that improvements and enhancements are appropriate or even necessary.

I find the greatest benefit of being an independent consultant is that I am able to serve the best interests of my clients free from political pressure or influence, and to report my findings to executive management based solely on the facts as I see and understand them—not on conjecture, political correctness, or political favor. This independence of action and thought is contrary to what most governing authorities can or will report on the nature of specific security problems: Why did the problem occur? What has been done to solve the problem? What impediments were encountered in solving the problem? What additional steps need to be taken to prevent reoccurrence? My obligation is to be objective, candid, truthful, and focused, and to give useful and meaning real-time advice. I cannot do this unless I:

- pay attention to the surroundings of those I advise
- ensure executives get the information they need to better judge the present and future
- judge the capabilities organizations and the competencies of those running them

Corporations across America could be equally independent and objective (if they chose to be) in serving the best interests of their clients, customers, stockholders, employees, and the communities they serve. Left unattended, the conditions, circumstances, and situations that create vulnerability creep-in can lead us down the road to "the many faces of vulnerability creep-in." I carry through with this viewpoint in the next chapter by introducing strategies that can save the day.

Strategies That Create Your Life Line

2

Strategies push an organization in a forward direction—always into tomorrow and beyond.

John Sullivant

Top Takeaways

- Discover the importance of creating a uniform set of security strategies
- Learn the guiding principles behind security strategies
- Understand the importance of communicating and interfacing with other agencies

Overview

Strategy provides positive energy that drives business and organizations, guides leadership, and directs people to move in the same direction. Strategy pushes, pulls, and adjusts the security organization in the larger context of its operations, and always in a forward direction—into tomorrow and beyond.

Strategy shapes the future by achieving desirable goals with available resources that ensure long-term success. A useful and meaningful strategy has three parts: (1) a diagnosis that defines or explains the nature of the challenge, (2) a guiding policy for dealing with the challenge, and (3) coherent actions designed to carry out the guiding policy (Rumelt, 2001, pp. 123).

The strategies introduced in this chapter and throughout the pages of this book encompass a series of top-level "battle plans" designed, either singly or collectively, to achieve one or more goals under conditions of uncertainty. Strategies are important because recourses and funding to achieve stated security goals are usually scarce commodities.

A Need Exists to Create a Set of Uniform Security Strategies

A corporation must recognize the need to establish and maintain a set of uniform security strategies, protocols, and best practices that foster a corporate security culture that optimizes the building of security resilience that is consistent with community service and public safety. The strategies offered in this section achieve this goal and are essential to the integrity, reliability, image, and reputation of any security organization, large or small, public or private. The listing is categorized into two parts.

Part I: General Security Strategies

- Ensure public safety, public confidence, and services
- Encourage and facilitate partnering internally and externally
- Interface with other corporate programs
- Encourage and facilitate meaningful information sharing
- Safeguard privacy and constitutional freedoms
- Security policy
- Security authority, responsibility, and accountability

Part II: Special Security Strategies

These strategies are addressed separately in other chapters:

- Chapter 6: Establishing a Security Risk Management Program Is Crucial
- Chapter 7: Useful Metrics Give the Security Organization Standing
- Chapter 8: A User-Friendly Security Assessment Model
- Chapter 9: Developing a Realistic and Useful Threat Estimate Profile
- Chapter 10: Establishing and Maintaining Inseparable Security Competencies
- Chapter 11: A User-Friendly Security Technology Model
- Chapter 12: Preparing for Emergencies
- Chapter 13: A User-Friendly Protocol Development Model
- Chapter 14: A Proven Security Organization and Management Assessment Model
- Chapter 15: Building Competencies That Count: A Training Model
- Chapter 16: How to Communicate with Executives and Governing Bodies
- Chapter 17: A Brighter Tomorrow: My Thoughts

Security Strategies and Guiding Principles

Implementing security strategies is a never-ending process. It requires a unifying organization, a clear purpose, a common understanding of roles and responsibilities, accountability, and well-disciplined determination. Since a corporation must perform its business mission with diligence and dedication to the communities it serves, all employees—in particular those assigned to and who directly support the staff of the security director—must endeavor to perform at the highest competency levels. These strategies can include one or more of the strategies described in the subsequent sections.

Ensure Public Safety, Public Confidence, and Services

Anticipate that widespread or large-scale business disruptions will undermine employee and public confidence in the corporation's ability to provide essential services. By making strategic improvements in security and emergency and business continuity planning, a corporation reduces vulnerability from physical attacks, particularly those involving catastrophic consequences. Providing corporate resources and assets with reasonable and prudent protection increases the organization's ability to withstand an attack and reduce the likelihood of sustaining significant losses and consequences. Effective security, emergency preparedness, and business continuity planning make the corporation's resources, assets, and functions more resilient, allowing for the quick restoration of critical services to minimize the detrimental effects to the corporation and the community.

Implementing and exercising a well-developed public safety and confidence strategy includes decision-making activities to:

- develop a risk management framework to guide prevention and protection programs and activities
- identify and regularly update the status of prevention and protection programs
- conduct and update security assessments and the corporate threat estimate profile
- update the security and emergency response plan and associated appendices, as required
- implement new security technologies to enhance and improve the productivity and competency of the security organization
- harden assets to the extent economically feasible to reduce risk exposure
- interdict human threats to prevent potential attacks
- respond rapidly to disruptions to limit the impact on public health and safety and corporate functions
- ensure rapid restoration and recovery from those events that are not preventable
- develop and implement a corporate-wide alert and notification system that notifies employees and others in times of emergency

This strategy is the key to shaping employee and public expectations and instilling confidence in the organization's ability to manage the aftermath of a major terrorist attack, natural disaster, industrial mishap, or weather-related calamity, as well as its capability to restore services in a timely manner.

Encourage and Facilitate Partnering Internally and Externally

Protection of company resources and assets is a shared enterprise responsibility that entails integration, organization, and collaboration skill sets. Every business disruption is initially a corporate and community problem with potential regional, national, and international repercussions. Corporate leaders should implement preventive and protective measures and emergency response plans to foster an environment in which all employees can better carry out their security responsibilities. Organizing may involve:

- identifying and ensuring the protection of those resources and assets that are most critical in terms of production capacity, economic security, public health and safety, and public confidence. Develop a comprehensive security assessment to prioritize threats and vulnerabilities across the corporation to establish an independent and adequate security budget to facilitate the allocation of security resources, facilities, and equipment.
- providing timely warning and alert notification to ensure that assets receive timely protection against specific or intimate threats.

- ensuring the protection of other resources and assets that may become attractive targets by pursuing specific initiatives and enabling a collaborative environment in which federal, state, and local governments working with the enterprise can better protect those resources and assets. The enterprise should remain cognizant that criticality varies as a function of time, risk, and market changes. Adversaries are known to shift their focus to targets they consider less protected and more likely to yield the desired shock effect at a particular point in time.
- reviewing operations that are critical to the business unit mission to establish security priorities and ensure adequate security and redundancy for all identified critical facilities and services.
- creating and implementing comprehensive multitiered security practices that could include:
    - developing essential protocols,
    - organizing and coordinating security emergency preparedness and business continuity planning integral to the overall security program,
    - developing security protocols for information technology, telecommunications, and cyber security, and
    - developing security event–driven emergency response and recovery procedures corresponding to varying ranges and levels of threat and alert conditions.

Successful collaborating activities may involve:

- developing a process to identify and monitor external first responders entering company property
- improving the corporation's ability and commitment to work with federal, state, and local responders and service providers
- exploring potential options and incentives to encourage stakeholders to devise solutions to unique security impediments
- exploring options for incentives to increase the security budget, including government grants, if applicable
- elevating awareness and understanding of threats, vulnerabilities, and risk exposure to corporate critical assets through the promotion of corporate-wide security awareness and other security education programs
- seeking legislation to apply sabotage laws to corporate activities.

Interface with Other Corporate Programs

Corporate security programs complement and support other major corporate programs such as safety, human resources, business continuity, capital improvement efforts, and the security engineering and design development process. A clear understanding of these relationships and interfaces is vital because there is a degree of common interest and mutually shared responsibility among these programs.

Safety Program

In many situations, safety and security protocols complement each other; both emphasize the protection of employees and property. The corporate safety program is an Occupational Safety and Health Administration compliance requirement that protects the workforce. In most instances, safety and security protocols can and do complement each other. For instance, security officers are often in a position to observe compliance with corporate operating protocols and safety procedures. While security officers can help management enforce certain safety compliance issues, they do not direct their entire attention on monitoring employees' behavioral patterns to prevent safety infractions. Instead, their primary focus is to protect employees from injury, death, assault, or attack resulting from the damage or destruction of assets.

Since the rise of terrorism during the 1970s, the primary focus of security has changed from physical asset protection to protection of individuals from thieves and an occasional disturbed assailant to protection from terrorist attacks. When guarding against these evolving threats, security planners and designers need to guard against installing protective materials, barriers, or systems, or establishing protocols that are in direct conflict with existing codes or standards that focus on life safety, fire prevention, and other dangerous hazards. Where a conflict exists between safety and security protocols, the protocol that provides the safest work environment should prevail until the conflict can be resolved.

Human Resources and Capital Investment

Human resources are the most important commodities of a corporation. Attracting, recruiting, and keeping good people are solid investment strategies that include:

- hiring practices and attracting, recruiting, and keeping motivated and dedicated people, which helps to reduce risk exposure from the insider threat
- developing corporate-wide criteria for background checks, screening, and positive identification of employees
- developing certification criteria for background screening companies
- participating in the establishment, maintenance, and evaluation of security training programs and certification standards for the security staff
- participating in the development, conduct, and evaluation of a corporate-wide employee security awareness training program

Business Continuity Planning

The business continuity planning effort is (or should be) an integral part of the security planning process. Much of the research and data needed for business continuity planning process are based on the framework of the security risk management program, security strategies, and security practices. For example, business continuity planning strategies embrace the same risks, threats, and hazards discovered through a security assessment as well as identified in the corporate threat estimate profile. This research and analysis does not have to be duplicated, but only applied to specific continuity goals and objectives (if they are different from existing security goals and objectives).

Capital Improvement Program

Security design architecture must be considered in the planning, design, engineering, and construction of new facilities, systems, networks, and functions early in the developmental phase. The security engineering and design development process must always directly support security operational performance requirements.Explore the hardening of critical facilities against risk exposure with security construction technology, crime prevention through environmental design, and state-of-the-art technology applications.

Use Unique Criteria Associated with Protection

Inherent program constraints and limitations must be recognized at the outset. To frame the initial focus of the protection effort, you must be prepared to acknowledge that not all assets that comprise the corporate infrastructure are uniformly "critical" in nature, particularly within a corporate-wide context. Therefore the following suggestions may be helpful in your security planning efforts:

- Priority 1: Identify and ensure the protection of those resources and assets designated as most "critical" to mission operations.
- Priority 2: Identify and ensure the protection of those assets that face a specific, imminent threat.
- Priority 3: Pursue measures and initiatives to ensure the protection of other potential business operations that may become attractive targets.
- Priority 4: Pursue the advancement of concepts, practices, and technologies that increase the security program effectiveness of all resources and assets across all business boundaries.

Such activity may include the following:

- For new or modified facilities, redesign technology-based equipment to significantly lower the costs of existing capabilities.
- Design new facilities that provide cost benefits, state-of-the-art solutions to safety, and security requirements that can benefit all business operations.
- To the extent feasible and practical, use technology that results in better efficiencies such as monitoring, surveillance, and assessment, and the enhanced use of scarce resources.
- Search out technology pilot programs used to solve security problems that have passed the research and demonstration stage, such as the Constellation Automated Critical Asset Management System of the City of Los Angeles, the South Florida Coastal Surveillance Prototype Test Bed, and the National Capital Region Rail Security Corridor Pilot Project in Washington, DC.

Exploring Methods to Authenticate and Verify Personnel Identity

The security director should create more effective and positive means of identifying people requiring access to critical assets and functions, including establishing ways and means to control access to and egress from the scene of an emergency, to maintain the integrity of the site boundary, and to protect first responders. This includes a uniform and rapid means of identifying and monitoring first responders reporting to the site of an emergency.

Coordinating Interoperability Standards to Ensure Compatibility of Communication Systems

To the extent practical, the security director should strive to create standard communication protocols to enable secure and assured interoperable communications among the various company C^3 which stands for Command, Control and Communications centers, security operations centers, and community first responders. Standardized communication systems enhance the security response and promote efficient planning and training at all levels. The ability to establish and maintain efficient communications between security and community first responders is essential to ensure the effectiveness of the response and recovery processes.

Security Technologies and Expertise

Science and technology are key elements in protecting resources and assets. A corporation should fully leverage its technological advantages to improve the monitoring of assets and functions to reduce labor-intensive monitoring and surveillance activity. Pooling corporate scientists, engineers, and security professionals can increase the overall understanding of the threat and risk exposure. It also fosters collaboration between the various disciplines and enables the corporation to capitalize on emerging technologies and facilitate security and emergency preparedness planning, decision-making, and resource allocation. This includes, but is not necessarily limited to, coordinating interoperability standards to ensure performance compatibility during both routine day-to-day operations and emergency situations, and implementing best practices.

Encourage and Facilitate Meaningful Information Sharing

A corporation that participates in the community information sharing process tends to formulate better security policies and protocols, and make informed security investments and decisions in an accurate and timely manner. This includes:

- understanding effective information sharing processes among security partners
- providing protocols for real-time threat and incident reporting, alerting, and warning
- establishing effective coordinating structures among security partners
- enhancing coordination with the local, state, and federal communities
- building public awareness
- analyzing, warehousing, and sharing security assessment data in a secure manner that is consistent with relevant legal requirements and information protection responsibilities

Accordingly, the security director adopts measures to identify and evaluate potential impediments or disincentives to security-related information sharing among business units and between the entity and federal, state, and local governments. This allows for the formulation of appropriate strategies to overcome these barriers and to establish and maintain reliable, secure, and efficient communications and information systems to support meaningful information sharing. This may involve:

- defining security-related information-sharing needs and establishing effective, efficient information-sharing processes to ensure that appropriate users can access needed information in a timely manner
- expanding voluntary security-related information sharing among business units, as well as between federal, state, and local governments and industry
- facilitating the sharing of industry best security practices and processes
- improving processes for the collection and analysis of threat information needed for strategic security planning, prioritization, resource allocation, and budgeting

- improving the company alert advisory system and identifying appropriate actions that correspond to the various threat levels
- ensuring that the public affairs office develops a comprehensive communications plan for notifying the news media and the public of emergency conditions and situations

Safeguard Privacy and Constitutional Freedoms

Most corporations are a tapestry of diverse races, ethnicities, cultures, religions, and political ideologies. This pluralism and a company's ability to accommodate diversity significantly contribute to its strength as an enterprise. This diversity, however, can also be an inherent vulnerability by possibly exposing employees to propaganda and other influences.

Notwithstanding achieving security, a corporation must accept some level of risk as a persisting condition in the daily lives of the workforce. The challenge is finding the path that enables the corporation to mitigate risk and protect resources, assets, and functions while respecting privacy and the freedom of expression, and upholding federal and state labor laws. The security director collaborates with the director of human resources and other staff agencies, as appropriate, to develop and implement this strategy.

Security Policy

A corporate security policy commits the organization to protecting its employees and assets from acts that would:

- undermine the corporation's capacity to deliver minimum essential water and power services to the communities it serves,
- undermine the public's morale and confidence in the corporation's capability to deliver services, and
- impair the corporation's ability to ensure the public's health and safety with respect to products and services provided.

To achieve these goals, it is necessary to develop, monitor, and maintain threat-level information and to combine the results of threat analysis information with the elements of security planning, emergency planning, and business continuity planning into a cohesive program in which all elements are compatible and interoperability is achieved across the company.

Security Authority, Responsibility, and Accountability

All enterprise business units have an important role to play in protecting resources and assets. This necessarily encompasses the mechanisms required to coordinate and integrate security policies, planning, resource management, and performance measurement across the entire spectrum of the company. It includes a coordinated and integrated process for security program implementation that:

- supports prioritization of security programs and activities
- helps to align the resources of the corporate budget to the protection mission
- enables tracking and accountability for the expenditure of allocated security funds

- takes into account federal, state, and local government considerations related to security planning, programming, and budgeting
- draws on expertise across organizational boundaries
- shares expertise and advances in implementing security best practices
- recognizes the need to build a business case based on business and security values

The key component of this strategy is the delineation of security roles, responsibilities, and accountability against established performance expectations.

Conclusion

A large capital investment is required to acquire and hold onto human resources. Assets are expensive to acquire, install, and maintain, and intellectual property and other confidential and sensitive information is vital to corporate operations. In addition, business operations are dependent on the integrated systems and processes that make up the infrastructure; these can potentially disrupt or shut down operations, turning into unnecessary costs, delays, backlogs, and, in some instances, loss of revenue or disgruntled employees. Finally, the laws and best practices of the industry require the protection of resources, assets, facilities, systems, networks, functions, and information so that if they are compromised, disrupted, injured, damaged, or destroyed, there is the potential for criminal consequences and civil liability.

The Many Faces of Vulnerability Creep-in

Vulnerability creep-in simply does not happen. It is created! It is a cancer of inexperience, a weak management knowledge base and the inability to grasp the basic but crucial principles and philosophies of security. This cancer hibernates in the bowels of organizations—sometimes for years. It stays dormant and undetected in the darkest corners of a corporation until a major disruptive event occurs.

John Sullivant

Top Takeaways

- Understand management decisions and other actions that influence security resilience
- Understand the implications of weak management and leadership
- Discover the impact deficiencies and weaknesses have on security operations
- Uncover performance weaknesses that influence security abilities and capabilities
- Learn how human and technology performance inadequacies degrade security operations

Overview

Vulnerability creep-in should never happen, but it does, and it appears throughout the industry with overwhelming regularity. This cancer not only encompasses security hardware and software technology deficiencies but also canvases a management culture that stifles creativity, initiative, modernization, and competency.

Vulnerability Creep-in Eludes Many Security Professionals

Vulnerability creep-in comes in various disguises and forms. Its many faces shock the very fiber of security practices and make it extremely difficult for many security professionals to recognize and detect its presence, even under the healthiest work relationships with executives and staff. It also defines where security sits on the executive management agenda.

Vulnerability creep-in presents a "triple threat" to security resilience. This axis comprises strategic security deficiencies, programmatic security weaknesses, and security competency inadequacies, as highlighted in Fig. 3.1. The listings represent the most frequently observed frustration-inducing behaviors I have seen in all my years of consulting, staff, and operating responsibilities. I find no industry sector or enterprise to be immune to this phenomenon.

At the very least, vulnerability creep-in holds the promise of damaging an organization's image, brand, and reputation. At the far end of the spectrum, vulnerability creep-in represents wave after wave of degradation of security resilience, and it has had that affect on many security organizations.

The grouping of an activity under a particular category is subjective, and it can easily qualify for placement in any one of the three main categories—as a strategic security deficiency, a programmatic security weakness, or a security competency inadequacy—or appear in more than one category depending on the conditions and circumstances during discovery. There is no doubt that, after reviewing the

Categories of Vulnerability Creep-in	Executive Summary Description of Less-Than-Acceptable Competencies
Strategic security deficiencies	▪ Actions that compromise the ethical behavior of people or the quality of services and products ▪ Belittling or humiliating those who suggest ethical standards or creative ideas ▪ Contradictory, conflicting, or confusing guidance ▪ Creating feelings of dread, helplessness, even betrayal in professional relationships ▪ Deliberately withholding information, support, admiration, cooperation, or collaboration ▪ Disrespect for others, leading to discomfort, frustration, anger, and more negative behavior ▪ Disruptive influence of inexperienced executives in security activities ▪ Failing in doing whatever it takes to achieve business and financial goals ▪ Executives struggle to grasp the essential principles of security planning ▪ Failing to accurately and realistically identify faulty thinking, mistakes, or stupidity ▪ Ignoring rogue behavior ▪ Intentionally misleading through acts of omission, commission, or negligence ▪ Lack of tough, appropriate, centralized compliance ▪ Leadership that allows managers and supervisors to overlook bad behavior ▪ Many executives exhibiting little knowledge of the "duty to care principle" ▪ Permitting shortcuts to be taken for a variety of obviously questionable reasons ▪ Senior management disengaging from its own leadership group ▪ A "shoot the messenger" mentality ▪ Some executives have no clue what security is about ▪ Staff remain loyal to executives for reasons other than objectivity ▪ Toleration of management decisions ▪ Weak security managers must enhance skill sets to match business culture ▪ Weak management and leadership
Programmatic security weaknesses	▪ Shifting blame, creating separation, distance, and disappoint ▪ Corporate culture influences security practices and competency ▪ High turnover takes a toll on historical perspective ▪ Ineffective planning and development plagues many security organizations ▪ Failing or refusing to acknowledge mistakes and errors in judgment ▪ Making unilateral engineering decisions without input or approval from security ▪ Many security professionals lead from behind ▪ Poor decision making based on fallible, erroneous, or incomplete data, or misguided analysis ▪ Protocols are poorly constructed, poorly written, and difficult to understand and follow ▪ Security compensatory measures are not widely used ▪ Security creditability and competency hang in the balance ▪ Security design, engineering, and technology application need improvement ▪ Security planning, policies, and practices lack strategic vision, balance, and purpose ▪ Security organizations are vulnerable to poor leadership and management ▪ Security roles, responsibilities, and accountability are often blurred
Security competency inadequacies	▪ Equipment and facility shortfalls degrade security capability ▪ Immature security design development practices ▪ Security force and other personnel inadequacies ▪ Security technologies and their applications that hinder security capabilities

Figure 3.1 Categories of vulnerability creep-in and an executive summary description of less-than-acceptable competencies.

lists and assessing your own unique organizational business relationships with other business units, you may consider placing selected topics under a different category.

While conventional problem-solving approaches mostly focus on external sources to identify problems, I suggest that in many instances we should turn our focus inward to address crucial factors associated with "insider threat" probabilities. In chapter The Cyber Threat Landscape, I talk about human fallacies. Fallacies may include one or more of the following:

- Processes, protocols, and security practices
- Responsible managers and decision makers who guide, direct, and control the destiny of corporate security
- Individuals who lack the ability to fully grasp the essential principles of security
- Leadership that constantly disengages from the problem-solving process
- Gatekeepers who are bottlenecks to progress and who either delay or block security improvement initiatives or prevent access to chief executives; these gatekeepers often are ignored or discarded as root causes
- Disgruntled, bored, or unhappy employees, and those with a misguided ego, who want to gain attention and demonstrate their capacity to do harm

In the next three major sections I summarize some of the most prominent case histories that directly create tension, uneasiness, and distrust within many security organizations. I have witnessed and reported on these observations throughout my career, counseled executive management on the affect these issues have on security operations and performance, and lectured on these topics at various forums. These topics include:

- strategic security deficiencies, which top the list as the most frequently occurring,
- programmatic security weaknesses, which rank second place, and
- human and technology inadequacies, which place third in the ratings.

Strategic Security Deficiencies Top the List

Strategic security deficiencies consist mostly of senior management decisions that demonstrate a narrow strategic vision and the exercise of leadership that is not clearly understood by others. They occur more frequently throughout the industry than do the other two categories, which I address shortly. These deficiencies have the potential to degrade security programs and often place enterprises in jeopardy with regulators, governing bodies, stakeholders, the community, or even the courts. Some case histories that fall within this category are described in what follows.

Some Executives Have No Clue What Security Is About

At several locations, chief executive officers had the perception that the corporate security program was effective, but in reality, these organizations were some of the worst ever seen (*lack of understanding or disinterest*). At many locations, a number of those in upper management had repeatedly opposed measures to improve various aspects of security initiatives (*inexperience or indifference, arrogance*). At yet other locations, systemic problems existed for years without executive management intervening to correct the situation. Failure was predictable—and should have been expected by management (*poor leadership and management interest, disengagement from the staff and operating managers*).

Some enterprises did not have in charge of security anyone with the competencies to bring all elements of a corporate-wide security program to bear. There were no clear lines establishing who was in charge of security (*weak leadership, poor management, acceptable business culture, lack of security principles and practices*).

The challenge here is to educate C-suite executives, their senior staff, and senior security professionals on the fundamental mission, purpose, and benefit a competent security organization has to offer, reinforcing basic principles of security management and leadership, as well as advanced management theories and best practices.

Executives Struggle to Grasp Essential Principles of Security Planning

The lack of executive leadership and weak management coupled with too many instances of poor competencies and judgments was sufficient cause to examine some organizations further. Areas preliminarily uncovered included integrity, ethics, subpar oversight of activities and the staff, and poor planning and capability to achieve expectations of what a professional security organization should look like and be (*poor management skill sets*). Little evidence was found to suggest that the current strategies adopted by several enterprises had or would lead to fundamental improvements to security (*poor management oversight, analytical skills*).

Executives Exhibit Little Knowledge of the "Duty to Care Principle"

Across the country, a strong defense team can argue that many enterprises exhibit a disregard for the "duty to care principle."[1]

Federal and state courts, including the U.S. Supreme Court, hold to this principle. These rulings hold organizations responsible and legally accountable for failing to take measures against acts or omissions that could cause harm, injury, or death within the workplace, thereby failing to provide a safe and secure work environment for employees. The principle not only applies to public and private enterprises alike, but also to individuals such as lawyers, doctors, accountants, police, and engineers, as well as to binding agreements between contracting parties.

---

[1] Because each of the 50 U.S. states is a separate sovereign free to develop its own tort law under the Tenth Amendment, there are several tests in each State for finding a duty of care in United States tort law. Several tests of agreeing or disagreeing with lower court rulings may also be found in U.S. Supreme Court rulings. Employees who have been assaulted on company grounds bring a large amount of lawsuits upon a corporation claiming insufficient or no security was available to provide for a safe and secure environment. Other leading tort actions include malfunctioning security technology, poor lighting, signage, inconsistent security practices and enforcement.

The standards of acceptable performance issued by the courts are measured by specific actions taken or not taken by business owners or those in charge of reducing risk exposure from foreseeable threats and hazards. The courts have ruled that the degree of care taken must be reasonable and prudent. Some unacceptable security practices declared by the courts include:

- not enforcing published safety and security guidelines, standards and other directives in a uniform or consistent manner
- providing a false sense of safety and security by posting signs containing false, erroneous, or misleading information
- installing security equipment that provides a sense of a safe and secure environment but is actually an inert component or not in a serviceable condition
- failure to maintain installed security systems to their design performance standard
- not using security equipment as it was intended

Of importance to chief executive officers is being given notice of a security condition by a consultant, auditor, or inspector and failing to take corrective action—until someone was harmed, injured, or killed, or until an employee lodges a complaint against the company; this has often been the basis for many lawsuits. Equally important, courts are increasingly holding corporate officers and even department managers personally liable for neglecting to take a proactive stance in developing and implementing reasonable and prudent measures to protect the workforce. The following paragraphs describe some case histories involving the duty to care principle.

In at least five Fortune 500 corporations, independent and separate consultants completed three to five security assessments and audits within a 5-year period. None of the recommendations received serious consideration by executive management, even though several recommendations from each security consultant were similar in nature (*arrogance, indifference, not important to management*).

At several locations, corrective actions were not based on complementing security operation–sensitive reporting timelines or on feedback from security practitioners and others having specialized expertise in sound research and security engineering principles (*arrogance*).

Five years after deferring the implementation of over 300 recommendations presented by 3 separate security consultant firms, one particular enterprise still had no timetable to even start planning and developing a sound security program (*indifference, lack of understanding of security needs*).

Many enterprises failed to move swiftly to correct previous security deficiencies. Several did not act in earnest until external political pressure was exerted (*not important to management*).

The Disruptive Influence of Inexperienced Executives in Security Activities

The inexperience of executive management and many senior staff members in security matters fosters a narrow and perhaps misguided application of security principles, techniques, methods, protocols, and technology. This in turn creates a corporate culture that builds barriers to carrying out effective security strategies. In my view, this situation implants unintentional (and undetectable) gaps in security programs. Here are some case histories to support this perspective.

Bottlenecks created through bureaucratic inefficiencies, insufficient follow-up, and weak management caused delays, slowed things down, and prevented the completion of actions that could have been done in a reasonable time, but were not (*poor management, inexperience, indifference*).

At some locations, most corrective actions were only symbolic in nature and did not contribute to enhancing security resilience. Other actions were implemented only because of external political pressure from city officials and community groups, and this distracted the enterprise from pursuing practical and workable security solutions (*weak management and leadership*).

Failure resulting from underestimating the range and difficulty of obstacles that were encountered suggested a lack of strategic vision and expertise to manage security activities at many locations (*inexperience, poor planning*).

Many Security Professionals Lead from Behind

At many locations, a clear trend of ineffectiveness, inefficiency, and lack of security leadership became detrimental to the security organization. Many security strategies lack purpose and consistency, and were doomed to fail from the start, which should have been obvious (*inexperience, lack of professional development, weak visionary skills*).

Weak Security Managers Must Enhance Skill Sets to Match the Business Environment

I have always had a concern for security directors and security managers who lack the basic skill sets to influence, coach, and teach decision makers and staff, and those who are not fully delegated the authority or given the resources and funding to carry out the corporate security charter. In several instances the security organization's inability to complete actions because of dependent internal departments was a factor contributing to delays in completing many initiatives. In many enterprises a strong, clear, and distinct security policy outlining business unit responsibilities, coupled with executive management support, could have prevented all, if not most, of the findings we reported.

Programmatic Security Weaknesses Rank Second Place

Programmatic security weaknesses reflect weak leadership, incomplete or poor planning with no vision for program or system integration, and poor decision-making based on fallible, incomplete, or outdated information. Programmatic security weaknesses rank number two as the most frequently reoccurring observations. These weaknesses:

- affect the ability and capability of a security organization to perform its critical operational tasks—deterrence, delay, prevention, protection, detection, assessment, response, and recovery—and contribute to the weakening of security resilience more than any other security activity
- may place entire enterprises in jeopardy with regulators, governing bodies, and the courts or result in stakeholders loosing confidence in an enterprise's ability to provide a safe and secure environment and protect their capital investment
- are often caused by actions that are outside the reach of the security director to resolve without external support and cooperation

Security Units are Vulnerable to Poor Leadership and Management

I was astonished that so many security organizations lack the ability and capability to fulfill their charter. In general, too many corporate security organizations are a mess, and leadership does not show much resolve to fix things. One particular organization was "in crisis."

- There were numerous management deficiencies in employee discipline, and the simplicity of directions given required improvement.
- Too often, the organization transitioned back and forth between policy fads and the excessive and unnecessary pressuring influence of the "political climate."

Security Creditability and Competency Hangs in the Balance

Those enterprises without a security leadership element assigned responsibility, authority, and accountability for planning, coordinating, developing, and implementing an integrated security program could not demonstrate the ability and capability to:

- exhibit strong security leadership
- perform adequate security assessments and threat and vulnerability analyses
- design, develop, coordinate, and implement next-generation security strategies
- identify and correct ineffective security practices
- develop and implement workable and practical security emergency response plans
- effectively measure and evaluate security performance

Moreover, these organizations have non-security-type personnel planning, developing, and implementing security programs, including writing security plans, policies, and protocols that do not meet acceptable industry standards. Many of the security missions had become muddled over the years and suffered from poor leadership, a lack of accountability, and an inefficient organizational structure. Strong executive leadership to reestablish credibility could have solved many security problems, both actual and perceived, at these locations.

High Turnover Rates Take a Toll on Historical Perspective

Change in management or high employee turnover has reached critical mass for many security organizations. It is difficult for these enterprises to hold onto good people for an extended time, and at times it is equally difficult to rid the ranks of subpar performers. With a rush of new blood into an organization, several trends begin to appear.

- One is the gradual loss of corporate memory and experience, or the value of lessons learned.
- Things get lost in the shuffle or forgotten.
- New blood is eager to establish a "stake" in the organization and the focus is on a personal agenda, discarding protocols, processes, and practices that have served organizations well.

The restructuring of several enterprises involving changes in the business culture and its goals, or changes in processes and protocols, may create anxiety, tension, and even mistrust among and between managers and the workforce, and, in particular, between the security organization and other departments.

At several sites, collaborating with the security organization early in the decision-making process would have given the security staff time to evaluate the impact of decisions on preserving the integrity of corporate security, and to design security strategies and solutions to accommodate changes in a timely and orderly manner without jeopardizing overall corporate security.

Ineffective Planning and Development Plagues Security Organizations

At many locations, improvements had not created the anticipated results, and no midcourse corrective actions were introduced in the hope of finding something else that might work (*poor management and planning*). In addition, security planning, coordination, development, and implementation were weak or lacking across a wide spectrum of security activity (*poor planning*).

The security planning effort should be led by a senior security professional who works in concert with operational personnel and those in other disciplines. For large corporations, the enterprise security director should take advantage of the skill sets a qualified security consultant brings to the table. This was not the case in many security organizations. To correct this situation, a security-conscious planning strategy is indispensable to interfacing all the aspects of security enhancements in an orchestrated and deliberate manner. This could have best been achieved if security planning involved:

- the act of viewing or envisioning the physical arrangements and functional interfaces of resources, activities, processes, facility space planning, and security design planning into an integrated whole to support security operations;
- a balanced mix of physical, electronics, information, cyber security, personnel, communications, operations and security principles that encompass prevention and protection techniques, as well as detection, assessment, response, and recovery capabilities; and
- identifying and determining the applicable standards of performance, regulatory mandates, and other obligations enterprises voluntarily subscribe to or are obligated to subscribe to.

These cumulative operational benchmarks are what build the platform on which security design planning[2] begins.

Security Planning, Policies, and Practices Lack Strategic Vision, Balance, and Purpose

At a few locations, some managers spend more time defending the status quo than explaining processes and their rationale; or they take more time to answer questions from or collect data for the investigative team to review, and less time implementing what may be valid recommendations for improving their operations (Broder, 2007, pp. 251).

Recommendations implemented in a piecemeal or indiscriminate fashion rather than in a systematic and logical manner lead to the continuing deterioration of program effectiveness, produce significant cost overruns from original project estimates, and eventually become counterproductive to achieving security strategies, goals, and objectives (Sullivant, 2007, pp. 206).

Protocols are Poorly Constructed, Poorly Written, and Difficult to Understand

In this category, I most often see obsolete and cumbersome protocols and incomplete and ineffective security plans—particularly security emergency plans—and virtually no formal security event-driven response and recovery procedures (*poor management and communications skills*). At most locations, security plans and security emergency response plans lack specified actions to be taken (*poor management & planning skills*).

Security Compensatory Measures Are Not Widely Used

I am convinced that few industry leaders have no firm grasp of the security compensatory measures concept or the options available to implement them. An experienced security director, however, does (or should) possess this knowledge and knows (or should know) instinctively how to help the corporation benefit from the use of such actions. Whenever security is significantly degraded, corrective actions should be implemented to reduce the vulnerability gap created by such loss.

For example, if automated access controls at a particular entry point malfunction, placing a guard or area representative at the entry checkpoint to verify the identity of persons before they enter the area is a comparable temporary compensatory measure until the system can be repaired. Another alternative may be closing the portal pending equipment repairs and diverting the population to another entry point.

Another example is providing portable emergency lighting systems for high-security areas to compensate for the loss of perimeter or area lighting, should standard

---

[2] Security planning and security design planning are often inappropriately used as synonyms when in fact each represents different disciplines and education, significant variances in competencies and different responsibilities, as well as authority and accountability.

backup power supplies or emergency generators not be available. Most sites visited did not have a compensatory measures program (*inexperience*).

Security Design, Engineering, and Technology Application Need Improvement

In several instances, in-house engineering departments made unilateral design decisions without the input or the approval of security organizations. After reviewing schematics and other engineering data, and running several functional tests on particular security systems, I am convinced that design teams could have produced reliable, quality designs to support operational needs had design groups "teamed" their way into the final decision-making process, rather than arbitrarily make unilateral design decisions of their own accord. I was shocked to discover the number of security managers who admitted they were not given the opportunity to participate in the design review process or sign off on the design, or who had not seen the design before construction began. In most instances I find that design development and the installation of security systems begin without the benefit of defined formal security system parameters, performance standards, training, and logistics and maintenance considerations (*poor management skills, inexperience*).

At several locations, the practice of installing security systems in piecemeal fashion, with system integration scheduled to be completed in future years as a retrofit project, was the norm. This strategy—approved by executive management—did not consider the impact this installation approach would have on the ability and capability of the security organization to perform its critical mission. The unilateral decision by the engineering department (without the approval of the security director) placed affected enterprises and security organizations in great jeopardy, ignoring the primary reason for the urgency behind the security upgrades (*poor management and planning skills*).

Corporate Management Culture Influences Security Practices and Competencies

Many diversified enterprises practice a management approach in which each division, directorate, or department is a separate operating entity within the corporation, with significant autonomy to conduct its business affairs, including security, as it sees fit. This management approach is sometimes referred to as the "stovepipe mentality" or "silo management" approach.

These organizations are hierarchical in nature and operate in "silos." They seem reluctant to report problems up the chain of command, are skittish about putting security concerns in writing, and have a general bureaucratic resistance to change (*corporate business culture*).

- Decisions must percolate up the chain of command. These are discussed and analyzed at varying levels of management, and then a decision is handed down. The process is time-consuming and often cumbersome, with little direct interaction between the "doer," the planner, and the decision maker(s).

- Under this management model, security is the inherent responsibility of selected staff members—none of whom are security professionals or have any background in the application of security principles, techniques, methods, or technology. In almost all cases executive management has even less experience and expertise to pass judgment on the staff's security work—a recipe for predictable failure.
- Typically, these corporations have no formal corporate security organization in place with the proper authority, responsibility, and accountability to execute leadership, direction, and oversight of security programs or to provide guidance on security matters to respective business units. Under this management approach:
  - The significance of threats are usually minimized or underestimated because there is no corporate threat profile or corporate-wide priorities to establish, develop, and implement security strategies or to prioritize the allocation of resources and funding to protect the most critical assets. Management actions to implement protective measures often are based on incomplete or erroneous information or misguided analysis.
  - Security and security-related roles and responsibilities are often blurred and may be duplicated or most likely overlooked, creating cascading ineffective or inappropriate results, including contradictory, conflicting, and confusing guidance.
  - Many enterprises require the respective business units to pay directly for security services provided. This approach is often doomed to fail—and this should have been obvious to executive management from the start.

Human and Technology Inadequacies Rate Third Place

Human and technology inadequacies rank third in the most frequently noted observations. These inadequacies can taint a corporation's brand, stain its image, blemish its reputation, and cause stakeholders to lose confidence in the entity's commitment to excellence. While these inadequacies occur less frequently than strategic deficiencies and programmatic weakness, they do represent the "public face" of a security organization and a corporation. They have a much larger influence in protecting image, brand, and reputation than strategic deficiencies and programmatic weaknesses because they directly influence the overall standing of corporate security programs and relate to operational matters that are easily visible to the public and the news media.

The following sections describe case histories that highlight some of the most prominent inadequacies I have observed.

Security Force and Other Personnel Shortcomings

In several instances, responsible individuals in the security organization ignore or even cover up security breaches and other inappropriate behavior simply to reduce the need to report incidents and prepare reports (*ethical and integrity issues*). Office checks completed after hours are either ineffective or are not being performed, even though they were reported as accomplished (*poor management oversight*).

Several guard service agreements are written in broad general terms and failed to address essential elements of the services to be performed (*weak contract administrative and management skills*). In addition, many contract guards fail to meet stated minimum employment requirements, including qualifications, education, and competencies to perform to expectations (*weak management and leadership skills*).

Security Technologies and Applications Hinder Security Competency

Disparate security systems exist throughout the industry in all business sectors, making detection, assessment, and response difficult, and in many locations making it impossible to accomplish this in a timely manner (*budget constraints, poor technical management oversight*). At some locations CCTV cameras are not synchronized for call-up and recording when sensors and access control devices are activated (*ineffective technical management oversight, poor design*).

Security Design Development Practices are Immature

The goal of the security design phase is to develop sufficient technical and engineering data to demonstrate that the physical features, infrastructure, electronic security systems, and other support elements integral to the security design meet the established system design and performance specifications. These elements include human-factors engineering, technical interfaces, interoperability, supportability, dependability, control room and console layout, and other crucial system features and capabilities such as system integrity and survivability.

The prime objective of security design planning is to ensure that it supports time-sensitive and time-dependent security operational requirements. Security matters are urgent when time is the driving force or is used as one, when the loss of time has real consequences, or when time may be running out. For instance, it is important for senior management and engineering staff to acknowledge that the display, announcement and assessment of alarms create a nonnegotiable, distinct, time-sensitive demand window (3–5 s) for a system operator to react to the validity and severity of an event or transaction that triggers an alarm. This time demand calls for the finite integration of design deployment and technology application that does not hinder, hamper, or slow the capability of a security organization to detect, assess, and respond to security events. Few security systems have this performance capability (*poor design & design management*).

A qualified engineer with previous experience in developing security designs should lead the design-planning phase. This engineer must work under the guidance and oversight of a security professional and must interact with the security staff.

Equipment and Facility Shortfalls Degrade Security Capability

Many older security facilities were designed using some combination of volunteer security design criteria, except for compliance with the National Electrical Code and other municipal codes. Most remaining design criteria are based on design features adopted from similar facilities or offered by the security organization and accepted by the design engineer. Newly constructed or recently modified facilities show evidence that designs incorporated information gleaned from open-source general threat statements and appropriate industry facility design criteria.

Conclusions

Vulnerability creep-in is a cancer of inexperience, a weak management knowledge base, and the inability to grasp the basic but crucial principles of security. It exists for many and varied reasons but mostly results from the cumulative effects of the festering consequences of management's actions:

- Inability to recognize the diversified threat, vulnerability, and the consequences of loss
- Inability to grasp essential principles or prevention and protection concepts, as well as time-sensitive and time-dependent security conditions
- Fallible decision-making and poor or near-reckless security planning
- Exercise of weak or poor security leadership or negligent management
- "Head-in-the-sand syndrome" whereby management ignores security issues or fails to act on security matters

Many factors affect the semblance of vulnerability creep-in: apathy, arrogance, conceit, complacency, indifference, insensitivity, and ignorance, among others. The phenomena of strategic deficiencies occur more frequently throughout the industry than do programmatic weaknesses and performance inadequacies. A major strategic deficiency can degrade a security program and place an enterprise in serious jeopardy with regulators, governing bodies, stakeholders, the community, or even the courts.

Programmatic weaknesses, while equally important, rank as the second most frequently reoccurring observations. Programmatic weaknesses affect the ability and capability of a security organization to perform its critical operational tasks (deterrence, delay, prevention, protection, detection, assessment, response and recovery) and, more than any other security activity, contribute to the weakening of security resilience.

Competency inadequacies rank third among the most frequently noted observations. These inadequacies can taint a corporation's brand, stain its image, blemish its reputation, and cause stakeholders to lose confidence in the entity's commitment to excellence. While these inadequacies occur less frequently than strategic deficiencies and programmatic weakness, they do represent the "public face" of a security organization and a corporation. In many instances, these inadequacies have a much greater impact on protecting image, brand, and reputation than strategic deficiencies and programmatic weakness because they directly influence the overall effectiveness of corporate security programs. Operational matters are easily visible to the public and the news media.

A security-conscious planning strategy is indispensable to interfacing all the aspects of security enhancements in a deliberate manner. The approach involves security planning, facility space planning, and security design planning. Security planning and security design planning are often inappropriately used as synonyms, when in fact each represents different disciplines and education, significant variances in competencies and different responsibilities, as well as authority and accountability.

The challenge for executive management is to remove the barriers and obstacles that impair the modernization of security programs and commit to advancing corporate security, with the aim of providing a more safe and secure work environment for employees, visitors, and the general community.

The Evolving Threat Environment

4

Because variables differ from one asset to another, and from one location to another, and from one business interest to another, and from time to time, no one set of security solutions can apply to the protection of all assets.

John Sullivant

Top Takeaways

- Advance your knowledge of the global, national, and local threat environments
- Understand the complexities of an all-hazards threat environment
- Become familiar with threats of significant concern to both the United States and U.S. corporations and other entities
- Distinguish between international, domestic, homegrown, and insider threats
- Recognize the merging threats from transnational criminal organizations and insider threat
- Become familiar with significant modes of attack

Overview

Understanding the Business Environment and Its Challenges

In today's risk-averse business world, the dynamics of evolving threats to critical infrastructure and key assets have proven to be daunting. Since businesses have unique characteristics and requirements, they also have unique assets that contribute to business operations. In high-threat environments, these threats are fluid and can worsen rapidly (Sullivant, 2007 pp. 55–84).

Understanding the Threat Environment and Its Challenges

In the post–Cold War environment, terrorist activity has moved away from government targets and has placed its sights on commercial targets. Business infrastructures and assets are much softer targets than government facilities, and adversaries see them as attractive targets that require little investment but produce massive destructive affects. The economic and psychological impact of destroying the civilian elements of the national infrastructure is more devastating than damaging a single government or military facility. Large numbers of people and business establishments become the victims of a single attack, and cascading collateral damage can be significant (Sullivant, 2007 pp. 19).

Most recently, activists and terrorists minded individuals and groups have selected even softer targets such as elementary schools, college campuses, sports arenas, open plaza's and shopping malls, drive by shooting of restaurants, stores, and other places of public gathering, and even business holiday parties. The only rule these perpetrators have is cause dramatic death and havoc of their choosing, timing and place.

The horrific terrorist attacks in Paris and San Bernardino, Calif., have vaulted terrorism and national security to become the American public's top concern. As the global Islamic Jihad movement expands, Americans continue to fear that the United States is becoming more vulnerable to jihadist attacks. FBI Director James Comey has said the Bureau is investigating ISIS-related activity in all 50 states—and that ISIS is recruiting here "24 hours a day."

What You Should Know About Terrorist Plots

James B. Comey, Director of the FBI testified before the Senate Committee on Homeland Security and Government Affairs on October 8, 2015 that the threat of terrorism to the United States is diversified and more aggressive as in previous years. Here are some recent examples of uncovered plots.

- Mexico–Texas border: At least 10 Islamic State of Iraq (ISIS) fighters were caught crossing the Mexican border into Texas in October 2014. Four were arrested.[1]
- A sophisticated international narco-terror ring with national connections from El Paso to Chicago to New York was uncovered in October 2014. Undisclosed numbers were arrested. These men met with two others in Anthony, New Mexico, to discuss the movement of drugs, money, and people in the United States in March 2014. Two men connected to the narco-terror ring had planned in 2009 a Chicago truck bombing that was thwarted. In 2010–2011 they planned two additional bomb plots targeting oil refineries in Houston and Fort Worth. Fellow conspirators at three mosques in El Paso further planned the plots. One of the men smuggled explosives and weapons from Fort Bliss in concert with corrupt U.S. Army soldiers and government contractors.[2]
- New York: a plot to make explosives was foiled in 2015
- Minneapolis, Minnesota: a local mosque bred homegrown terrorists to fight for ISIS, 2014
- London, England: plot to behead British citizens in public, 2014
- Washington, DC: plot to destroy the capitol building, 2011
- New York City: plot to explode a car bomb at Times Square, 2010
- Detroit, Michigan: plot to blow up Northwest Airlines Flight 253, 2009
- London, England: plot to bomb underground subway and bus, 2005
- Newark, New Jersey: plot to buy a "dirty bomb" and smuggle hand-held missiles into the United States, 2005

[1] Judicial Watch, Vol., December 20, 2014, Washington, DC.
[2] Ibid.

- New York City: plot to blow up the subway station at Herald Square, 2004
- New York City: plot to use tourist helicopters to attack city, 2004
- Britain, United Kingdom: plot to attack Heathrow International Airport, 2004
- Madrid, Spain: plot to blow up a high-speed train, 2004
- Madrid, Spain: plot to blow up the city's main subway station, 2002
- Los Angeles, California: plot to attack Los Angeles International Airport during the millennium, 2000
- Los Angeles, California: plot to destroy the U.S. Bank Tower building by aircraft, 1995
- Los Angeles, California: plot to blow up 12 U.S. aircraft over the Pacific, 1995
- Chicago, Illinois: plot to destroy the Sears Tower building by aircraft, 1995
- Paris, France: plot to fly a jet airliner into the Eiffel Tower, 1994
- New York City: plot to blow up tunnels and bridges throughout Manhattan, 1993

Additional Facts About Other Terrorist Activities (2013–2015)

- The FBI reports that more than 400 Americans are fighting on the battlefield for ISIS.
- ISIS killed 39 on the beaches of Tunisia and another 27 in Kuwait.
- ISIS beheaded two Frenchmen in France.
- Conspirators were arrested in Canada for accessing computer networks of Boeing, Lockheed Martin, and other defense contractors and stealing secret military aircraft and weapons systems data.
- Walter and Christina Liew and retired DuPont engineer Roger Menagerie were convicted of selling DuPont trade secrets; 20 additional defendants pleaded guilty to the same charges.
- Radicals were arrested in London, accused of trying to recruit westerners to join ISIS.
- A 19-year-old woman was sentenced to 4 years for helping a terrorist group.
- Three men were charged with serving as secret agents for Russia.
- A CIA officer was convicted of espionage.
- Yemen fell to terrorist attacks; the president and cabinet members resigned.
- Major portions of Syria and Iraq are occupied by ISIS terrorist insurgents.
- Two New York Police Department officers were killed in a parked patrol car.
- A man with an axe attacked four New York Police Department officers in public.
- A lone gunman shot two Seattle police officers.
- A gunman killed two deputy sheriffs and wounded one in California.
- A Seattle student killed one student, wounded four others, and killed himself.
- Terrorists assassinated French cartoonists and killed several others in Paris.
- Terrorists were arrested in London and Paris.
- Women were beheaded in the workplace by a disgruntled coworker.
- A terrorist was caught at the U.S./Canadian border driving a vehicle loaded with explosives.
- Weapons and explosives were found buried on two nuclear power plant sites.
- A California power grid was attacked by armed adversaries.

In the last month (November, 2015) terror attacks that left 130 dead in Paris and hundreds wounded, 43 dead in Beirut and took down a Russian airliner with 224 people aboard in addition to at least 20 hostages killed and injured numerous in an attack on a luxury hotel in the capital of Mali, Bamako, and most recently San Bernardino, California, have made the entire world horribly aware that the Islamic State does not only seek to establish a caliphate in Syria and Iraq, but also is beginning to export its monstrous savagery across Western civilization.

The Threat Landscape Is Diversified and Sophisticated

Protecting Critical Infrastructure and Key Assets Remains a Pressing Concern

During the past three decades security professionals have focused on traditional threats such as joyriding, petty thievery, opportunistic crime, planned criminal activity, the protection of assets and people, and special threats by relying on a token physical security presence backed up by insurance coverage to recoup losses. Since the events of 9/11 and the more recent rise of transnational criminal organizations, activists, extremist and hate groups, terrorist and criminal activities have become more complex, daring and unstable and are a growing threat to our national economy and national security.[3]

Globalization presents a new dynamic of hard-to-imagine threats: transnational organized crime and domestic crime; domestic and international terrorism, including state-sponsored cyber crimes, cyber terror, and cyber warfare; weather-related catastrophes; and pandemics and civil unrest, to mention a few.[4]

Today's challenges call for diversified strategies to guard against multiple threats to reduce business risk exposure. Today, the corporate security organization must protect against traditional threats as well as high-technology data and economic information; competitive business strategies and safeguarding proprietary information; and new levels of terror, brutality, and intimidation dominated by chaos, hidden and diverse enemies, and ongoing threats in our society.[5] In spite of distinct differences in the nature of threats, knowledge, and experience, proactive and preventative security planning can strengthen resilience in many areas, including the use of effective and enforceable protocols, human factors training, abnormal behavior patterns, and understanding adverse conditions and events. Chief executive officers (CEOs) are counting on their security directors to guide them through inevitable risk-prone situations and offer practical and workable security solutions.

The foundation of all prevention and protection programs is based on the analysis of reliable and dependable intelligence information and professional security experience. This platform is the threat estimate profile (or threat forecast) that essentially guides the decision-making process for selecting mitigation strategies and solutions to counter specific threats. Understanding the threat environment and how it influences the business operating environment is crucial if CEOs are to make the tough choices for their companies.

The FBI and Homeland Security officials predict that the 21st Century will usher in new threats. At this moment, from a national perspective, the two most likely and serious threats are cyber threats and biological and chemical threats.[6] In this chapter

---

[3] The National Strategy for Homeland Security: U.S. Department of Homeland Security, Washington, DC, 2007.

[4] Szady, D.W., Vice President, Guardsmark (FBI Assistant Director, Retired), Security Management, April 2014.

[5] The National Strategy for Homeland Security: U.S. Department of Homeland Security, Washington, DC, 2007.

[6] U.S. Department of Homeland Security, Washington, DC, 2013.

I talk about biological and chemical threats, as well as other significant threats and share some case histories. In chapter The Cyber Threat Landscape, I talk about cyber threats.

Biological and Chemical Threats Are a Great Concern to the United States

Seized ISIS Laptop Reveals Terrorist Group's Bio Weapons Attack Plan

In 2014, a captured ISIS laptop revealed documents expressing ISIS's biological weapons attack plan.[7] Hidden in several folders on the laptop were 35,347 files containing documents and speeches of leading jihadi clerics, videos of Osama bin Laden, and practical training on how to carry out deadly campaigns. The laptop also contained documents about how to build and use biological weapons.

Following the attacks on September 11, 2001, in October and November 2001, anthrax was distributed in envelopes through the U.S. postal system, causing 5 deaths and 21 injuries (Sullivant, 2007, pp. 25). In March 2002, U.S. Special Forces discovered a partly constructed laboratory in Afghanistan, in which al Qaeda planned to develop anthrax and other biological assets, including how to use these as weapons (Sullivant, 2007, pp. 26).

Of special note, the result of a naturally spreading disease and bioterrorism are the same. Most frightening to law enforcement officials is the fact that deadly biological agents can be delivered across international boundaries with little or no chance of detection. A few ounces of smallpox virus—or worse, a genetically altered, highly contagious virus for which there may be no known vaccine—can kill thousands if not millions of people in only days (Sullivant, 2007, pp. 27).

Terrorist Groups Want Chemical Weapons Capability

Security analysts have concerns about terrorist groups that continue to seek castor beans to make the poison ricin or obtain sarin, which might be used in subway attacks in America and other countries, and possibly combined with explosives to disperse the toxins.

In 1995, the Aum Shinrikyo Japanese doomsday cult used sarin in a Tokyo subway, killing 13 people and injuring 5,000, causing widespread pandemonium. In 1994 and 1995 the cult used VX to assassinate four enemies of the cult, but only one of the individuals died (Sullivant, 2007, pp. 26). In 2014 Syria used chemical weapons on its own population in the midst of its civil war, and in 2015 ISIS used captured chemical weapons on the Syrian population.

Nuclear Weapons May Go to the Highest Bidder

Terrorists continue attempts to acquire the means to make or buy nuclear weapons through their own resources and underground connections (Sullivant, 2007, pp.

---

[7] Seized ISIS laptop reveals terror group's bio weapons attack plan, August 30, 2014: dnaindia.com.

26–27).[8] In 1993 al Qaeda agents tried repeatedly and without success to purchase highly enriched uranium in Africa, Europe, and Russia, and in particular from Pakistani scientists and a nuclear power plant in Bulgaria.[9]

The Russian Mafia has masterminded the theft, diversion, transportation, and distribution of nuclear materials outside the former territories of the USSR. Security agents in Turkey, Morocco, and South Africa seized weapons-grade nuclear materials known to belong to Russia. Relaxed border crossing in European countries has made the movement of nuclear materials from former Soviet territories through these nations easier to accomplish and more difficult to detect. Hospitals in Eastern Europe have reported alarming rates of radiation poisoning and death among smugglers trafficking in nuclear materials (Sullivant, 2007, pp. 25).

As early as 1981, Iraq's drive to obtain nuclear weapons was set back when Israeli jets destroyed the Osiris nuclear reactor outside Baghdad. When United Nations inspectors dismantled a revitalized Iraqi nuclear weapons program in 1991, they found that Iraq was probability within 2 to 3 years of having enough highly enriched uranium to build a nuclear bomb (Sullivant, 2007, pp. 25).

In January 2003 British officials found documents in the city of Heart, Afghanistan, that described al Qaeda's nuclear aspirations along with their desire to obtain dirty bombs (Sullivant, 2007, pp. 26).

International Terrorism

ISIS or the Islamic State of Iraq and the Levant

The terrorists known as ISIS—the Islamic State of Iraq and the Levant (ISIL)—are the greatest international terrorist threat the world faces today. ISIS emerged a decade ago as a small Iraqi affiliate of al Qaeda, one that specialized in suicide bombings. Today it is the largest, richest terrorist organization in history. Its rise in Iraq and Syria, Boko Haram in Nigeria, al-Qaeda in the Islamic Maghred (AQIM) in Mali, and al Qaeda in the Arabian Peninsula (AQAP) show that the jihadist movement is a relentless enemy that is constantly finding new ways to cause massive harm and destruction. ISIS is engaged in ethnic cleansing, imminent genocide, dividing captured families, forcing men to choose between conversion and execution, raping women or taking them into slavery, and performing beheadings and mass executions, bank robbery, kidnapping, extortion, and black market oil sales. ISIS followers are ruthless, and their fanatical belief that they are the true leaders of the Muslim world and the head of all jihads makes them a formidable threat in the Middle East and a severe threat to the Western world. They want to create an Islamic state that includes all Muslims as a part of it, covering every aspect of life—a totalitarian project imposing its extreme version of Sharia law on subject populations. They are intolerant of all other views—including al Qaeda's—of how this should be accomplished. Their battleground has been in Syria and Iraq as they—unlike al Qaeda—have conquered and hold land. Their attacks have spread to Africa, Central Europe and the United States.[10]

---

[8] Szady, D.W., Vice President, Guardsmark (FBI Assistant Director, Retired), Security Management, April 2014.

[9] Ibid.

[10] Lipman, I.A., Founder and Chairman, Guardsmark, The Lipman Report, August 15, 2014.

al Qaeda

After 15 years, al Qaeda is well and still considering attacking America again. Top U.S. intelligence officials warn that al Qaeda poses an even greater challenge today because its franchises are much more globally dispersed and the organization recently has benefited from the massive leaks of U.S. intelligence information. These leaks, created by former National Security Agency contractor Edward Snowden, who is now a fugitive, provided al Qaeda, other terrorist groups and adversaries and Russia insight into U.S. intelligence sources, methods, and tradecraft.[11]

Cells and Sleeper Cells

The ranks of ISIS are filled with thousands of radicals from all over the world and from the remnants of al Qaeda and other terrorist groups who are willing to join their efforts to form an Islamic state, including radicals holding Western passports. At this time, recruitment of these individuals creates the ominous threat of "lone wolves" acting on their own initiative or at the behest[12] of ISIS to attack the West, its organizations, and its corporations at home and abroad. We have seen the testaments of this goal in the most recent Paris and San Bernardino attacks. In the wake of U.S. prisoner swaps with the Taliban, militant jihadism has been on the rise worldwide. Expect sleeper cells to get a wake up call. Attacks across the globe are expected, as mentioned in the chapter opening (Sullivant, 2007, pp. 20–22).

Numerous sleeper cells have been discovered in Great Britain, France, and other countries. Over 30 Islamic training compounds exist across the United States. Sleeper cells, consisting of people who have returned home after training with ISIS overseas, and fighting in Iraq and Syria are hiding in all parts of the country. These camps teach jihad against America, harbor fugitives, build weapon stockpiles, and train fighters. It is suspected that the Boston bombers were part of a 12-member terrorist sleeper cell.[13]

Every major terrorist organization in the Middle East has created significant infrastructure networks across America, Canada, Mexico, Europe, and Asia. The activities of these groups include recruiting, weapons training, bomb making, robbery, extortion, assassination, counterfeiting money and documents, and other criminal activities.[14]

Currently, the FBI has thousands of individuals in all 50 states either under surveillance or investigation for terrorist activity or for supporting terrorist groups.

Domestic Extremist Groups

The FBI's top six domestic extremists groups at this time are the Sovereign Citizen Movement, militia groups, white supremacy groups, abortion groups, animal rights groups, and environmental groups.[15]

---

[11] Lipman, I.A. Founder and Chairman, Guardsmark, The Lipman Report, September 15, 2014.

[12] Number of Jihadist Fighters Has Doubled Since 2010, Rand Corporation, June 4, 2014.

[13] The People, London, England, April 21, 2013.

[14] Patterns of Global Terrorism, U.S. Department of State, Washington, DC, 2004.

[15] Lipman, I.A., Founder and Chairman, Guardsmark, The Lipman Report, September 15, 2014.

The Sovereign Citizen Movement

This movement is a loose grouping of American complainants and financial scheme promoters who take the position that they are answerable only to their particular interpretation of common law and are not subject to any statutes or proceedings at the federal, state, or municipal levels. They do not recognize U.S. currency, and they believe they are free of any legal constraints.[16–19] They especially reject most forms of taxation as illegitimate.[20] Many members of the movement believe that the U.S. government is illegitimate.[21]

The Southern Poverty Law Center estimates that approximately 100,000 Americans are "hard-core sovereign believers," with another 200,000 just starting out by testing sovereign techniques for resisting everything from speeding tickets to drug charges.[22] A 2014 report by the National Consortium for the Study of Terrorism and Responses to Terrorism reported that a survey of law enforcement officials and agencies across America concluded that this movement was the single greatest threat to communities. Islamist extremists and militia/patriot groups round out the top three domestic threats to communities in America.[23–26]

Militia Groups

Militia organizations include paramilitary or similar groups organized to defend their rights and property against a tyrannical government.[27] While groups such as the Posse

---

[16] https://www.fbi.gov/news/stories/2010/april/sovereigncitizens_041310/domestic-terrorism-the-sovereign-citizen-movement.

[17] Johnson, Keven, "Anti-government 'Sovereign Movement' on the rise in U.S.", USA Today, March 30,2012.

[18] "Sovereign Citizen Suing State Arrested Over Traffic Stop", April 6, 2012, WRTV Indianapolis.

[19] https://en.wikipedia.org/wiki/Sovereign_citizen_movement.

[20] Carey, K., "To Weird for The Wire": How black Baltimore drug dealers are using white supremacist legal theories to confound the Feds," The Washington Monthly, Washington, DC (July 2008).

[21] MacNabb, J.J., "Context Matters: The Cliven Bundy Standoff–Part 3," Forbes Magazine, May 16, 2014.

[22] MacNab, J.J., "Sovereign Citizen Kane," Intelligence Report. Issue 139, *Southern Poverty Law Center*. Fall 2010.

[23] Parker, J., "Study: Greatest Terrorism Threat In America Not Al Qaeda, It's Right-Wing Sovereign Citizens," *addicting info.org*, August 3, 2014,

[24] Jessica R., "Sovereign citizen movement perceived as top terrorist threat," July 30, 2014, National Consortium for the Study of Terrorism and Responses Terrorism, College Park, Maryland, July 30, 2014.

[25] David C., Steve C., Jeremy C., Jack D., "Understanding Law Enforcement Intelligence Processes: Report to the Office of University Programs, Science and Technology Directorate, U.S. Department of Homeland Security," 4 July 2014, National Consortium for the Study of Terrorism and Responses to Terrorism (College Park, Maryland). The Consortium is a grant foundation funded by the U.S. Department of Homeland Security and various other federal agencies, private foundations and universities.

[26] The Ku Klux Klan (KKK) or just the Klan is the name of three distinct movements in the United States. They first played a violent role against African Americans in the South during the Reconstruction Era of the 1860s. The second was a very large controversial nationwide organization in the 1920s. The current manifestation consists of numerous small but unconnected groups that use the KKK name. They have all emphasized secrecy and distinctive costumes, all have called for purification of American society and all are considered right wing. All groups are classified as hate groups. It is estimated to have between 5,000 and 8,000 active members as of 2012.

[27] Mulloy, D., 2004. American Extremism: History, Politics and the Militia Movement, Routledge, U.K.

Comitatus existed as early as the 1980s,[28] the movement gained momentum after controversial standoffs with government agents in the early 1990s. By the mid-1990s, groups were active in all 50 states, with membership estimated at between 20,000 and 60,000.[29]

In April 2013 a militia group attacked a power grid in California.[30] The group entered an underground facility and vault of a power station through manholes, just off a freeway in San Jose, California. Strategically cutting telecommunications, telephone lines, and Internet cables, their objective was to sabotage communications, which would then delay response by authorities. Thirty minutes later, snipers opened fire on oil-filled cooling systems, and subsequently 17 transformers that funnel power to Silicon Valley began to fail. Electric-grid officials prevented a blackout by rerouting power around the downed station. It took crews a month to repair the station and get it up and running again.

White Supremacy Groups

White supremacists believe that white people are superior to people of other racial backgrounds and that whites should politically, economically, and socially govern nonwhites.[31] Different forms of white supremacism have different conceptions of who is considered white, and different white supremacists identify various racial and cultural groups as their primary enemy. In the United States the Ku Klux Klan (KKK) and other white supremacist groups such as Aryan Nations, The New Order, and the White Patriot Party are considered antisemitic.[32] The groups mentioned above and similar ones reside in the "twilight zone" between a conventional terrorist group and a conventional hate group (Sullivant, 2007, pp. 23).

Abortion Groups

The abortion extremist movement consists of a loosely affiliated network of individuals involved in criminal activity or advocating the use of force or violence in the furtherance of an ideology based around the issue of abortion rights and practices.[33] Abortion rights movements advocate for legal access to induced abortion services. Groups have demonstrated against clinics, bombed facilities, and killed employees and patients (Sullivant, 2007, pp. 23).

Animal Rights Groups

The primary organization leading this movement is the Animal Liberation Front, an international, underground, leaderless resistance that engages in illegal action in

[28] Pitcavage, M., 2001. Camouflage and Conspiracy: The Militia Movement From Ruby Ridge to Y2K, Institute for Intergovernmental Research. American Behavioral Scientist, http://abs.sagepub.com/content/44/6/957.abstract.

[29] Berlet, C., Lyons, M., Right-Wing Populism in America: Too Close for Comfort, Guilford, U.K. 2002.

[30] FBI Terrorist Task Force, FBI Field Office, Los Angeles, CA, April 2013.

[31] Wildman, S.M., Privilege Revealed: How Invisible Preference Undermines America, 87. New York Press, NY.

[32] Flint, C., Spaces of Hate: Geographies of Discrimination and Intolerance in the U.S.A. Routledge, London, England, 2004.

[33] Abortion Extremism: FBI Domestic Terrorism Operations Unit, Washington, DC, December 12, 2011.

pursuit of animal liberation. Activists remove animals from laboratories and farms, destroy facilities, arrange safe houses and veterinary care, and operate sanctuaries where the animals subsequently live. Within the United States, attacks in 2001 included the firebombing of a primate laboratory in New Mexico and a federal horse corral in California (Sullivant, 2007, pp. 23).

Environmental Groups: Case Histories

Environmental groups target logging facilities, real estate developers, and other organizations perceived to engage in activities that are detrimental to the environment. In 1998 the Earth Liberation Front firebombed a ski resort in Vail, Colorado, destroying $12 million in property. In 2003 it targeted car dealerships in California, damaging and destroying 125 sport utility vehicles. The Earth Liberation Front is a collection of autonomous individuals who use economic sabotage and guerrilla warfare to stop activities they perceive as exploiting and destroying the environment (Sullivant, 2007, pp. 23).

Transnational Criminal Organizations

Transnational criminal organizations have infiltrated every fiber of America's infrastructure and most other countries. They are the world's largest illicit social networks and present a clear and present danger to the national economy and national security of all governments. These criminal networks not only are expanding their operations, they also are diversifying their activities, resulting in a convergence of transnational threats that are becoming more complex, explosive, and destabilizing. Transnational organized crime is a cooperative activity between criminal groups in various nations, estimated to be a $2 trillion industry.[34]

Transnational Criminal Organization Structure

Transnational criminal groups include politicians, government officials, and executives who are nothing more than a new bread of sophisticated gangsters, mobsters, thugs, dope dealers, and terrorists who now seek to obtain global power, influence, and monetary and/or commercial gain by illegal means - rather than regional control of territory while protecting their activities through a transnational organizational structure and the exploitation of transnational commerce. The organization comprises countless international executives from varying backgrounds. A representative listing of the organization's membership includes:

- Russian mobsters who emigrated to the United States in the wake of the Soviet Union's collapse
- U.S. criminalheads
- groups from African countries
- Chinese tongs, Japanese boryokudan, and other Asian crime rings
- enterprises based in Eastern European nations such as Hungary and Romania

[34] Lipman, I.A., Founder and Chairman, Guardsmark, The Lipman Report, April 15, 2013.

- Mexican and Columbian drug cartels

Some of their criminal activities focus on:

- attempts to gain influence in government politics and transnational commerce
- buying off corrupt officials. Corruption is any abuse of power for private gain. It includes political wrongdoing, bribery of officials, mispresentation, fraud, procurement manipulation, and wrongful reporting. Bribery, corruption, and other white-collar crimes are not solely legal issues; they can have damaging effects on business organizations. This is why security must be the first line of defense of an organization's image, brand, and reputation.
- forging alliances with corrupt elements of governments to threaten governance
- influencing governments to exploit these relationships to further their interests
- penetrating state institutions to exploit differences between countries
- defrauding millions each year through various stock and financial frauds
- manipulating and monopolizing financial markets, institutions, and industries
- crime–terror–insurgency nexus, intimidation, kidnapping, and assassination
- disguising the pattern of corruption and violence through legitimate businesses
- trafficking drugs, humans, body parts, and endangered species
- trafficking weapons and nuclear materials
- money laundering and prostitution
- stealing intellectual property and cyber crime exploitation
- using power and influence to further criminal activities
- isolating themselves from detection, sanction, and prosecution

Radicalization Is a Growing Concern

As of this writing, more than 1500 Americans have crossed the threshold of American values to battle in the name of Islam. These American citizens operate under the radar and take on roles as clandestine "lone wolves" or join small groups, giving renewed emphasis to the insider threat. Some of these individuals have committed horrific crimes: killing police officers, beheading an Oklahoma woman, shootings at Fort Hood and in Chattanooga and Huston, and the bombing of the Boston Marathon, to mention only a few.

Since 9/11 more than 50 major plots involving 190 homegrown terrorists with ties to international terrorist groups have been exposed.[35] In July 2015, just before the Fourth of July weekend, the FBI reported arresting more than 20 individuals associated with a plan to attack New York City and several other cities. This radicalization process is gaining momentum and represents the greatest current challenge to counterterrorism we face today (Coolsaet, 2011, pp. 85). Most recently, the director of the FBI testified before Congress that the agency has on-going investigations in every state on the radicalization of U.S. citizens and others.

The Insider Threat

The insider adversary can be any trusted individual filling any position: managers, administrative staff, operations and maintenance personnel, security personnel,

[35] Szady, D.W., Vice President, Guardsmark (FBI Assistant Director, Retired), Security Management, April 2014.

vendors, and even part time workers. These persons may be active or passive, violent or nonviolent, and motivated by financial, vengeful, egotistical, psychotic, voluntary, or coercive considerations.[36,37]

The passive insider adversary commits no acts; he or she merely provides information to outsiders. The active insider adversary may be nonviolent and unwilling to use force against others, or be violent and willing to actively use force. Various insider abilities and capabilities can be used:

- Ability to perform routine tasks or to get authorization to perform special tasks
- Authority to exploit and influence processes, practices, and protocols
- Authorized access to work schedules and employees as sources of information
- Capability to use tools available in the work place
- Characteristics of critical assets, including asset vulnerability
- Supervision of or control of others
- Knowledge of security/control systems, work schedules, and assignments
- Known weaknesses and gaps in security planning, response, and recovery
- Opportunity to choose the time and place to commit an act over a span of time
- Opportunity to recruit and collude with others, both insiders and outsiders
- Specific details of enterprise operations, processes, practices, and policies

Attack Modes Make Planning and Response a Challenge

In this section I describe some threat modes to consider when planning your security activities as well as your event-driven emergency response and recovery procedures and training.[38]

Conventional Attacks Are the Preferred Method to Wreak Havoc

Improvised explosive devices; bomb attacks, assassinations, kidnappings, or ground assault attacks are normally referred to as conventional attacks.

Nonconventional Attacks Are in Their Embryonic Stage

Nonconventional attacks range from the use of weapons of mass destruction, such as anthrax and radiological materials, to cyber crimes, cyber terror, and cyber warfare. Attacks staged by hostile nation-states are aimed at damaging or destroying economic, trade, currency, and military stability. Transnational groups are bent on controlling the commercial or financial markets, including criminal activities such as corruption, extortion, and fraud.

---

[36] James, P. Chapter 22, "Insider Analysis." The Nineteenth International Training Course for the Physical Protection of Nuclear Facilities & Materials. Sandia National Laboratories & The International Atomic Emergency Agency, Albuquerque, NM, 2006.

[37] Murray, D.W., DOD Security System Analysis Department, Sandia National Laboratories, Albuquerque, NM; Biringer, B.E., Security Risk Assessment Department, Sandia National Laboratories, Albuquerque, NM: Defending Against Malevolent Insiders Using Access Controls (contributing authors). Wiley Handbook of Science & Technology for Homeland Security, John Wiley & Sons, NJ. 2008.

[38] Szady, D.W. Vice President, Guardsmark (FBI Assistant Director, Retired), Security Management, April 2014.

Vehicle Bombs

Vehicle bombs are the preferred weapon of use. Terrorists have been successfully using explosives in cars, trucks, and boats for years. In 1995, McVeigh and Nichols used a truck bomb to kill 168 people and injure 680 others in the Oklahoma City bombing. The blast destroyed or damaged 324 buildings within a 16-block radius, destroyed or burned 86 cars, and shattered glass in 258 nearby buildings, causing at least an estimated $652 million worth of damage. Faisal Shazhad attempted to detonate a vehicle bomb in Times Square in 2010.

Train Bombs

Train bombs have been used successfully in Madrid (2004), London (2005, 2013, 2014, and 2015), Mumbai (2006), and Egypt (2014). Muslims helped to foil a train bomb plot for U.S. Canadian-bound rail lines in 2013. Authorities foiled several suspected bombing plots against New York City subways.

Airplanes Used as Weapons of Mass Destruction

On September 11, 2001, terrorists hijacked four commercial aircraft and used these planes as weapons of mass destruction against the World Trade Center and the Pentagon. The attacks resulted in more than 3000 deaths and thousands of injuries, catastrophic losses in terms of property destruction and economic effects, as well as profound damage to public morale and the confidence of the nation. In addition to the loss of life and damage and destruction of property and buildings, thousands of vehicles and utility, transportation, telecommunications, and government services throughout the northeastern part of the nation sustained collateral damage. When the seven buildings that made up the World Trade Center complex collapsed, more than 29 surrounding high-rise buildings were either severely damaged or later condemned. Many stand empty to this day. Approximately 34,000 businesses and residences, and hundreds of government agencies, lost the capability to function and communicate for extended periods. The wave of destruction took with it over 300,000 voice lines and over 3 million data lines. Disruption of services occurred because various carriers had equipment collocated at the site that linked their networks to Verizon and other providers. In addition, a considerable amount of telecommunications traffic that originated and terminated in other areas but passed through this location was disrupted. AT&T's local network service in lower Manhattan was significantly disrupted following the attacks, which directly affected the operations of the world financial district, the stock exchange, and international banking operations. Electricity, water, and other services also were knocked out. Satellite links and underground cables were severed, disrupting communications for millions of other users in the northeast and mid-Atlantic states.[39]

---

[39] The National Strategy for the Physical Protection of Critical Infrastructure & Key Assets, U.S. Department of Homeland Security, Washington D.C. February 2003.

Piracy

During the 21st century, more than 2000 cases of piracy have been committed on the high seas. A single piratical attack affects maritime security, an economic interest of all nations, including the flag state of the vessel, the various nationalities of the seafarers taken hostage, regional coastal states, owners' states, and cargo destination and transshipment states. Such attacks undermine confidence in global sea lines of communication, weaken or undermine the legitimacy of states, threaten the legitimate revenue and resources of nations, cause an increase in maritime insurance rates and cargo costs, increase the risk of environmental damage, and endanger the lives of seafarers who may be injured, killed, or taken hostage for ransom.

Kidnapping

Kidnapping for ransom or assassination is a common occurrence across the globe, creating an enormous threat to American citizens and corporate executives. It is believed that in 2013 the Boko Haram was paid nearly $17 million in ransom from the French government. The U.S. Treasury Department estimates that $120 million in ransom flowed to such groups from 2004 to 2012.[40] The top countries for kidnapping and ransom are Mexico and Colombia. Mexico City ranks number one in the world, whereas Phoenix, Arizona, takes second place globally. Ransoms have become the main source of funding for terrorist groups.

Small Aircraft With Explosives

Rural airports are left largely unguarded; great destruction could be caused if airplanes are packed with explosives and flown into crowds or buildings.

Suicide Bombers

This mode of attack creates fear, panic, and death across the globe. A backpack or vest bomb in a concert, shopping mall, movie theater, restaurant, or other places where large groups gather would cause widespread panic and have a sizable financial impact because people may begin to avoid these destinations. Suicide bombers are a common weapon across the Middle East and bordering countries. This phenomenon, until recently, has not reached the shores of Western countries. During the November attack in Paris, three of the terrorists were suicide bombers, and exploded their vests. The San Bernardino attackers also had in their arsenal suicide vests. I am convinced that this tactic will soon come to the shores of the United States.

Radiological Bombs

A radiological weapon, or "dirty bomb," combines radioactive material with conventional explosives. Such bombs can be miniature bombs that fit in a suitcase or big bombs

[40] Lipman, I.A., Founder and Chairman, Guardsmark, The Lipman Report, August 15, 2014.

that fit in trucks, and they are designed to injure or kill by creating a zone of intense airborne radiation that could extend several city blocks. People in the immediate area would be killed, and radioactive materials would be dispersed into the air and reduced to relatively low concentrations. Jose Padilla, a U.S. citizen who trained in Pakistan with al Qaeda, attempted to build one in 2002. He was convicted of aiding terrorists.

According to a United Nations report, Iraq tested a one-ton radiological bomb in 1987 but gave up on the idea because the radiation levels it generated were not deadly enough. We know that the late Osama bin Laden attempted to purchase several suitcase bombs from contacts in Chechnya and Kazakhstan. Several international intelligence agencies have also reported that about 100 of these dirty bombs disappeared from Russian stockpiles in the early 1990s and have yet to be found.[41]

Other Criminal Activity Is Also a Threat

Threats to Personnel Safety

There are about two million assault incidents every year. According to the FBI, general assaults account for 42% of all crimes in the United States.[42] Every day an estimated 16,400 threats are made against someone in the workplace or against the workplace itself. Every day over 700 workers are attacked on the job—an excess of 200,000 per year. This equates to nearly one worker assaulted every minute. Every day nearly 44,000 workers are harassed, and every year about 1000 workers are victims of a workplace homicide. During the year 2000 there were over 23,000 reported violent acts committed against management-level personnel in all areas of employment in the United States. Here are some targets of assault:

- Executives, officers, or other key personnel who are vulnerable by virtue of their positions and actual or perceived responsibilities, for which some employees, customers, or others find "cause" and attempt to injure or kill them. According to the Justice Department, men are victims of 80% of all workplace violence. Most are executives, managers, or other key personnel.
- Human resources personnel and managers are susceptible because of their role in employment terminations.
- Managers are potential victims of violence connected with personal relationships.
- Women comprise 50 percent of the workforce and share an increasing vulnerability in management positions. Their death in the workplace exceeds the industry index for wrongful deaths.

In-house Employee Terminations

Anger or rage is one of the most common sources of workplace violence. "Roller coaster" employment and layoffs can leave discharged employees feeling disrespected and unfairly treated. The combined fear of being unable to support themselves or their families, insult to their capabilities, embarrassment of termination, a question of

[41] Terrorism & National Security, U.S. Department of State, Washington, DC, 2003.
[42] Lipman, I.A., Founder and Chairman, Guardsmark, The Lipman Report, August 15, 2014.

"Why me, not him or her?," and wondering where and when their next job will come can fester into a strong resentment and a desire for retribution. A discharge for cause can be even more likely to breed resentment, which may result in a violent act against the employer or company representative. The target can be anyone from the CEO to part-time employees.

I believe termination or separation interviews conducted by people trained in dealing sympathetically with both downsizing and for-cause terminations can prevent a large portion of retaliatory assaults against physical or intellectual property or systems. The "clean out your desk while I watch" approach always ignites a firestorm of resentment.

Insult and Emotional Trauma

Incidents such as being passed over for promotion or having requests for a transfer to a new position denied can cause deep-seated resentments. More common is the persistent demeaning of an individual by a superior. These conditions can be difficult to discern, frequently continuing for years out of the victim's fear of retaliation or discharge. Skilled interviewers can often unearth these conditions through annual reviews or recognition of frequent requests for transfer. Not only can these conditions become dangerous, but certain behavior such as persistent harassment of one employee by another (especially a superior) is illegal. In these days of frequently impersonal relations between management and workers, the human resources, health and safety, and security divisions would do well to work together to prevent not only legal action but also the potential for violent incidents.

Theft of Property

Theft may occur from one of two sources: those within the organization and outsiders. Theft can occur when there is a conspiracy between an insider and someone on the outside. It can be motivated by economic gain, a desire for retaliation, or as a means of gathering information. Corporate theft is a situational, opportunistic, and seasonal phenomenon.

Stockroom and Inventory Threat

Stockroom and inventory theft frequently involves more than one individual. Collusion between someone on the inside and someone on the outside is the most common method and may involve criminal partnerships, such as between a cashier and a customer, a receiving clerk and a truck driver, or an employee and someone on a cleaning crew. The types of property in stock or on hand frequently determine the type of thief and the type of crime. Materials that are easily disposed of, such as televisions, computer equipment, weapons, drugs, tires, or cigarettes, and that can be sold on the street are most often stolen by gangs and organized crime groups who have ready outlets for the stolen goods. Weapons, chemicals, or other dangerous substances can be targets of terrorists, extremists, or organized crime groups, as well as professional thieves stealing for pure profit. Common thieves often steal relatively low value items because they are usually easy to steal and remove from the property, and can be easily be discarded if thief is about to be caught attempting to leave the property.

Competitors and Espionage

Practiced internally, nationally, and internationally, espionage may involve hiring away a key employee or planting a spy within a company or organization. Activities may include pouring through forms filed with the Securities and Exchange Commission and pirating trade secrets, advertising programs, strategic business plans, football playbooks, music, videos, computer software or hardware, or weapon designs. Espionage, especially economic and competitive espionage, is practiced on a huge scale. Nearly every business enterprise does whatever it can to learn everything possible about its competitors. From a security perspective, however, the release of inside information to a competitor is a real loss and one to be prevented. Most significant losses of this type occur because of someone on the inside selling information for either money or personal gain. Today, given the global use of e-mail, the Internet, fax machines, and scanners, the transfer of a company's confidential or proprietary information can occur in seconds, often not being discovered until it is too late. Stealing, selling, or leaking trade secrets or insider information is an increasing problem in the business world.

Vandalism and Sabotage

Security people are just beginning to address the tip of the iceberg in the areas of vandalism and sabotage. Physically booby-trapping computers with explosives or other harmful devices is a frequent strategy of terrorists. While vandalism and sabotage may derive from different intentions, the results are the same: property or operations are destroyed or damaged. Saboteurs have a desire or motive to cause damage. They may not necessarily select a target that would cause the greatest harm, but rather one that seems to afford the greatest chance for success or symbolism. Vandalism, on the other hand, is more often an act of opportunity and may be performed by someone who is merely angry or bored. This person may be a thrill- or power-seeker, whether by wielding a can of spray paint or hacking into a computer. The target may be important only as an opportunity, test, or challenge.

Conclusions

A big challenge for organizations is prioritizing, understanding, and addressing threats in a business context. The threat of international terrorism remains at a significantly high level, and those with the desire, intent, and means to do us harm continue to demonstrate that they are both highly determined and persistent. Right now, ISIS is the greatest terrorist threat facing not only America, but the entire world. Second to ISIS is al Qaeda. Al Qaeda poses an even bigger challenge today than in previous years because its franchises are "much more globally dispersed," and the organization recently has benefited from the massive leaks of U.S. intelligence information.

The insider threat is by far our greatest challenge. Security measures must aim, in part, to minimize the potential of hiring an adversary and to deter individuals from becoming an adversary once they are hired. Such measures must compel the workforce to do the right thing and cause them to take high risks of exposure to do the wrong thing. If an insider chooses to do the wrong thing, security measures must detect such actions early enough and delay the insider long enough so that a response can interrupt the action before it is completed.

Current threats are escalating faster than we are able to identify, and they know no geographical boundaries. They can occur at any moment, anywhere—in areas from urban centers to Main Street, targeting small businesses and major corporations, and people regardless of age, economic status, or social position, from high-profile individuals to any parent, child, grandparent, friend, or coworker. Corporate America's answer to these threats must be an unyielding resolve to remain relentlessly proactive, followed by reasonable and prudent actions to reduce risk exposure.

The biggest change in industry during the past two decades has been technology. Technology continues to grow and advance beyond our present-day imagination and will do so well into the future. This phenomenon creates an ongoing demand to protect corporate America and its business operations from the rising threats of transnational organized crime and terrorist activities. Change, of course, has always been a management challenge, but change today has taken on an entirely different meaning. Today, it is more rapid and more complex to manage.

The challenge for CEOs is to focus on possessing in a timely manner the whole set of disciplines, expertise, experience, and capabilities to keep up with the fast pace of continual change, while not loosing sight of quality high-performance results within the fog of evolving and emerging security threats. This challenge calls on CEOs to muster a dedicated security organization comprising of staff who are knowledgeable and experienced in dealing with diversified threats, ensuing consequences, and emergency response planning, and who have the expertise to lead prevention, deterrence, and protection initiatives. Lacking this capability, they must seek professional consulting expertise to achieve goals and objectives.

The Cyber Threat Landscape

The cyber threat has pushed security planning and protection from an operational concern of corporate security and IT departments onto the strategic agenda of CEOs and Boards at many enterprises across America. But many Board directors are dissatisfied with both the quantity and quality of information offered [to] executive decision-makers about cyber security and cyber risk. These executives want changes in how security oversight responsibility is invoked, improved incident response means and competency that stop breaches.

John Sullivant

Top Takeaways

- Discover who is behind all the data breaches and who is being targeted and why?
- Understand the perceptions of executive management, information technology security professionals, and employees
- Uncover the truth about employee dependability, reliability, and trustworthiness
- Gain an understanding of constraints in dealing with, detecting, and responding to breaches
- Determine the effectiveness of cyber protocols, budgets, and training

Overview

Spies have been damaging U.S. interests since the American Revolution. But today's world makes it easier to commit espionage because of the increase in the number of people who now have access to sensitive information, the ease of transmitting information, and the growing demand for sensitive information from end users.

Some of our most trusted people have crossed the line to perpetrate the most damaging U.S. counterintelligence failures. In each case these individuals had exhibited the identifiable signs of being a traitor, but those signs went unnoticed or unreported for years because of the unwillingness or inability of colleagues and managers to accept the possibility of treason. Another reason is the fear of being sued for defamation of character. Insiders convicted of stealing information had been doing so for a long time before being caught. Here are five important case histories:

- Army PFC Bradley Manning leaked the largest cache of classified documents in U.S. Army history when he disclosed restricted military records to the Wikileaks website. He was sentenced in 2013 to 35 years in prison.[1]

[1] United States versus Manning, August 21, 2013.

- Former National Security Agency (NSA) contractor Edward Snowden perpetrated the biggest NSA intelligence leak in U.S. history. In 2011 Snowden leaked millions of documents to the Wikileaks website, revealing numerous NSA global surveillance programs. He devastated the entire country and its national security, degrading the United States' capability to gather intelligence information.[2]
- Former FBI counterintelligence agent Robert Philip Hansen provided highly classified national information to Russia and the former Soviet Union. Hansen provided the KGB and its successor agency, the SVR, with top secret and "code word" documents from 1985 through 2001.[3]
- The biggest espionage leak in U.S. Navy history was the Walker family spy ring. This group gave the Soviets information from 1968 to 1985, which allowed the Soviets to access weapons data, naval tactics, and surface, submarine, and airborne readiness capabilities. It was later discovered that the Walkers' activities enabled North Korea to seize the USS Pueblo and capture a significant amount of classified information. The information cache shared by the Walkers with the Soviets enabled the Soviets to build replicas and gain access to U.S. naval communications systems, which continued into the late 1980s.[4] North Korea still has possession of the USS Pueblo.
- Daniel Ellsberg, a senior research associate at the Massachusetts Institute of Technology's Center for International Studies, strengthened public opposition to the Vietnam War in 1971 when he leaked the Pentagon Papers to the *New York Times*. The documents contained evidence that the U.S. government had misled the public and Congress regarding the country's involvement in the war, including the years leading up to the war.[5]

While terrorism continues to dominate our national discourse, the global threat landscape has been transformed, with terror networks using new technologies and strategies to carry out attacks at home and abroad. The cyber terror threat has become more sophisticated and more deadly with the advent of social media and mobile networks.

Who Is Responsible for Today's Cyber Attacks?

Threats come from terrorists, hackers, disgruntled employees, individuals specifically engaged in corporate and economic espionage, professional spies, state-sponsored terrorists, and transnational organized crime operations. The expertise of cyber attackers varies from small-time hackers with minimal capabilities to national intelligence agencies with thousands of software engineers exploiting the latest techniques. Experts divide cyber culprits into four categories based on their capabilities.[6]

- Group 1 consists of "hacktivists," such as Anonymous, and terrorist groups such as al Qaeda, Hezbollah, Hamas, and ISIS.
- Group 2 consists of cyber criminals. The capabilities of these criminals vary, but their motivation is primarily financial gain. Their goal is not destruction but acquisition of information.

---

[2] https://en.wikipedia.org/wiki/Edward_Snowden.

[3] FBI National Press Office Release, Washington, DC, February 21, 2001.

[4] https://en.wikipedia.org/wiki/John_Anthony_Walker.

[5] https://en.wikipedia.org/wiki/Daniel_Ellsberg.

[6] Szady, David, W., FBI Assistant Director, Retired. Security Management, The Time for Urgency Is Now, September 2013.

- Group 3 is nation-states performing cyber espionage for technology transfer. These adversaries are infinitely more insidious and damaging to the U.S. economy than cyber criminals, hacktivists, or terrorists, and include China, North Korea, Russia, and Iran.
- Group 4—the most formidable group—is destructive foreign military operatives. Their goal is to shut down the systems of national critical infrastructures. Such attacks would cause widespread chaos and damage, and diminish the country's capability to defend the nation from an all-out military invasion. Agents from China, North Korea, Russia, and Iran are among this group.

The Cyber Threat Continues to Devastate the U.S. Economy and National Security

Cyber intrusions into corporate networks, personal computers, and government systems are occurring every day by the thousands. Cyber attacks include cyber crime, cyber terror, and cyber warfare.[7]

- Cyber crime involves phishing, extortion, fraud, theft, and other crimes. This crime is rampant and is growing in scale and sophistication.
- Cyber terror involves attacks on critical computer-controlled infrastructure such as water, energy, telecommunications, transportation, and banking. Cyber terror is also expected to grow in scale and sophistication.
- Cyber warfare involves the theft of sensitive information and espionage used by one nation-state against another. China and Russia have engaged in cyber warfare on at least two occasions: China's reprisals against U.S. government information networks after the May 1999 accidental bombing of the Chinese embassy in Belgrade, and Russia's distributed denial of service attacks against Estonian computer networks in May 2007—though both countries deny involvement.[8]

The cyber threat is not defined by a single event such as an attack on an electric grid; rather, it is the ongoing onslaught and the transfer of wealth from our economy and national security—thus a cyber "death by a thousand cuts."

Computers and servers in the United States are the most aggressively targeted information systems in the world. These attacks threaten the nation's public works, communications systems, computer networks, and commerce. Cyber crime is emerging as one of the most daunting threats faced by the nation today. More than 100 countries, including some major U.S. allies, are deeply involved in cyber espionage and have been for several decades. Examples of such threats include:

- shutting down systems or simply generating fear
- altering air traffic, train, and subway data and controls to create mid-air collisions and crashes
- causing havoc with financial institutions, creating bank and credit fraud
- disrupting communication and transportation systems and services
- disrupting power grids, gas and oil pipeline flow, and water and sewer supplies
- disabling or hacking into sensitive computer systems
- making services unavailable to users
- manipulating computers to cause explosions or environmental contamination
- violence against persons or property

[7] See footnote 7.
[8] See footnote 7.

- sending a wireless virus out to computers and phones, rendering them useless
- stealing money, intellectual and proprietary information, and identities

Cyber espionage is intensifying in frequency and severity, doing horrendous damage to our national economy and security. Iran, China, North Korea, and Russia are the leading international cyber hackers.[9]

Hackers have penetrated, taken control of, damaged, and/or stolen sensitive personal and official information from computer systems at many government departments and agencies[10]:

• Commerce	• Justice
• Commodity Futures Trading Commission	• Labor
• Environmental Protection Agency	• NASA
• Defense	• National Weather Service
• Energy	• Nuclear Regulatory Commission
• Federal Reserve	• Office of Personnel Management
• Food & Drug Administration	• States
• Homeland Security	• U.S. Copyright Office

We know that China operates the largest covert electronic espionage spy network in the world. They have been spying on the United States and stealing our secrets since the early 1970s. French companies have been stealing American trade secrets since the early 1960s.

Thousands of prominent U.S. corporations have also been penetrated, systems damaged, and proprietary, sensitive, and confidential information stolen. In fact, in 2013 the FBI notified more than 3000 U.S. companies that they had been hacked.[11] That number reflects only a fraction of the true scale of cyber intrusions into the private sector by criminal groups and foreign governments and their proxies—particularly China, Iran, North Korea, and Eastern Europe; it is impossible to detect all such breaches. Here is a sampling of some of the corporations penetrated:

• Automatic Data Processing	• JPMorgan Chase & Company
• Boeing Aircraft Company	• Lockheed Martin
• Citigroup	• Major government contractors[12]
• CrowdStrike Company	• Michael's
• Dairy Queen	• NASDAQ
• EMC Corporation	• Sony
• Epsilon Data Management	• Target
• Home Deport	• Wal-Mart
	• U.S. Investigative Services (USIS)[13]

[9] Szady, David, W., FBI Assistant Director, Retired. Security Management, The Time for Urgency Is Now, May 2014.

[10] The Federal Government's Track Record on Cybersecurity and Critical Infrastructure. A Report Prepared by the Minority Staff of the Homeland Security & Government Affairs Committee. Senator Tom Coburn, MD, Ranking Member (3), February 4, 2014.

[11] https://www.washingtonpost.com/world/national-security/2014/03/24/74aff686-aed9-11e3-96dc-d6ea14 c099f9_story.html.

[12] Thousands of companies having prime contracts, many classified are continuing targets of espionage spying by China, North Korea, Iran, and other countries.

[13] Retrieved from: http://www.reuters.com/article/2014/08/22/us-usa-security-contractor-cyberattack-id USKBNOGM1TZ20140822.

It is not surprising to discover that 80 percent of most U.S. companies have experienced at least one breach, with most of them achieving "veteran status" for numerous attacks. It is equally disturbing to learn that most of the breaches are not reported to the government. And, 40 percent of these companies do not interact with the FBI, U.S. Secret Service, or other agencies on such cyber breaches. Their reasoning is that they will lose market share, stock prices will drop, prosecutions will make their trade secrets public, and they do not want to be embarrassed.[14]

Trusted Insiders Bear Watching

Of all the methods for obtaining a company's intellectual and proprietary information or classified government information, the most effective is the use of the trusted insider—one who volunteers or is successfully recruited or sent by an intelligence service or corporation. 93 percent of U.S. organizations are vulnerable to such insider threats.[15] While businesses are growing increasingly aware of insider threats, they still lack enforcement controls to stop perpetrators and the will to punish them. Businesses take little action to mitigate the insider threat.

Motivational Factors Shed Insight on Undesirable Employee Behavior

Many motivational factors explain why an employee would decide to steal a company's intellectual or proprietary information, or sensitive or classified government information, and give it to a competitor or another organization. Lipman identifies 16 factors, and a good account of these motivational factors is given in "The Lipman Report" of March 15, 2014.

• Alienation	• Organizational drift
• Drugs	• Money
• Emotional involvement	• Messiah complex
• Family problems	• "My generation"
• Hatred and revenge	• National pride
• Hostage situation	• Sense of adventure
• Idealism and beliefs	• Threat/blackmail
• Ingratiation	• Weak ego

Some actions that may suggest an individual is involved in unauthorized, illegal, or unethical activities may include:

- accessing restricted websites
- a disregard for policies on installing personal software or hardware
- asking to use others' passwords

[14] The Lipman Report, March 15, 2014, Exclusively for Management; http://www.guardsmark.com/files/crime/TLR_Mar_14.pdf.
[15] https://www.nsi.org/Security_NewsWatch/NewsWatch/1.21.15.html.

- doing unauthorized work at home
- downloading documents that are unrelated to their responsibilities
- indifference to coworkers or supervisors
- suspicious personal contacts with competitors or unauthorized people
- unexplained affluence
- unreported foreign contacts
- use of a personal computer at work
- working odd hours

We Can Learn From Our Mistakes and Bad Experiences

One of the legacies of Edward Snowden's treason[16] is that many companies are now concerned about the insider threat more than they have ever been, but fewer are taking any serious action to do something about it.

- Snowden demonstrated that a trusted person with the most stringent security measures could devastate an entire organization, or in Snowden's case the entire nation.
- While technology and security practices should have caught Snowden, there is also the realization that his coworkers and managers should have noticed indications of unusual behavior.
- The damaging leakage of national top secret information by Snowden serves as a wake-up call not only for government agencies but private employers as well.
- Snowden's actions provide a clear example of what can happen, even for some of the most security-conscious organizations, when the insider threat is not taken seriously.

A legacy of betrayals by the Walker family, Hansen, Ellsberg, and Manning is that people with boundless access to sensitive data present the greatest risk of misusing that privilege. Wrongdoers are able to cover their actions very well, but the reality is that just about every malicious insider shows some indications of their intent. Managers and coworkers are in the best position to see those indications.

State-Sponsored Cyber Attacks Create Havoc With Our Economy and National Security

Sponsored cyber attacks[17] are becoming the method of choice for foreign governments to infiltrate and steal information and intelligence from the U.S. government and American businesses, and we are unprepared to stop them. We have suffered breaches involving:

- credit card information[18]
- critical national infrastructure intelligence[19]

---

[16] Retrieved from: http://nsi.org/SecurityNewsWatch/NewsWatch/4.16.14.html.
[17] Retrieved from: http://venturebeat.com/cagtegory/security/.
[18] Ibid.
[19] Retrieved from: http://venturebeat.com/2014/09/03/victim-to-a-mysterious-cyber-attack-home-depot-struggles-to-find-out-what-went-wrong?/.

- employer data[20]
- patient health records[21]
- personal financial information[22]

Collectively, these breaches demonstrate both the diversity of targets and their shared vulnerabilities. Here are three case histories of major concern to our national security:

- USIS[23] is the largest government contractor conducting background investigations for the U.S. Department of Homeland Security. A single USIS data breach involved the theft of personnel information for 25,000 federal employees and contractors seeking clearance for access to U.S. government classified information. While this breach represents a second black eye for USIS—it was the firm that performed the background check for Edward Snowden and the U.S. Navy Yard shooter—the broader implications of this attack are serious and highly concerning. Experts advise that this type of attack is usually intended for the purposes of identifying potential recruitment candidates for intelligence purposes. By collecting such information, the sponsors behind this attack can identify which members of the U.S. security clearance population might be suitable for targeting by a foreign power.
- The Nuclear Regulatory Commission[24] suffered three major attacks in as many months. These breaches seem to have been designed to gather information on the capabilities of U.S. nuclear assets and to probe the cyber readiness of the Commission's workforce.
- A U.S. defense contractor who smuggled classified F-35 design plans for China. This theft remained undetected until the design architecture was noticed on China's stealth bomber.

58 percent of senior information technology (IT) security professionals believe the industry is losing the battle against state-sponsored attacks. 30 percent say they are not even confident that foreign state-sponsored hackers have not breached their own corporate network. 96 percent believe that the hacking landscape is going to get worse over time.[25]

Cyber Practices and Incident Responses Need Improvement

No corporation or government is exempt from cyber attacks, yet many organizations are not clear-eyed about their cyber security resilience. Several prominent research firms and institutions report a telling story about America's cyber

---

[20] See footntoe 21.

[21] Retrieved from: http://venturebeat.com/2014/08/18/hackers-stole-data-from-4.5-million-u-s-patients/.

[22] Ibid.

[23] Retrieved from: http://www.com/azrticle/2014/08/22/us-usa-security-contrazctor-cyberattack-idUSKB-NOGMITZ20140822.

[24] Retrieved from: http://venturebeat.com/2014/07/30/Canda-Says-China-Guilty-Of-Cyber-Attack-On-To Research-Organization/.

[25] Lieberman Software Corporation, Black Hat USA 2013 Conference, Las Vegas, NV. E&T Magazine, September 14, 2013. Retrieved from: http://nsi.org/SecurityNewsWatch/NewsWatch/6.4.14.html/.

security capabilities and the character of those charged with planning, development, implementation, and monitoring for success. Security practitioners, executive management, and governing boards that face cyber security challenges can greatly benefit from understanding the impact of cyber crimes on their organizations and act accordingly.

Below is a selection of case histories from recent surveys, which will give you a sense of the magnitude of the problem, including system vulnerability, that security professionals face on a daily basis. This information can be a useful tool for developing prevention and protection strategies, emergency response plans, cyber incident response plans, and protocols to strengthen cyber security operations. This information can also offer insight into fostering business relations, establishing and maintaining dialog with upper management, and structuring awareness training programs. The case histories are divided into five groups:

- Perceptions of executives, IT security professionals, and employees
- Employee dependability, reliability, and trustworthiness
- Capability to detect and respond to breaches
- Usefulness of cyber policies, plans, and procedures
- Budget, time, and training

Executives, IT Security Professionals, and Employee Perceptions Are Cause for Alarm

A recent Cisco study revealed that complacency, ignorance, and low levels of security awareness among corporate senior management staffers contributed to major insider threat vulnerabilities. The study found that staff were becoming a big part of the insider threat problem.[26] 58 percent of staffers were aware of security threats and the risk they pose to corporate information. Disturbing as this finding is, one would hope that, upon reading the report findings, C-suite executives took immediate steps to change the attitudes and behavioral work habits of their senior staff members or, lacking success in that, found quality replacements who really understand and demonstrate their individual responsibilities about security. It seems that neither action was taken.

Similar survey findings suggest that the biggest cyber security threat firms face is not state-sponsored, geopolitical, or clandestine, but much closer to home: employees. Internal security breaches, including accidental ones, are caused by careless employees, and results are indicative of noncompliance, misunderstanding of protocols, and failure to communicate effectively with security departments.

- 55 percent of Department of Defense officials surveyed identified careless and untrained insiders as the greatest source of (IT) security threats at their agencies.[27]

---

[26] Retrieved from: http://nsi.org/SecurityNewsWatch/NewsWatch/1.14.15.html/.
[27] SolarWinds Survey, 2015. Retrieved from: http://nsi.org/SecurityNewsWatch/NewsWatch/1.25.15.html/.

- One study reported that almost all (91 percent) of the companies surveyed had at least one external breach in the past 12 months.[28]
- Another study addressed management's knowledge of security vulnerabilities and attacks. In this study, 35 percent of the respondents said that they had experienced an insider attack, whereas 34 percent indicated that the threat was not even a management priority.[29]
- Yet another survey[30] of 240 senior IT decision makers found that hackers were present on a network for an average of 229 days before being discovered. This is more than 7 months.

While most C-suite executives agree that protecting their company's confidential data and trade secrets from the prying eyes of competitors is important, 55 percent of senior IT security executives said they had discovered an insider taking information from the company's computer systems to use in a competing business.[31]

Other studies show similarly disturbing results[32]:

- 40 percent of CEOs believe they are making the wrong level of security investment or are unsure whether their investment is appropriate.
- 30 percent of board members understand or are aware of specific cyber security threats.
- 27 percent of CEOs cite cyber criminals as the most prominent threat.[33]
- 12 percent of CEOs cite state-sponsored cyber attacks as the greatest threat.[34]
- 8 percent of CEOs cite competitors as the biggest single security peril.[35]

One particular study focused on workforce behavior patterns and CEOs' confidence level regarding their employees:

- 75 percent of CEOs consider data leaks or malicious behavior by insiders as their number 1 risk.[36]
- 53 percent of CEOs say the main risk to corporate data and computer systems is human error, carelessness, or ignorance among their own employees.[37]
- 50 percent of CEOs worry more about their own employees turning rogue than about external cyber threats.[38]

---

[28] eSecurityplanet.com. Retrieved from: http://nsi.org/SecurityNewsWatch/NewsWatch/6.4.14.html/, (accessed 02.09.14.).

[29] Retrieved from: http://venturebeat.com/2014/09/03/victim-to-a-mysterious-cyber-attack-home-depot-struggles-to-find-out-what-went-wrong?/.

[30] Itgovernance.com.uk/boardroom-cyberwatch.aspx. Retrieved from: http://nsi.org/SecurityNewsWatch/NewsWatch/7.9.14.html/.

[31] Courion Corporation, Annual User Conference, May 2014, Boston, MA. Retrieved from: http://nsi.org/SecurityNewsWatch/NewsWatch/6.4.14.html/.

[32] IT Governance's Boardroom Cyber Watch 2013 Survey. Retrieved from: http://nsi.org/SecurityNewsWatch/NewsWatch/10.10.13.html/.

[33] Ibid.

[34] Ibid.

[35] Ibid.

[36] Retrieved from: http://nsi.org/SecurityNewsWatch/NewsWatch/4.23.14/.

[37] IT Governance's Boardroom Cyber Watch 2013 Survey. Retrieved from: http://nsi.org/SecurityNewsWatch/NewsWatch/10.10.13.html/.

[38] Ibid.

Despite this, 61 percent of companies breached take no disciplinary action against employees.[39]

• When questioned, 79 percent of employees admit that their illegitimate actions had never been discovered.
• 47 percent of the workforce admits to removing confidential files and information from the workplace.
• 41 percent of employees admit to giving their password to coworkers and family friends.
• Of those employees who were caught:
   ◦ 67 percent said they were spoken to but no action was taken, and no report of their behavior was entered in their personnel file.
   ◦ 25 percent said nothing happened.

Other surveys revealed other statistics:

• 50 percent of security experts said their agency was likely to be a target of a denial-of-service attack in the next 12 months.[40]
• 40 percent of IT professionals said the increase in breaches had not changed the level of attention CEOs give to security or any budget increase for additional resources to handle the influx of hackers.[41]
• 36 percent believe employees can access or steal confidential information.[42]
• 32 percent of IT security professionals said they had never spoken to their CEO. Of those who did, 23 percent say they speak to the CEO only once a year.[43]
• 30 percent of U.S. CEOs said they are prepared to meet the growing threat of a major cyber attack.[44]

Few would argue that many companies are blind to data breaches, are complacent in their security measures, and have little or no contact with board members, local law enforcement, or the FBI regarding these matters.

Employee Dependability and Reliability Cannot Be Trusted

Human error looms large. From misconfigurations and poor patch management practices to the use of insecure or default credentials and the loss of equipment to the

---

[39] Retrieved from: http:/nsi.org/SecurityNewsWatch/NewsWatch/4.16.14.html/.

[40] Meritalk surveyed 100 cyber security professionals and 100 employees within the federal government. Survey results are indicative of noncompliance and failure to communicate effectively. Meritalk.com/cyber-security-experience-register.php. Retrieved from: http://nsi.org/SecurityNewsWatch/NewsWatch/10.17.13.html/.

[41] Atomic Research surveyed 102 financial organizations and 151 organizations in the United Kingdom, all of which process card payments. Government Security News, June 25, 2014. Retrieved from: http://nsi.or/SecurityNewsWatch/NewsWatch/6.25.14.html/.

[42] LogRhythm survey of 1000 IT professionals. Retrieved from: http://nsi.org/SecurityNewsWatch/NewsWatch/4.16.14.html/.

[43] Retrieved from: http://nsi.org/SecurityNewsWatch/NewsWatch/7.23.14/.

[44] Retrieved from: http://nsi.org/SecurityNewsWatch/NewsWatch/8.13.14.html/.

disclosure of sensitive information through careless mistakes—human error accounts for 95 percent of security incidents.[45]

The cyber threat from within is the number 1 concern of most chief executives. Surveys reveal many telling conditions among the workforce. A study of breaches, commissioned by Cisco, revealed that many employees deliberately fail to adhere to security policies because of a lack of understanding and poor communication from their security department. A complementary study by Xerox also found that 54 percent of employees did not always follow their company's security polices, leaving the security of sensitive data at heightened risk.[46]

- 49 percent of employees said security breaches are caused by a lack of user compliance.[47]
- Another 49 percent of employees said compromises occur when other employees bypass security measures.[48]
- 36 percent of employees said breaches result from employee errors.[49]
- 25 percent of employees said breaches are caused by malicious insider behavior.[50]

Within the U.S. government, the biggest source of cyber threats is inept coworkers, rather than intentional leakers.[51]

- Careless or poorly trained employees account for 53 percent of security breaches.
- Foreign governments account for 48 percent of cyber invasions.
- General hacking accounts for 35 percent of security breaches.
- Terrorists account for 31 percent of security breaches.
- Employees bypassing security measures create 40 percent of security breaches.[52]

Employee dependability and reliability will continue to be a challenge for CEOs until they take responsible action to implement clear and distinct guidance regarding employee behavior and have the courage to consistently enforce violations of security practices.

Ability to Detect and Respond to Breaches Requires Significant Improvement

No doubt, CEOs take a dim view of people who damage the company's image, brand, and reputation. I argue that inadequate qualifications, training, and budgets are the lead contenders responsible for performance ineffectiveness and inefficiencies. A

---

[45] 2014 Cyber Security Intelligence Index, IBM, NY, 2014.
[46] Retrieved from: http://nsi.org/SecurityNewsWatch/NewsWatch/9.13.14.html/.
[47] Meritalk.com/cyber-security-experience-register.php. Retrieved from: http://nsi.org/SecurityNewsWatch/NewsWatch/10.17.13.html/.
[48] Meritalk study. Retrieved from: http://nsio.org/SecurityNewsWatch/NewsWatch/8.21.14.html/.
[49] Ibid.
[50] Forrest study. Retrieved from: http://nsi.org/SecurityNewsWatch/NewsWatch.8.21.14.html/.
[51] Retrieved from: http://nsi.org/SecurityNewsWatch/NewsWatch/4.3.14.html/.
[52] Retrieved from: http://nsi.org/SecurityNewsWatch/NewsWatch/10.17.13.html/.

recent study by the Sans Institute[53] found that poor or no integration between security products had a tendency to negatively affect a response to cyber attacks. IT security professionals said they needed better, more compatible tools and a faster response to defend against cyber attacks. Key results of this study found that broad definitions of an incident place a strain on incident response (IR) teams, and that a lack of formalized IR plans and dedicated IR staff plagues most organizations.

Another Sans Institute study[54] found that:

- 62 percent of responders said there is no time available to review and practices procedures.
- 60 percent of responders said key impediments hinder an effective response.

75 percent of responders indicated they did not have the ability to detail the human behavioral activities of an insider threat.[55]

The Ponemon Institute study found that 47 percent of IT security professionals felt frequently disappointed with the level of protection their security program offered their customers.[56]

A Meritalk survey concluded that detecting and responding to breaches requires significant improvement, whereas overall attitudes seem to indicate a high degree of overconfidence among many IT security practitioners.

- 95 percent of IT security professionals in these organizations are in agreement that they can detect a breach of critical systems within a week, but nearly all publicly disclosed breaches go for months without detection.[57]
- In that same Atomic Research study, 85 percent of IT security professionals report that point-of-sale intrusions take 2 weeks to discover.[58]
- 60 percent of IT security professionals believe their systems have been hardened enough to prevent breaches.[59]
- 43 percent of IT security professionals report that Web attacks take months to discover.[60]
- 40 percent of cyber security professionals said ensuring a user-friendly experience is a priority.[61]
- 35 percent of IT security professionals said it takes 2–3 days to discover a breach.[62]

---

[53] Threat Intelligence & Incident Response: A study of U.S., Europe, Middle East and Africa (U.S. & EMEA) Organizations, Sans Institute, IL, August 2014. Retrieved from: http://nsi.org/SecurityNewsWatch/NewsWatch/6.18.14.html/.

[54] Retrieved from: http://nsi.org/SecurityNewsWatch/NewsWatch/8.14.14.html/.

[55] Retrieved from: http://nsi.org/SecurityNewsWatch/NewsWatch/9.1.14.html/.

[56] Ponemon Institute surveyed more than 160,000 security professionals in 15 countries to determine the challenges they face in dealing with cyber security threats. Retrieved from: http://nsi.org/SecurityNewsWatch/NewsWatch/7.23.14.html/.

[57] Atomic Research surveyed 102 financial organizations and 151 organizations in the United Kingdom, all of which process card payments. Government Security News, June 25, 2014. Retrieved from: http://nsi.or/SecurityNewsWatch/NewsWatch/6.25.14.html/.

[58] Ibid.

[59] Meritalk study. Retrieved from: http://nsi.org/SecurityNewsWatch/NewsWatch/8.21.14.html/.

[60] Ibid.

[61] Meritalk surveyed 100 cyber security professionals and 100 employees within the federal government. The survey results indicate noncompliance and a failure to communicate effectively. Meritalk.com/cyber-security-experience-register.php. Retrieved from: http://nsi.org/SecurityNewsWatch/NewsWatch/10.17.13.html/.

[62] Ibid.

Other studies report similar types of statistics:

- 74 percent of IT security professionals said their agency is not ready to support secure access from mobile devices.[63]
- 74 percent of IT security professionals said preventing theft of information is their top priority.[64]
- 67 percent of IT security professionals said their agency is not ready to fend off hackers.[65]
- 60 percent of IT security professionals are confident that security controls protect individuals' account information.[66]
- 38 percent of the IT security professionals surveyed said they do not have, or know of, any systems in place to stop employees from accessing unauthorized data.[67]

In another survey, 60 percent of IT security professionals indicated they are not prepared to respond to insider attacks.[68]

In yet another survey, 30 percent of U.S. companies reported that they have no system in place to stop employees from accessing unauthorized data. 48 percent of the companies said they changed passwords to stop former employees from gaining access to their systems.[69]

Based on survey findings, it might be in the best interests of these organizations to consider performing a formal assessment of their cyber security programs against these survey findings to enhance security resilience.

Cyber Security Protocols Lack Clarity, Substance, and Usefulness

In Chapter A User-Friendly Protocol Development Model I talk about the many facets that contribute to poor clarity, consistency, and organization and, often, ineffective protocols. In that chapter I also emphasize that most protocols are cumbersome, outdated, and not user friendly.

Several Meritalk, Atomic Research, and Forrester studies reveal telling employee concerns regarding the effectiveness and user-friendliness of IT security guidance.

- 80 percent of users said security protocols distract from productivity.[70]
- 66 percent of employees viewed security directives as time restrictive.[71]
- 66 percent of users said security protocols are burdensome and time-consuming, and they cannot complete their work because of the security measures.[72]

---

[63] Meritalk.com/cyber-security-experience-register.php. Retrieved from: http://nsi.org/SecurityNewsWatch/NewsWatch/10.17.13.html/.
[64] Ibid.
[65] Ibid.
[66] Ibid.
[67] LogRhythem survey of 1000 IT professionals. Retrieved from: http://nsi.org/SecurityNewsWatch/NewsWatch/4.16.14.html/.
[68] Retrieved from: http://nsi.org/SecurityNewsWatch/NewsWatch/9.1.14.html/.
[69] Retrieved from: http://nsi.org/SecurityNewsWatch/NewsWatch/4.16.14.html/.
[70] Meritalk.com/cyber-security-experience-register.php. Retrieved from: http://nsi.org/SecurityNewsWatch/NewsWatch/10.17.13.html/.
[71] Meritalk study. Retrieved from: http://nsi.org/SecurityNewsWatch/NewsWatch/8.21.14.html/.
[72] Ibid.

- 60 percent of employees said work takes longer because of security protocols.[73]
- 54 percent of users said they struggle to keep track of their passwords.[74]
- 51 percent of IT professionals are somewhat confident in their security plan.[75]
- 36 percent of IT professionals had no confidence in their security plan.[76]
- 50 percent of employees said they were not aware of their company's current security protocols.[77]
- 48 percent of 1000 IT professionals included in a LogRhythm survey regularly changed passwords to stop former employees from gaining access.[78]

While protocols have their place, they are of little value unless employees understand their responsibilities and the rationale behind the rules, and are properly trained to use them quickly when responding to a cyber breach, or detecting it and stopping further future damage. Study findings strongly point out that security protocols do not meet these expectations.

So, how do you make sure that your organization's information assets are protected? The first line of defense is to develop clear, distinct, and user-friendly protocols with employee buy-in. The second line of defense is employee awareness. A more security-aware workforce can mean the difference between an employee preventing the next data breach and an employee becoming the next breach. The third line of defense is proper training and quality management oversight of workforce behavior trends.[79]

Users Say Budget, Time, Resources, and Training Are Insufficient to Thwart Cyber Threats

- In a 2013 survey, Global Corporate IT Security Risks reported 60 percent of IT decision makers believe they are not given enough time or funding to develop effective IT security policies. 49 percent said they did not feel they had organized, systematic processes to deal with IT risks.[80]
- 28 percent of educational institutions said they are confident they had sufficient investment. In this same survey, only a third 34 percent of government and defense organizations said they have enough time and resources to develop security protocols.[81]

---

[73] Meritalk study. Retrieved from: http://nsi.org/SecurityNewsWatch/NewsWatch/8.21.14.html/.

[74] Ibid.

[75] Atomic Research: Government Security News, June 25, 2014. Retrieved from: http://nsi.org/Security NewsWatch/NewsWatch/6.25.14.html/.

[76] Ibid.

[77] Forrester study. Retrieved from: http://nsi.org/SecurityNewsWatch/NewsWatch/8.21.14.html/.

[78] LogRhythem survey of 1000 IT professionals. Retrieved from: http://nsi.org/SecurityNewsWatch/News-Watch/4.16.14.html.

[79] Retrieved from: http://nsi.org/Securitysense/what-is-security sense.shtml.

[80] Szady, David, W., FBI Assistant Director, Retired. Security Management, The Time for Urgency Is Now, December 2013.

[81] eSecurityPlanet.com. Retrieved from: http://nsi.org/SecurityNewsWatch/NewsWatch/6.4.14.html/, (accessed 02.09.13.).

- 52 percent of the companies surveyed did not provide cyber security education to their employees.[82]
- 42 percent of employees said they receive adequate training.[83]
- Another study reported that respondents attributed their failure to respond to insider attacks to both a lack of training (55 percent) and budget (51 percent).[84]

Providing an adequate budget, resources, and time to prepare procedures and train personnel in these procedures must be a high priority of every CEO. Without this support from upper management, nothing will ever be accomplished.

Monetary Consequences of Cyber Crime Have Reached a New High

The United States averages 5.7 million cyber attacks annually, and those are only the breaches we know about. Here is some interesting cost data that may make you raise your brows:

- The FBI estimates that American companies have lost a staggering $1.2 trillion (roughly $100 billion more than drug trafficking or heroin, cocaine, and marijuana) to theft of intellectual and proprietary information over the past decade. Currently, the FBI is prosecuting over 50 economic espionage cases a year and has seen a 300 percent increase in economic espionage investigations over the past 5 years.[85]
- Daily attempted or actual cyber attacks number in tens of thousands, costing corporations an average of $1.5 million a day in lost revenue.[86]
- System repairs resulting from cyber attacks exceed $130.1 million per year.[87]
- Only 3 percent of total breaches are classified as "noteworthy" (meaning significant). These breaches account for 75 percent of the total costs for security incidents and 95 percent of all costs related to image, brand, and reputation damage.[88]
- Costs to repair damage to image, brand, and reputation average $5.3 million per substantial event.[89]
- Those surveyed say a serious security incident costs large companies an average of $649,000 and small to medium-sized companies an average of $50,000.[90]
- In 2013, the U.S. government spent $11.6 billion to protect classified information.[91]

---

[82] Ponemon Institute surveyed more than 160,000 security professionals in 15 countries to determine the challenges they face in dealing with cyber security threats. Retrieved from: http://nsi.org/SecurityNews-Watch/NewsWatch/7.23.14.html/.

[83] LogRythem survey of 1000 IT professionals. Retrieved from: http://nsi.org/SecurityNewsWatch/News-Watch/4.16.14.html/.

[84] Retrieved from: http://nsi.org/SecurityNewsWatch/NewsWatch/9.1.14.html/.

[85] Szady, David, W., FBI Assistant Director, Retired. Security Management, The Time for Urgency Is Now, May 2014.

[86] Retrieved from: http://nsi.org/SecurityNewsWatch/NewsWatch/3.27.14 html/.

[87] See footnote 88.

[88] 2014 Cyber Security Intelligence Index, IBM, NY, 2014.

[89] Ibid.

[90] eSecurityplanet.com. Retrieved from: http://nsi.org/SecurityNewsWatch/NewsWatch/6.4.14.html, (accessed 02.09.14.).

[91] Retrieved from: http://nsi.org/SecurityNewsWatch/NewsWatch/7.9.14 html/.

- The estimated cost to US companies and consumers to defend against cyber attacks is up to $100 billion annually.[92]
- The growing cost of cyber crime on the global economy is $575 billion a year—more than the value of many countries' economies.[93]
- The average cost of cyber attack clean up after each serious breach is $1 million.[94]
- The average cost of cyber crime is 11.6 million per US company.[95]
- Breaches and damages caused by employees reach $3 million to $4 million per year,[96] yet, as reported earlier, insiders who threaten the entire corporation are seldom disciplined, fined, demoted, or fired from their jobs.[97]

Conclusions

Today, more information is carried or sent out the door on removable media in a matter of minutes than the sum of what was given to America's enemies as hard copies throughout history. Consequently, the damage done by malicious insiders and hostile nation states will likely continue to increase unless we create effective threat detection programs and enforce the implementation of such programs so cyber threats can be proactively identified and mitigated before they fully mature.[98]

Public and Private Sectors Struggle to Build Security Resilience

Our understanding of cyber threats is limited because available statistics on cyber security are poor, contradictory, and sporadic at best. Compilations of cyber attacks and violations within the private sector rely on voluntary reporting and surveys. Interviews with chief information officers and other security officials indicate a widespread reluctance to report most intrusions, even attempted ones. Unfortunately, CEOs and other decision makers have the tendency to look at cyber security as just another expense. From a risk-management perspective, many CEOs simply do not see cyber protection as a bottom-line activity.[99]

However, costly and devastating cyber attacks continue to plague both public and private sectors and individuals, suggesting that the present cyber security strategies are not very effective.[100] As a nation, our cyber security responses have failed to address the extent and nature of cyber threats. Even though we have the technology to eradicate the problem, the politicians in Washington view political correctness as a sound

[92] Retrieved from: http://nsi.org/SecurityNewsWatch/NewsWatch/3.27.24.html/.
[93] Retrieved from: http://nsi.org/SecurityNewsWatch/NewsWatch/1.14.15.html/.
[94] Retrieved from: http://nsi.org/SecurityNewsWatch/NewsWatch/10.10.13 html/.
[95] Ibid.
[96] Ibid.
[97] Lipman, Ira, A., Founder & Chairman, Guardsmark. The Lipman Report (pp. 2–5), March 15 2014.
[98] Szady, David, W., FBI Assistant Director, Retired. Security Management, The Time for Urgency Is Now, December 2013.
[99] Szady, David, W., FBI Assistant Director, Retired. Security Management, The Time for Urgency Is Now, May 2014.
[100] Szady, David, W., FBI Assistant Director, Retired. Security Management, The Time for Urgency Is Now, April 2013.

strategy. This is a good example of politicians (from both parties) not doing what they are elected and paid to do.

We Are Dealing with Outside Experts and Cunning Insiders, Not a JV Team

Well-funded and businesslike adversaries using extremely sophisticated, targeted attacks dominate the cyber threat landscape,[101] as do malicious and negligent employees who victimize their own organizations by continuing to put them at grave risk.

The increase in foreign state-sponsored cyber breaches illustrate an important and alarming shift in the cyber threat landscape as these global adversaries increasingly leverage cyber strategies to exploit vulnerabilities to further their own national interests. State-sponsored data breaches should serve as a wake-up call for organizations of all sizes and in all industries, public and private, to act in a responsible manner to preserve and protect not only their current investments, but also future aspirations to grow and prosper.

Our Approach Is Not Working: We Need to Change Our Strategy

While companies and governments spend billions on technology solutions to deter, detect, and deflect unauthorized access and network intrusion, breaches keep happening. Why? Clearly, our efforts are not working. We are not keeping pace with the threats we face. We need to change how we think about and approach cyber security. We need to think outside the box, abandon self-interest and personal agendas, and start thinking "total quality management" [102] for the betterment of the entire organization and the nation. I encourage the reader to consider these ideas when developing your cyber security plan.

- Stop thinking about data breaches as external threats. More than 90 percent of all reported breaches are attributed to the actions of a trusted insider, and 90 percent of those could have been prevented if established protocols were in place and management did its job.[103] It is time to design a better-quality workforce.
  - We need an in-depth screening process. While organizations work to screen out applicants with specific stability issues, the absence of these traits does not ensure that the individual is not predisposed to compromise national security after being hired. Those who act because of conscience issues and moral ambiguity—traits that are not so easily detected—demonstrate this. Current investigation techniques and even polygraphs can only bring to the surface past nefarious behavior. They cannot predict future malicious behavior. The best weapon to ferret out undesirable and unethical employees, in addition to an intensive background investigation, is a penetrating interview to detect personality traits that would lead one to question whether the individual can be entrusted with serious

---

[101] 2014 Cyber Security Intelligence Index, IBM, NY, 2014.

[102] Total quality management presents a dramatic rethinking about how decisions are made, how work is evaluated, and how communication is conducted in the workplace. Schmidt, Warren, H. and Finnigan Jerome, P. Finnigan, TQ Manager, Jossey-Bass Publishers, San Francisco, 1993.

[103] http://nsi.org/SecurityNewsWatch/NewsWatch/1.21.15.html/.

secrets.[104] However, industry leadership is not yet ready to "intrude" on potential hires in this manner.

- Conscientious and quality supervision must include enjoining supervisors and managers at all levels of hierarchy to monitor employee anomalies and, when necessary, take immediate reasonable and prudent steps to safeguard business investment and interests. Such intrusiveness is viewed by many as "spying" on employees rather than overseeing social behavior and work patterns.
- While we must accept that traditional IT security measures are essential, it is also time to embrace a more comprehensive philosophy that views security through a holistic lens that incorporates the physical, technical, and administrative risks across the entire organization, including third-party threats and the insider threat lurking within. Only through this approach can we identify vulnerabilities and prevent a serious data breach from occurring in the first place.
- Organizations must create a security culture and encourage vigilance across the entire spectrum of the company. Every employee, from the janitor to the CEO, must receive frequent, up-to-date security awareness training. Specialized cyber training for employees on phishing attacks, anomaly detection, and other techniques used by hacker groups is essential so they can perform their jobs more efficiently.

Since most data breaches occur because of inept, careless, or resentful employees, an "insider threat program" must include:

- continuous monitoring and evaluation of personnel
- procedures for reporting anomalous behavior
- assessment of individuals' reliability and trustworthiness
- establishment of an integrated capability to monitor and audit computer network user activity
- implementation of the "two-person rule" for access to the greatest level of sensitive information and system activity

Today's harsh realities require organizations to have comprehensive cyber IR plans ready to execute at a moment's notice. IR plans, in concert with the other security emergency response plans and procedures that are custom designed to meet the security needs of each organization, are undeniably a critical component of an organization's security strategy to establish and maintain security resilience.[105]

American "Exceptionalism" Is Disappearing: We Must Take It Back

Corporate espionage is the highest that it has ever been in the history of the United States, and cyber intruders are using every unethical and criminal means to acquire data that will give them a competitive or financial advantage over their competitors. Cyber spies are stealing valuable trade secrets, intellectual property, and confidential

---

[104] Szady, David, W., FBI Assistant Director, Retired. Security Management, The Time for Urgency Is Now, April 2013.
[105] http://nsi.org/SecurityNewsWatch/NewsWatch/1.14.15.html/.

business strategies. Top-secret defense information and other U.S. classified information have been stolen over the past decade, and this crime is spiraling at a rapid pace. Despite the efforts of corporations and the government, cyber attacks and cyber espionage continue to grow at an exponential pace, and cyber intrusions into corporate networks, personal computers, and government systems are occurring every day by the thousands. The threat of state-sponsored attacks is extremely serious for all entities, public and private, with attacks being launched on a regular basis, 24/7. And the trusted insider who wishes to steal information is in a key position to obtain it.

Human Fallacy Is Our Greatest Weakness: Let Us Do Something About It!

One of the greatest challenges CEOs face is managing the human side of the enterprise. Today there are more threats, more vulnerabilities, more portable storage devices, and increased mobility. That means that educating employees about security is more difficult, demanding, and necessary than ever before. Employees are the weakest link in the security chain because they are not trained to be security-conscious, are not responsible and accountable for their actions, and are not properly supervised. A report by Ernst & Young found that "security awareness programs at many organizations are weak, half-hearted and ineffectual." As a result, employees ignore them.[106] The best strategy is to teach employees on a continual basis the perils of human error and inattention to security protocols (Sullivant, 2007, pp. 14–44).

We Must Act Responsibility and Be Accountable for Our Actions

Chief executives can no longer ignore the possibility of cyber attacks. Five critical elements are essential in establishing a successful cyber security program.

1. CEOs must aggressively enforce a vigorous information and cyber security program.
2. CEOs must allocate the necessary resources and funding to support the program.
3. Everyone from the CEO down must get involved and buy in to the program.
4. All individuals must be adequately trained and their performance continually monitored.
5. No program can be successful without the collaboration of security, legal, human resources, and the user departments.

Companies have gone out of business because of economic espionage, and large companies are losing billions of dollars. The economic espionage problem is serious, and corporations have a responsibility to deal with it in a responsible manner.

---

[106] Szady, David, W., FBI Assistant Director, Retired. Security Management, The Time for Urgency Is Now, May 2014.

Only Our Willingness Stands in the Way of the Sharing of Intelligence Information

Not only are thieves learning to steal millions of credit card numbers and email addresses, they have access to elaborate pieces of malware that are capable of spying on whole organizations for long periods of time, capturing computer screens, key strokes, and data, and transmitting it all to distant servers without being detected.[107]

Because of this emerging threat, federal agencies, particularly the FBI, now believe sharing information with the public is more important than ever before. The FBI recently announced that it cannot fight this new cyber threat effectively without help from the private sector, and it is looking to share threat information with companies and to get companies to share intelligence from their product divisions and from their general employee population.[108]

We Must Gain Executive Management's Trust, Get in Front of the Issues, and Stay There

In the world of IT security, threats are constantly evolving and shifting. It is critical to stay abreast of the current emerging threat landscape. Keeping up to date with security threats helps you to mount defenses that are more effective and to educate your users. User education is important, yet is an often-overlooked element of IT security. Users must avoid being easy prey, especially in the case of phishing fraud.

CEOs Face Great Challenges and Must Rise to the Occasion

The challenge for CEOs is formidable. They must:

- recognize emerging cyber threats and allocate sufficient resources, training time, procedural development time, and funding to stay ahead of new threats
- create an awareness of the company's weaknesses and the insider threat through enhanced security awareness training
- make cyber security risk management decisions based on the corporation's best interest to advance the bottom line, with no guarantee of being successful
- establish rules of behavior, codes of conduct, and ethic principles for the workforce
- acquire, equip, and train a staff that is technically and professionally skilled to design, develop, and implement cyber security measures, or, lacking that capability, seek professional security consulting expertise to achieve these goals and objectives
- foster a culture of security awareness throughout the company

The challenge for security professionals is equally formidable. They must:

- develop comprehensive yet simple cyber security procedures and incident response procedures and then train the workforce to use them effectively and efficiency
- adhere to best practices and hold employees accountable for their actions

---

[107] See footnote 108.
[108] WSJ.com, http://nsi.org/SecurityNewsWatch/NewsWatch/9.17.14.html/, (accessed 15.09.14.).

- foster a culture of security awareness throughout the company

Employees must also accept inherent challenges, such as:

- complying with all security procedures
- accepting individual responsibility and accountability for their actions, particularly when they willfully ignore standards and acceptable practices or stray from fundamental and time-honored principles of security
- participating in fostering a culture of security awareness throughout the company and reporting security violators to supervisors

Establishing a Security Risk Management Program Is Crucial

Where no performance measurement standard exists, there can be no meaningful evaluation of mission ability and capability, and mission effectiveness, efficiency and productivity. Without these measurement criteria to baseline an endeavor, any investigative process such as a security assessment, audit, or inspection is just an exercise in the waste of time, money and resources, producing embarrassing personal opinions and speculation rather than objective analysis, defendable facts and professional judgments.

John Sullivant

Top Takeaways

- Learn the purpose and need for a risk management program
- Learn how to measure security organizational performance
- Understand how measurement and evaluation establish organizational creditability
- Learn how to use a successful risk management framework and architecture platform

Overview

Did you know that nearly two-thirds of upper management believes that security is stronger than it actually is, whereas only less than a quarter of top executives are aware of their company's true security resilience posture?[1] Costly cyber attacks are not almost routine for businesses, but while many organizations are focusing on external attackers, companies may want to know that the largest single cause of confidential data loss is due to employees—more than 42%. Nearly three out of four companies have suffered an insider threat event. According to the "IT Security Risks Survey" conducted by Kaspersky Lab and B2B International, 73% of companies have been affected by both intentional and unintentional internal information security incidents. Out of those, more than 21% of companies also lost valuable data that subsequently had some sort of negative effect on their business. Fraud committed by employees is a major issue. The survey found that 15% of organizations encountered situations where company resources were used by employees for their own purposes. The losses caused by these incidents exceeded the

[1] https://www.nsi.org/Security_NewsWatch/NewsWatch/11.18.15.html.

damage caused by confidential data leaks for enterprises by outsiders. As you will recall, in both Chapters The Evolving Threat Environment and The Cyber Threat Landscape, I talked about the perceptions of several chief executive officers (CEOs) many years before the survey cited above was conducted. My findings, and those of many of my colleagues, refute the majority of CEO beliefs expressed in that survey. I find it astounding that almost two-thirds of the nation's top CEOs are in the dark about the true security readiness[2] of their corporations. This gap in perceptions, knowledge, and understanding of the strengths and weaknesses of a security organization by respectable top management should be great cause for alarm. It is time for executive management and top security professionals to bridge the gap between "what is" and "what is not," and to earnestly work together to develop an executive and security management communications plan to narrow this gap. Nothing is more discouraging than having your ideas ignored, your presence taken for granted, or failing in your attempt to be successful (Schmidt and Finnigan, 1994, pp. 1). The secret to being successful is picking yourself up when you fall, picking up the pace should you slow down, and believing in yourself when others do not.

Risk management is a strategy of security activity and the cornerstone of security governance. It is important for every security organization to have in place a realistic risk management program that can show executive management how well the security organization is performing its prime mission or, conversely, where the organization fails to perform to expectations. The goal of a security risk management program is to help security organizations become more productive; to determine the effectiveness of security policies, procedures, practices, and security measures; to ascertain the readiness of critical operational abilities and capabilities; and to determine the quality of management, leadership, staffing, and training while reducing the level of risk exposure.

To be of value to an entity, the security risk management program must be based on a set of acceptable performance standards, rules of behavior, and expectations that service the security organization, with a focus on those areas that matter most to C-suite executives. In sum, risk management is the process of constructing, measuring, evaluating, selecting, implementing, and monitoring actions to alter the presence of risk.

Risk Management Measures and Evaluates Risk Exposure and the Ability to Deal With Threats

The management of risk requires effective measurement and understanding of what effect vulnerability has on the level of risk. Both risk and vulnerability constantly change in response not only to threats and hazards but also to the business objectives. Organizations need a mature risk and vulnerability identification, measurement, and management process. In Appendix A, I highlight a proven strategy and model that can be adopted by any security organization.

A well-orchestrated security risk management program reflects the culture and character of the corporation and its security organization. To determine the

---

[2] "Readiness" and the terms "ability" and "capability" are often used interchangeably and have the same meaning. Refer to Appendix A, Security Risk Management & Architecture Platform.

effectiveness of security abilities and capabilities, as well as performance expectations, measurement and evaluation must be grounded in critical security functions. A reliable and valid measurement and evaluation program permits you to speak to corporate leadership in a familiar business language.[3] A sound program is vital to any security organization and is an important element of overall security management responsibility and accountability. Measurement and evaluation play key roles in examining the effectiveness, efficiency, and productivity of security performance. Without a compelling program, security professionals and budgets will never achieve aspiring goals and objectives.

Purpose and Need for a Security Risk Management Measurement Program

Executive management has a right and need to know how effective, efficient, and productive his or her security organization is, but what does this really mean? Do you really understand the significance of this commitment and how it affects your organization? In a risk-based environment, a business-oriented audience wants to know:

- How well are things going? If not well, how long have conditions existed?
- What are our risks? What is our posture? What do we do about it?

Communicate well the answers to those questions and you have won the battle. Articulate what works and what does not work, and you have won the war.

Identifying Security Successes and Failures Is Crucial

Evaluating performance effectiveness simply identifies gaps in the security organization's ability and capability to accomplish its mission. It also helps to build a foundation for developing and implementing prioritized solutions (Sullivant, 2007, pp. 159). Such an effort may include any or all of the following:

- Analyze policies, processes, practices, protocols, training, prevention, and protection measures to determine the effectiveness of the security program, including its dependency partners, in preventing undesired security and risk-based events and their consequences from occurring.
- Identify the strengths and weaknesses of the security organization, its leadership, and staffing, as well as any corporate culture barriers that degrade performance.
- Analyze data collected, conduct interviews, and perform selected tests and exercises, including testing security systems.

The process focuses on answering the following questions and must be all-encompassing:

- What is the mission and overarching goals of the security organization?
- What assets, functions, and resources need to be protected?

---

[3] "Persuading senior management with effective, evaluated security metrics". Research funded by the American Society for Industrial Security (ASIS) Foundation 2014: Alexandria, VA.

- What threats, hazards, accidents, and disasters does the corporation face?[4] To identify these conditions, risk management and risk analysis must be all-encompassing. What I mean by that is that it should include all reasonable threats and hazards; not all security- and safety-related events might pose the greatest risk or the greatest opportunities for risk mitigation. Many risk mitigation actions can reduce the consequence of many threats and hazards and must be evaluated on that broader basis.
- Which physical, cyber, and procedural security measures must the inside/outside adversary defeat to successfully penetrate a sensitive area, reach a targeted asset, carry out the mission objective, and affect an escape?
- How well do enterprise institutional drivers and performance strategies contribute to the effectiveness of the overall security program?
- How well has the enterprise integrated its program, system, and operational capabilities into its routine?
- What are the restrictions, limitations, and constraints of protection?
- Who is imposing such obstacles or what circumstances and conditions threaten performance?

Subscribing to a Security Risk Management Program

Few security organizations adequately measure and evaluate performance, processes, and outcomes. Most have no clue how to accomplish this. The reoccurring deficiencies, weaknesses, and inadequacies I talk about in Chapters The Evolving Threat Environment and The Cyber Threat Landscape are testimonials to the inability of most organizations to measure and evaluate their own performance and to do so in an independent and objective manner. The consequences of not measuring or incorrectly measuring and evaluating security activity can be detrimental to an organization for various reasons. It could inhibit:

- Meaningful measurement and evaluation of the enterprise's security capability
- Executive management from holding the security organization accountable for effective performance and productivity
- The ability of security management to remain accountable for effective, efficient, and productive performance

These consequences could potentially create a management problem of the most fundamental nature; many security organizations do not formally measure performance because the resources, expertise, knowledge, and funding needed to do so are not readily available. Always remember that all problems are management problems before they become operating problems. Those measurement and evaluation programs that do exist are mostly presented at the conceptual level, with little or no guidance on how to effectively use them, how to ascertain what exactly needs to be measured, how to obtain measurements, and when and how measurement should be used. Two reasons exist for this condition.

---

[4] Threats are intentional manmade acts to harm and injury persons or damage and destroy property. Hazards and accidents are unintentional occurrences such as fire, explosions, oil spills, and production failures. Floods, tornados, hurricanes, earthquakes, and tsunamis are examples of weather related calamities and are a natural phenomenon, usually referred to as natural disasters.

First, there is no industry-wide standard for measuring and evaluating security organizations. Certainly, management is not in favor of allocating funds and resources for a noncompulsory program. Throughout the industry are several volunteer standards that have been developed by professional associations such as the American Society of International Security and the National Institute of Standards Technology, but few security organizations subscribe to these guidelines. Instead, they hazardously attempt to design their own programs, inventing the rules as they go along.

- At the very least, organizations typically pick and choose segments of these volunteer standards in an area of particular interest and attempt to perform in-house spot checks, convincing themselves they have properly measured and evaluated their security operations. However, they generally fail to separate critical activity from noncritical activity and to prioritize the most crucial functions.
- The regulated industries, such as energy, chemical, seaports, and civil aviation, have good measurement and evaluation programs, but these efforts fall under the purview of the regulators. Under this concept, the enterprise's and security organization's contribution to the overall process is to correct noted deficiencies or, alternatively, refute the findings. Few security organizations expend the energy, time, resources, and money to challenge a regulator's findings. Political correctness often embraces the status quo to maintain the peace with the regulatory agency and corporate senior management.

The second reason is that measuring and evaluating a security organization is time-consuming and requires unique talent and skill sets that are not normally available within a typical security organization. Most organizations simply fill out a checklist and file it. There are hundreds of checklists available—many are thorough and comprehensive, yet few are useful tools for measuring and evaluating performance. When the applicable blank sections of these checklists are filled in, one has only a document that shows compliance or noncompliance with a particular regulatory requirement, standard or code, or best practice. Checklists seldom touch on the human side of the enterprise. To find the answers you really need, more information and additional investigation are needed:

- Why particular items on the checklist were marked "NO"?
- How long have these conditions existed? Why do they exist in the first place? Why were these conditions not discovered earlier and are only now surfacing?
- Who approved these conditions and why? What are the root causes of the ratings?
- What actions could or should have been taken to prevent these unsatisfactory conditions?
- What was (or is) the impact of the unsatisfactory condition on up- and downstream operations, including dependencies and the supply chain?
- What security enhancements and improvements are needed? What steps are needed to prevent reoccurrence?
- Who needs to get involved in program fixes? Who needs to approve program fixes?

The crux of the matter is that you need more than a completed checklist to determine the performance effectiveness, efficiency, and productivity of any security organization. Unfortunately, many security professionals lack the time, expertise, or experienced staff to measure and evaluate their organization. Seeking outside consulting expertise can be extremely beneficial. For instance, a thorough and comprehensive performance, management, or financial audit could significantly increase your management knowledge base and minimize the damaging consequences of inadequate performance. It also offers opportunities to:

- Enhance corporate brand, image, and reputation
- Improve security management and leadership skills
- Improve work force performance, enhancing productivity and synergy
- Establish coherent, clear and distinct practices, and improve accountability

A Risk Management Program Establishes Creditability

What Are the Fundamental Aspects of a Risk Management Program?

Three of the many key aspects of risk management are performance, productivity, and risk.

- Performance is the measurement of the enterprise's ability and capability to achieve its critical operational objectives, usually stated in terms of accomplishment, such as planning and executing; the ability and capability to deter, delay, detect, prevent, protect, assess; security emergency planning; and the development of event-driven response and recovery procedures; as well as developing the capability to master these tasks.
- Productivity is the effort evolved and the cost incurred in achieving outcomes, usually stated in dollars or operational benefits, both tangible and intangible.
- Risk is the potential for injury or loss of life, or the damage or destruction of assets, functions, and other property. Risk has two parts: the likelihood of something happening and the consequence(s) of it happening.

You can do four things to improve and enhance the credibility and standing of your security organization: ensure quality service and performance, develop relationships, build teams, and continuously improve performance. Let us see how you might benefit from adopting each of these approaches.

Quality Service and Performance Must Be Your Number One Priority

In the overall scheme of things, your customers—both internal and external—are the people and organizations you service and perform for. You are responsible and accountable for setting the ultimate criteria for quality service. Satisfying the needs of your customers, including upper management, is your top priority. Lest the service you provide has slipped your mind, please recall that you engage in the greatest of tasks: *the saving of life and the protection of critical facilities and assets through the successful application of risk management principles, exceptional execution of security management oversight and leadership, and the dedication to advance the profession.*

Developing Relationships Is a Key Condition for Success and Your Second Priority

Your second priority is to establish and maintain a business climate of openness and trust. When a problem occurs, it is time to honestly state the facts. There is no time for hidden agendas. What should be in question is whether the root causes of the problem have been correctly identified and whether the fix is the right solution. Any other issues are secondary in nature; often they are not important enough to detract you from fixing the problem. Where trust is high, ideas and communications flow easily. Barriers between divisions and departments and people are minimized. More work is done in teams, many of which may be interdepartmental and multidisciplinary. Most important, teams view errors and problems as opportunities for learning, rather than blunders to be punished. Where trust is low, however, everything becomes more complicated. People hesitate to point out problems, suggest new ideas, or take responsibility for mistakes or omissions. The most critical element, of course, is the solid commitment of top management to embrace and participate in open communications and trustful professional relationships.

Building Teams for Creative Thinking and Achievement Is Priority Three

Priority three is to acquire new skill sets as well as to refine your current skill sets. The way of doing business as a "loner" has long passed—if ever it existed in the first place. There is no room in today's business world for the self-centered leader who expects sole recognition for all accomplishments, whether performed by others or not. Successful leaders seldom receive public recognition, and most of us seem to be fine with that. An occasional pat on the back, however, is nice. As an alternative, praise your people and recognize their contributions to the organization. Executive management will notice them, and you.

To be successful, build teams: Building skill sets is crucial to problem solving, planning, and learning. If workers are expected to behave differently, they have to be trained differently. They must feel comfortable with new protocols, processes, and practices, and understand their significance in a healthy work environment. When groups work well they provide a level of satisfaction and expertise that energizes and inspires others. When a team solves a problem, every member of the team is recognized. When a group achieves its goal, everyone celebrates. There is little doubt that the exhilaration that comes from being part of a successful team is different from the satisfaction that comes from individual achievement. Setbacks or disappointments are also easier to manage as a member of a team.

Continuously Improving Performance Is Priority Four

The quest to learn and improve performance is a work in progress—it never stops. Priority four is to keep up with industry and enterprise changes, and new practices and technologies. You cannot settle for just getting by. As long as things are not perfect, there is room for improvement. The singular standard operating procedure you should follow is that on the plaque hanging on your office wall behind your desk: "Keep doing better." If all things are perfect, then your standard operating procedure is to make sure they stay that way.

When to Measure and Evaluate Performance

One of the goals of any security assessment is to analyze (that is, to measure and evaluate) security performance. Such as assessment should be conducted at least every 24 months, or more frequently, when:

- Operational requirements or business goals and objectives change significantly
- Capital improvement efforts call for the security review of new facility security designs
- The level of threat, hazards, accidents, and disaster conditions change significantly
- A threat advisory notice calls for the assessment of security abilities and capabilities
- Existing processes, practices, and security technologies are no longer practicable
- A significant amount of the security workforce rotates or transitions to another organization, or its leadership element is no longer functional.

Inspections and audits are typically performed as mandated by law or industry standards, or to ease management and board anxieties to ensure operations are accomplishing their intended purpose. Measurement and evaluation can be accomplished either internally by the organization as a self-appraisal, or externally by a qualified security consultant.

While self-appraisals can be a good management tool, they have limited application and usefulness. I am not a fan of self-appraisals; they seldom produce intended results because they are generally biased, lack objectivity and independence of thought, and are usually influenced by "working politics."

Second, such appraisals are usually constraint by time and the availability of qualified resources. Since self-appraisals measure and evaluate one's own performance, in-house resources conducting them may not be clear about the root causes of any of the deficiencies, weaknesses, or inadequacies they observe, or they may be hesitant to document and report factual information that could embarrass the boss. When these conditions prevail, self-appraisals have a tendency to give executive management incomplete, outdated, or erroneous information. One can expect that such results often project a false sense of security and potentially lead to vulnerability creep-in downstream.

Conversely, an evaluation performed by a qualified security consultant could easily perform an in-depth, independent, and unbiased examination of the security organization that results in objective judgments free of any internal or external influences, including working politics. The metrics these professionals use have scientific merit and value to the organization, focus on the enterprise's risks and goals, and consider operating reasonableness. The results of such professional services show promise of significantly enhancing and improving security resilience. These services can entail all aspects of a security organization or be an endeavor focused on a particular area of interest to senior management. A clear and distinct request for a proposal and statement of work is the vehicle to use to obtain such services.

A Risk Management Program Is Key to Performance Success

Appendix A describes a proven integrated framework and architecture design that resonates with executive management. It can produce results. The framework consists of measurement and evaluation processes, and the relationship between measurement and evaluation. The architecture platform consists of risk-based metrics[5] that involve performance analysis,[6] risk analysis,[7] and diagnostic analysis,[8] as well as the evaluation tools used most by security organizations. The risk framework and architecture is not a one-size-fits-all solution using all elements, all the time. Tailoring the framework to a selected assessment methodology for a specific application can be useful in combining or eliminating tasks (for example, moving from a conceptual approach to a procedural one), providing clarity and detail to certain tasks. Conceptual frameworks may or may not explicitly specify an order for task activity or the flow of information between tasks, and they do not specify techniques or provide specifics with respect to data and measures. Procedural frameworks are more detailed and structured than conceptual frameworks and do indicate the order of tasking and the flow of information, and specify the techniques used to perform each task. They may or may not specify the data and measures used.

Executives Need Compelling and Persuasive Information to Make Sound Business Decisions

Chief executives need compelling and persuasive information to help them determine whether the security organization possesses the ability and capability to perform its critical task—information that tells them whether, and in what important ways, the security program or activity is working well or poorly, and why. *Attachment 1* further outlines some of the functional areas CEOs, boards, community

---

[5] Risk-based metrics gauge the value of both human and technology performance.

[6] Performance analysis examines the effectiveness, efficiency, and productivity of human, and technology performance, including compliance to laws, industry standards or other guidelines.

[7] Risk analysis is the process of dividing risk into its component parts: threat, vulnerability, and consequences. Risk analysis describes the nature and magnitude of risk exposure to critical assets from threats and hazards, and the likelihood of an occurrence and its consequences, including the relevant uncertainties.

[8] Diagnostic analysis examines route causes of events, trends, conditions and circumstances; analyzes the criticality of threats, hazards, and consequences and the rank orderings respective criticalities; and examines the technical interfaces and dependencies of security systems.

governing bodies, and emergency response agencies have expressed an interest in over time. This listing is not all-inclusive, nor is it static. I offer these topics as a "straw man" tool to help you tailor your own listing to meet the specific reporting requirements that matter to senior management, boards, and community governing bodies. To honor the total measurement philosophy, you may wish to measure and report all areas to management, but this is usually not possible, practical, or desirable. Ideally, you should close the gap as much as possible between what must be measured and what is desirable to be measured. The narrower this gap is, the more comprehensive measurement and evaluation program you have. Despite any appreciation that might exist for the total measurement philosophy, the scope of measurement is not usually governed by a commitment to this ideal, but rather by a combination of factors unique to your corporate culture. The most influential are likely to be:

- The desire to remain fully accountable
- The cost of measuring and evaluating "all" activity versus "indispensable" activity
- The degree of enthusiasm for and resistance to further measurement and evaluation
- The intensity of external pressure for more comprehensive measurement

In the final analysis the scope of measurement is likely to be a compromise between that which you would like to undertake and that which you can and must afford, financially and politically.

- The first step in the process is to determine which areas are to be measured.
- Then identify the activities not to be measured and document the rationale for your decisions.
- Prioritize the listing based on your mission statement and commitments.
- Add critical areas that may not be included in any program documentation.
- When you narrow down the listing to meet your specific needs, have a one-on-one sit-down session with your boss and the CEO to review the list. They will let you know what matters to them.

As mentioned earlier, the listing is not static. It often is seasonal and situational, depending on circumstances, conditions, and business activity.

Conclusions

A comprehensive measurement and evaluation program can identify and significantly reduce security deficiencies, weaknesses, and inadequacies. Experience shows that most litigation could be avoided with proper management foresight in planning and executing proactive security measures to minimize risk exposure.

One cannot expect either executive and security management decision makers to make sound security decisions if they are hampered by the lack of good information or lack of a solid management knowledge base. Decisions based on validated and reliable facts are usually the right choices.

Appendix A: Risk Management and Architecture Platform

Frameworks

Measurement

Measurement monitors productivity outcomes that support business goals and advance the security organization's progress in accomplishing its mission. It has value when an outcome is defined in absolute terms, not subjective or ambiguous descriptions. There are occasions, however, where outcomes such as "detect," "assess," and "respond" may be measured in relative terms because human behavior deals with abstract conditions, circumstances, and situations of uncertainty, the outcome of which is outside the control of, for example, a responding force. It supports policy decisions that improve security resilience. It can also serve as an early warning system to management and as a vehicle for advancing accountability. Measurement may address activities conducted (process), the products and services delivered (outputs), or the results of those products and services (outcomes).

Evaluation

Evaluation examines how well a program is working or not working. Evaluation examines the achievement of objectives in the context in which they occur; may assess a program's effects beyond its intended objectives or compare the effectiveness of alternative programs aimed at the same objective; and supports resource allocation and other policy decisions to enhance and improve productivity and security resilience.

Relationship Between Measurement and Evaluation

Measurement focuses on whether mission objectives, expressed as an acceptable measurable performance standard, have been achieved. Evaluation examines security operations, or factors in the operational environment that may impede or contribute to its success, or help to explain the linkages between security inputs, outputs, and outcomes.

Architecture Platform

The platform is made up of risk-based metrics and evaluation tools. Metrics establish the margin of expected human, technology, and process performance to achieve mission goals and objectives. Strategies address those critical areas requiring improvement or compliance that are most important to executive management.

Risk-based metrics measure security performance effectiveness and efficiency, and the productivity[9] of critical security activities and critical security programs. The means used to achieve these results is met using performance analysis, risk analysis, and diagnostic analysis—all key elements of a comprehensive security assessment. The areas described in what follows may provide value.

Performance Analysis

Performance analysis metrics measure the degree of effectiveness of various activities:

- Blast-resistant and fire-resistant structures
- Built-in security design for new or modified facilities and sites
- Capital improvement initiatives affecting security
- Compliance/noncompliance with regulatory requirements and other commitments
- Command, Control & Communications C^3 capabilities and coordination and interaction with others
- Cyber security effectiveness
- Effort/time spent on primary/secondary responsibilities
- Electronic security application, deployment, performance, and maintenance
- Emergency response forces (eg, police, fire, medical, mutual assistance agreements)
- Filtering air against known pathogens and chemicals
- Human resource capital investment and social behavioral issues
- Interface/coordination with local, state, and federal law enforcement/security agencies
- Management, leadership, organization structure, staffing, experience, and expertise
- Next-generation security systems and architecture
- Obstacles that hinder processes, practices, and performance
- Platform for making better security decisions and shortening the decision-making process
- Policies, plans, protocols, practices, and process progress or lack thereof
- Secured corporate-wide web for crisis management analysis, response, and recovery
- Security design and engineering strategy
- Security force qualifications/certifications
- Security management knowledge base and leadership
- Security systems, communications, equipment, and facilities
- Security system downtime and compensatory security measures
- Security training
- Threat estimate profile
- Supporting major HAZMAT accidents and disasters
- Synergy with senior staff, business units, and external organizations
- Time-sensitive assessment capabilities
- Time-dependent delay, detection, deterrent, prevention, and protection capabilities
- Time-sensitive assessment and, event-driven responses, and recovery capabilities
- Topics of which management has insufficient knowledge
- Work performance and termination standards

---

[9] Effectiveness, efficiency, and productivity standards or expectations differ among security organizations and are dependent on the specific mission, regulatory requirements, and the expectations of upper management.

Risk Analysis

Risk analysis metrics measure the probability that something will happen:

- Criticality of threats, vulnerabilities, and assets[10,11]
- Dedicated backup power systems for security facilities and security systems
- Dedicated network for security system is ensured
- Emerging technologies that enhance security posture
- Emerging threats and vulnerabilities
- Consequences of losing critical assets and resources
- Incidents affecting image, brand, reputation, safety, health, and security
- Increased insurance premiums/negative press resulting from occurrences
- Likelihood of insider threat
- Likelihood of security system success or failure
- Likelihood of successful adversary engagement
- Likelihood of a threat, hazardous condition, accident, or disaster occurring
- Methodologies to accurately identify and predict actors perpetrating cyber attacks
- Predictable paths and methods of currently undetectable food, water, and air alteration
- Prevention and protection measures
- Security force's ability and capability to respond to and recover from risk-based events
- Repeat findings of noncompliance/failure to meet performance expectations
- Residual risk tolerance versus consequence impact
- Results of most recent security assessments, audits, inspections
- Risk tolerance versus consequence impact of "no decision"
- Severity of threats, vulnerabilities, and consequences of loss

Diagnostic Analysis

Diagnostic analysis metrics measure the impact of functions:

- Business impact/performance costs
- Common business unit security areas that compliment/augment business activity
- Cost against budget/cost and risk reduction/performance/return on investment
- Cost–benefit analysis and cost estimating
- Employee and security force turnover rates and terminations
- Finance security impact on the bottom line
- Human and technology performance
- Prioritizing the allocation of resources and funding
- Prioritizing mitigation solutions
- Rank ordering of critical assets, processes, or functions
- Rank ordering of the criticality of threats, vulnerabilities, and consequences of loss
- Revising land use to compliment emergency planning
- Root causes of events or trends in activity
- Self-diagnosing and self-healing security systems

[10] Asset criticality and loss consequence are fundamental factors that weight on the types of solutions management considers, including prioritizing the allocation of resources and funding to those areas that require security the most.

[11] In determining the threat environment, Probability of Occurrence (P_A) is an important factor in the analysis and decision-making process.

- Spatial clustering of critical infrastructures and assets
- Trends affecting critical business operations, risk, threats, vulnerabilities and consequences

Evaluation Tools Mostly Used Within Security Organizations[12]

The Physical Security Assessment

The physical security assessment is the forensic holistic evaluation of the "state of operational security readiness." It centers on the protection, robustness, and assurance of mission continuity and workforce protection essential to mission execution. Activities may include:

- Analyze threats and vulnerabilities that attract adversaries
- Analyze the consequences of asset loss against threats
- Assess program effectiveness of proposed mitigation solutions
- Benchmark program effectiveness
- Communicate program risks to build understanding of and confidence in the results
- Conduct interviews, review program documentation, and collect and analyze data
- Define project boundaries and scope of analysis
- Deliver draft/final report
- Determine circumstances and conditions influencing performance
- Determine political and social tolerance for acceptable residual risk exposure
- Evaluate personnel and training
- Evaluate plans, protocols, processes, and practices
- Help decision makers make informed decisions to reduce program risk exposure
- Help to monitor system mitigation solutions for effectiveness and continual improvement
- Identify asset criticality
- Identify program performance strengths and weaknesses
- Identify project goals and objectives
- Perform a cost–benefit analysis of the proposed program mitigation options
- Perform gap analyses
- Perform key client orientation
- Plan and coordinate project activities
- Prepare cost estimate of mitigation solutions and milestone schedule
- Present briefings to management
- Produce prioritized suggestions to reduce risk and improve performance
- Select mitigation solutions to reduce risk exposure

---

[12] While audits and reviews are typically performed on a standalone basis, we have seen a trend whereas many security organizations consolidate particular aspects of a management audit or review into the statement of work for conducting a comprehensive security assessment, including a security technical assessment. This approach may be cost-effective because it eliminates duplication of research, interview, and analysis time, which would be required in all instances for independent reviews, audits, and some inspections. Regardless of the cost savings realized, many organizations prefer to keep these activities independent of each other, while other organizations are mandated by regulatory or industry standards to keep them separate. Absent the need to keep audits, reviews, and inspections as separate entities, a holistic approach to identify performance effectiveness, efficiency, and productivity is recommended whenever feasible and practicable.

The Cyber Security Assessment

The cyber security assessment is the forensic investigation of computer systems and networks. Cyber security assessments focus on the protection of system integrity from unauthorized access, misuse, or manipulation of hardware, software, and human interaction. Activities may include:

- Analyze the results of service denial or other consequences
- Analyze system threats and vulnerabilities that are attractive to adversaries
- Assess the acceptability of residual system risk exposure
- Assess the performance effectiveness of the proposed system mitigation solutions
- Benchmark system effectiveness
- Communicate system risks to build understanding of and confidence in the results
- Conduct interviews
- Define project boundaries and the scope of analysis
- Determine equipment change out, software updates
- Determine political and social tolerance for loss of data or services
- Determine system design modifications or acquisition of new systems
- Evaluate personnel and training
- Evaluate the physical and electronic security architecture
- Examine root causes of system breaches
- Help decision makers make informed decisions to reduce system risk exposure
- Help management monitor system mitigation solutions for continual improvement
- Identify critical cyber assets
- Identify project goals and objectives
- Identify system performance strengths and weaknesses
- Perform briefings
- Perform a cost–benefit analysis of the proposed system mitigation options
- Perform key client orientation
- Perform technical gap analyses of system controls, incident reports, and recovery plans
- Plan and coordinate project activities
- Prepared cost estimate of mitigation solutions & milestone schedule
- Produce prioritized suggestions to reduce risk and improve system performance
- Review system documentation and collect and analyze data
- Select mitigation solutions to reduce system risk exposure

The Security System Technical Assessment

The security system technical assessment is the forensic technical assessment of a security system. The technical analysis centers on system performance, features, and human interfaces. Activities may include:

- Analyze backup systems, redundancy features, and fail-safe capability
- Analyze the results of service denial or other consequences against threats
- Analyze man–machine interfaces
- Analyze technology constraints and cascading effects stemming from system failures
- Analyze system threats and vulnerabilities
- Assess the performance effectiveness of the proposed system mitigation solutions and the acceptability of residual system risk exposure

- Assess system reliability, maintainability, and interoperability characteristics
- Assess the availability of qualified system operators to acknowledge and assess the severity of the incident, to make the appropriate decision to "up-channel" the report, and to dispatch a response team that is capable of handling the situation
- Benchmark performance, including human engineering considerations and usability
- Calculate the speed in which transactions and detection devices activate, signal transmissions to a monitoring console, and acceptable time delay for camera call-up after sensor activation plus the time the video transmission takes to reach a monitoring location
- Collect and analyze data
- Communicate system risks to build understanding of and confidence in the results
- Conduct interviews
- Define project boundaries and scope of analysis
- Determine equipment change-out, software updates
- Determine political and social tolerance for weak system performance
- Determine system design modifications or acquire new systems
- Evaluate personnel and training, and recommend improvements to training program
- Evaluate system technology application and deployment
- Examine root causes of system breaches
- Help decision makers make informed decisions to reduce system risk exposure
- Help management monitor system for continual improvements
- Identify dependencies and interdependencies between subsystem components
- Identify project goals and objectives
- Identify system performance strengths and weaknesses
- Perform a cost–benefit analysis of the proposed system mitigation options
- Perform key client orientation
- Perform technical gap analyses of system controls, system management, and cyber security plan, and coordinate project activities
- Produce prioritized suggestions to reduce risk and improve performance including milestone schedule
- Present briefings
- Recommend prioritized mitigation solutions
- Review system specifications and plans
- Select mitigation options to reduce system risk exposure

The Technical Surveillance Countermeasures Inspection Review

The technical surveillance countermeasures inspection review is the technical forensic examination of selected offices, meeting areas, conference rooms, and other locations used to discuss highly sensitive business activities or confidential, proprietary, competitive-sensitive information; trade secrets and patients; and scientific data. The process uses technical sophisticated equipment to detect and find:

- Audio sounds and frequencies emitted by computerized technology
- Computer-related threats
- Electromagnetic spectrum, radiofrequency signals
- Hidden eavesdropping devices
- Hot spots inside walls
- Magnetic fields and electrical noise

- Objects inside walls
- Presence of technical surveillance devices
- Residual heat of a bug or power supply
- Technical security weaknesses
- Visual, electronic, and physical evidence of bugging
- Written report of findings , cost estimate of mitigation solutions and milestone schedule

The Organization and Management Review

The organization and management review is the forensic examination of the organization's ability and capability to perform its critical mission. The review:

- Analyzes management leadership and use of resources, staffing, and budget
- Analyzes what does and does not work
- Benchmarks performance
- Communicates organizational strengths and weaknesses to build understanding
- Determines political and social tolerance for acceptable performance
- Examines the mission statement
- Examines individual and group performance effectiveness, efficiency, and productivity
- Examines processes, practices, and protocols
- Evaluates organizational synergy and customer satisfaction
- Evaluates personnel qualifications, experience, and certifications
- Examines training programs to determine performance effectiveness
- Helps management to monitor system mitigation solutions for continual improvement
- Produces prioritized suggestions to enhance and improve organizational performance
- Performs a cost–benefit analysis of proposed recommendations

The Inspection Review

The inspection review is the forensic examination of a security organization to verify compliance with pre-established security standards and practices as described in policy and regulations in an effort to help maintain its security posture. Inspection teams use checklists to compare an organization's compliance with that outlined by an authoritative or regulatory body, the results of which are detailed in after-action reports provided to the responsible party. The inspection review:

- Determines whether program objectives, controls, processes, procedures, practices, and management are in place and report accordingly
- Examines plans, policies, and procedures
- Recommends corrective actions to be taken
- Reviews criteria to establish, check, maintain, and improve the management system against predetermined standards
- Tracks the status of improvements and their completion in a timely manner

The Compliance Audit

The compliance audit is the forensic examination of a security organization's compliance or noncompliance with regulatory requirements and adherence to protocols, standards, codes, and other commitments to better the understanding of costs and benefits. The audit:

- Compares "what is" with "what should be" and provides feedback for corrective action
- Examines activity to ensure that fundamental, task-unique conditions for success are met
- Identifies any looming impediments that might slow down, hold back, or delay progress
- Identifies the effectiveness and efficiency of operations, facilities, equipment, protocols, management, and leadership
- Recommends correct actions

The Special Study

The special study focuses on a concept of operation or the feasibility of an idea, process, or technology to support a broader range of goals and objectives. Research, development, test, and evaluation (RDT&T) activity is usually involved.

Quality Assurance: Zero Defects

The cornerstone of this framework and architecture platform is ZERO DEFECTS. This removes the emphasis on statistical quality controls used for hardware and software, and places responsibility and accountability for quality performance in the hands of those delegated the authority to oversee the various segments of a security mission on a personal basis.

The concept of zero defects:

- Aims at stimulating individuals and groups to care about accuracy and completeness, to pay attention to detail, and to improve work habits and social norms
- Emphasizes personal motivation and instills pride of work ownership
- Emphasizes reducing errors and omissions to Z-E-R-O

For ZERO DEFECTS to be of value, the measurement and evaluation process must:

- Have clear, concise, and distinct objectives that define value
- Identify exacting activity, process, practice, and protocols that capture the interest of decision makers and stakeholders

Goals and objectives must have value and meaning to decision makers and stakeholders. SMART goals accomplish this.

S	Specific	Clear and unambiguous language understood by management
M	Measurable	Visible to quality performance, progress, and productivity over time
A	Attainable	Realistic, practical, and reachable; reliable, dependable, and creditable
R	Relevant	Operating reasonableness, which is linked to business goals and objectives as well as business risk
T	Time-bound	Clear start and end points; have final closure

Useful Metrics Give the Security Organization Standing

Not having metrics to measure our progress and competencies is frustrating in proving our value to executive management.

__John Sullivant__

Top Takeaways

- Develop solid metrics that defend solutions
- Minimize when you or your boss is wrong or surprised
- Save time while increasing accuracy and reducing mistakes
- Help executive management make the right decisions
- Use risk-based metrics to measure critical security functions
- Protect against cognitive bias that leads to mistakes
- Justify your arguments and recommendations
- Use practical risk-based metrics that resonate with management
- Use metrics that are persuasive and matter to executive management

Overview

The basic security concept accepts the reasoning that no amount of security can keep a corporation or agency safe from every possible threat, hazard, accident, or disaster, and that all resources, assets, facilities, processes and practices cannot be given the same level of protection from such events. In other words, there is no such thing as perfect security, and there will never be such a scenario. Using risk-based metrics, C-suite executives can focus on key drivers and indicators of change to improve rigor, enhance understanding, and avoid pitfalls—always recognizing, acknowledging, and accepting the fact that there will always be a degree of residual risk, vulnerability, and consequences to deal with. We then enter the arena of prioritizing our prevention and protection actions, our detection and response and recovery capabilities, and our competencies.

Stakeholders in the information technology (IT)[1] parts of the business must also make these decisions and not leave it up to IT professionals to assume this awesome

---

[1] International Organization for Standardization (ISO) / International Electrotechnical Commission (IEC) 27,001 is a widely used, best practice certification that outlines mandated information technology security requirements surrounding the range of threats and vulnerabilities for cyber security, including related metrics.

responsibility. Doing so perpetuates the notion that IT risks relate only to IT. They do not. IT risks are only a portion of a much larger corporate integrated security risk management program.

Because of the diversity of security and its effect on the entire corporation or agency, security directors must adopt a provocative approach across the entire spectrum of security activity to determine the strengths and weaknesses of their organization. By default, this effort must focus on the capability of a corporation in general and a security organization in particular to perform its indispensable tasks—deterrence, delay, prevention, detection, protection, assessment, and response to and recovery from an adverse event—encompassed by the process of saving life and protecting assets. No other security mission task is more important than these. Embracing a set of risk-based metrics to address risk exposure and the performance effectiveness of these critical activities is fundamental to the creditability of a security organization.

Risk-based Metrics Are Often Underestimated

The vastness of security issues that need to be dealt with and the limited amount of resources and funding available make it critical that the security practitioner choose wisely how to manage risk and not be managed or influenced by it. I have found that most organizations have an array of operational metrics that they use to report basic law enforcement activity, such as the number of criminal acts, traffic accidents, traffic violations, personal assistance calls, population and vehicle throughputs, and a myriad of other behavioral social activity. While operational metrics can be of value internally to a security organization, they seldom resonate with chief executives because they are neither linked to, aligned with, or part of the larger enterprise risk process or corporate business goals and objectives, nor do they directly contribute to saving life and protecting critical infrastructure and key assets.

Conversely, risk-based metrics help executive management drive business and security decisions and behavior, and form the basis for long term capital improvements. They enable policies, processes, and practices to influence collaboration for corporate-wide benefits, drive investment decisions, and guide strategic and profit center alignment.

Measuring the performance of a security organization also identifies opportunities to help chief executive officers (CEOs) achieve company goals. Integrating security risk-based metrics into the corporation's overall risk management program offers a CEO and the leadership team a viewpoint from a different company perspective. This effort helps senior management to further understand security's contribution to the corporation and the important role it plays (Sullivant, 2007, pp. 72–73).

Here I deliberately avoid operational metrics and instead focus on presenting security risk-based metrics that address a security organization's ability and capability to perform its prime mission: saving life and protecting critical infrastructure and assets. Some elements of the management team may find this to be a provocative strategy foreign to the current culture. One can expect these forces to resist change, attempt to hold on to their own "turf" rules, and argue the basis of "old school" principles. A risk-based strategy fosters and promotes team building and shared security responsibility that provide a road map for change.

Setting the Metric Framework and Architecture Foundation

Sharing security responsibility punctures the "old school" concept and abandons the myth that responsibility is the internal province of the security organization. A well-designed metric can promote both a driving force and a starting point in determining the level of organizational security responsibility, and it can demonstrate how various organizations contribute to overall corporate security resilience.

Well-Designed Risk-based Metrics Resonate with CEOs

Embracing a set of risk-based metrics is fundamental to a security organization's credibility, reputation, and ability to perform. Risk-related metrics serve executives exceptionally well, but risk-based metrics are only an indicator, not an absolute value for measuring. They serve as the first step in guiding security professionals to meet acceptable competency standards and are a vehicle through which security programs can demonstrate their measurable influence on a company's strategic, organizational, financial, and operational risks and profits.

Risk-based metrics can gauge the effectiveness, efficiency, and productivity of the most critical security activities, programs, and competencies that are of interest to management. Such metrics may be quantitative or qualitative measurements, or a combination of both. Risk-based metrics focus on the actions (and results of those actions) that security organizations take to manage the risk of image, brand, and reputation; the protection of people, assets, and information; and conditions and circumstances that affect the well-being of the workforce, business operations, and corporate survivability. When a company uses these metrics to formulate conclusions, the decisions made are more likely to be the right ones since they are grounded in scientific merit, strategic relevance, and operational reasonableness.

Appendix A, "Metric Framework and Architecture Platform," illustrates how these characteristics create the foundation for meaningful and useful metrics that are simple and quick to complete, provide results that are easy to explain to senior management, and, most important, address those factors that matter most to C-suite executives. The framework and architecture are also important because they provide a roadmap to communicate with executives in a language they understand and embrace. I dedicate Chapter How to Communicate With Executives and Governing Bodies, to this very important topic.

Security organizations can effectively use two categories of measurement: the theory of probability and the theory of performance. This chapter focuses on the theory of probability, whereas the theory of performance is the main theme of chapter A User-Friendly Security Assessment Model, chapter Establishing and Maintaining Inseparable Security Competencies, chapter Preparing for Emergencies, chapter A User-Friendly Protocol Development Model, and chapter A Proven Organization and Management Assessment Model.

Theory of Probability

Probability theory is applied to the inseparable risk-based elements of the security risk management process (Sullivant, 2007, pp. 66–67):

- Serious damage to company assets, management, and business activities occurs.
- The life or the safety of the body or personal rights of management or employees is endangered by an incident or accident.
- The reputation of the company or the confidence in a brand is seriously damaged.
- Threat and vulnerability analysis is the probability that a specified threat, hazard, accident, or disaster may happen and the rank order of each outcome.
- Consequence impact analysis is the probability that an asset, facility, function, process, or resource may be injured, damaged, destroyed, or lost by a threat, hazard, accident, or disaster, and the rank order of the impact of each loss outcome.
- Competency analysis is the probability that a corporation possesses the ability and capability to perform its inseparable operational tasks to deter, delay, prevent, protect, and detect specified threats and other security-related functions; and to assess, respond to, and recover from such activity in a successful and timely manner.
- Shareholders, customers, business partners, and the public are seriously affected.

Probability is used to quantify some proposition, the truth of which we are not certain of. Certainty is described as a numerical measure, between 0 and 1, where 0 indicates impossibility and 1 indicates certainty. Thus the higher the probability of an occurrence, the more certain we can be that it will happen; it is thereby deserving of greater attention from management. While a lower rating also needs management's attention, it is not to be used as a tradeoff candidate for a higher rating. A proposition with a lower rating typically is considered for mitigation action as budgets and resources become available or is considered as residual risk tolerance.

This standard is useful in determining the degree to which critical infrastructures and assets need to be protected in an all-hazards environment that may affect business operations, should an incident occur. Here I offer a useful guideline for determining the process of ranking events and the protection of assets.

Probability of Occurrence (PA) Criteria

Probability of occurrence (P_A) criteria introduce planning variables into the decision-making process and add credibility to the analysis process (Sullivant, 2007, pp. 76–81). Fig. 7.1[2] graphically displays its integrated component parts.

---

[2] The application of Fig. 7.1 is shown in Chapter Developing A Threat Estimate Profile.

Likelihood of Occurrence	Likelihood Rating		Occurrence Measurement
	Numerical	Narrative	
High	0.90	H	Risk exposure is *high*
Moderate	0.60	M	Risk exposure is *moderate*
Low	0.30	L	Risk exposure is *low*
Not likely	0.10	NL	Risk exposure is *not likely*
Undetermined	0.00	I	Sufficient information is not available to make a determination

Figure 7.1 Business consequence analysis.
Source: Sullivant, J., 2007. CFC, CSC, CHS-IV, CPP, RAM-W, Diplomate, ABFET. Strategies for Protecting National Critical Infrastructure Assets: A Focus on Problem-Solving (Exhibit 7.7 Example Worksheet 18-Malevolent Acts & Undesirable Events by Los of Consequences and Probability of Occurrence (P_A) page 150). Wiley & Sons, New Jersey.

In Fig. 7.1, the likelihood that something will happen is ranked in column 1 as high, moderate, low, not likely, and undetermined. Columns 2 and 3 transcribe the likelihood rating into both numerical and narrative values. The numerical designation is helpful if you desire to measure the range in quantitative terms, whereas the abbreviated narrative value is helpful if you want to measure the ranges in qualitative terms. Caution is in order when using a quantitative measurement for security matters that are largely uncertain predictions as they could give executive management a false sense of security risk conditions. My rationale for this judgment is offered in the paragraph that follows. Objective (or quantitative) probability considers the relative frequency of the occurrence, whereas subjective (or qualitative) probability includes expert knowledge as well as quantitative data considering an occurrence. Column 4 describes the risk exposure occurrence measurement in narrative form.

Determining a realistic P_A is an important factor in the decision-making process. In the realm of security operations, analytical results, however, need not be based on the precision of a classical probability equation. As such, P_A contains wide latitude for variation. The advantage of using P_A is that absolute precision is not important nor desired. What is important is to identify specific threats, hazards, accidents, or disasters and associate their level of severity to business accomplishment or the consequences of business failure. Risk, then, is determined by applying a probability rating using accurate historical information; acceptable actuarial tables; established policy, standards, specifications, and procedures; and acceptable professional judgment. From a business perspective I have never been able to fully convince executive management that there is a 0.9 or 0.7 percent chance that something bad may happen. I learned that approach has little or no meaning or value to management, and it is difficult to ask management to allocate resources and funds to such a proposition. What has worked for me is building a business case on a "High" or "Moderate" likelihood that a specific event could occur, verified by a realistic forecast of potential business loss consequences. I have found management can relate to revenue loss, and if significant will act on any reasonable request to reduce business risk exposure.

When considering the effective performance of an electronic security system, determining the probability of security system success $(P_S)^{3,4}$ is based on quantitative measurement only. What I mean by this is that security hardware and software either works or it doesn't work. There is no room for shades of grey for technology to work only occasionally. When measuring technology performance and system capability you are addressing a simple pass/fail criteria. Nothing else is an acceptable alternative. Nothing else matters. As such, P_S encompasses the cumulative effect of the following activities measured against specified standards of time constraints and performance levels.

- Probability of detection is the activation of an intrusion detection sensor.
- Probability of CCTV camera call-up is the activation of one or more cameras integrated with a sensor, card reader, door, or other security device.
- Probability of communications is the time it takes for a signal to transmit from the sensor to the monitoring station, possibly through one or more control panels.
- Probability of video display is the time it takes a signal takes to display on the designated monitor.
- Probability of assessment is a human measurement function and is the degree of speed and accuracy with which an individual can respond to an alarm, which includes reacting to an announced alarm, performing an initial assessment, and notifying a responding unit of the crisis.[5]
- Probability of response force encompasses a combination of human and technology attributes that examine the ability and capability of the response force to act. This involves arriving on the scene within a specified time; tactically deploying adequately and in a timely manner; using available technical and human expertise to effectively contain or neutralize the adversary; and prevent him or her from achieving a targeted objective or completing his or her mission.[6]

---

[3] Few organizations, if any, have the technical expertise, time and technical resources available to perform a formal P_S specification test of their electronic security system to determine an exacting level of system performance to original equipment manufacturer specifications or a formal system acceptance test performed as part of the system turnover process during the acquisition phase. Rather, many organizations perform self-tests at the start of each shift and at other times, such as when maintenance on the system is performed. Such tests may include any or all of the following:

- A system diagnostic test to check for anomalies, system malfunctions, or inoperative alarm points.
- A physical inspection of visible system components to check for visible damage or tampering.
- Testing detection sensors for general operability but no formal Pd testing.
- Testing CCTV and communications for general operability but no technical testing.
- Testing of automated and manual barrier systems for general operability.
- Other system functions as applicable to user needs.

[4] Depending on the complexity of the system and mandated regulatory performance requirements, additional probability elements can be added to the representative listing to meet any unique local demands that may need to be addressed.

[5] Measurement involves a level of performance effectiveness and efficiency and other factors such as visibility, weather conditions, operation of equipment, and distractions.

[6] Measurement involves a combination of factors such as knowledge of route or routes to take, traffic congestion, weather conditions, condition of transport mode used, potential for being ambushed on the way to the scene, and other factors such as tactical knowledge, experience, and leadership.

| Likelihood of Consequence | Rating | | Consequence Analysis (C_A) |
	Numerical	Narrative	
Fatal to the business	0.90	F	• High potential for the effects of life and health, injury or loss of life, or economic, institutional, and social damage • Workforce is anticipated to exhibit widespread panic and confusion • A portion of the leadership element is expected to be included in workforce losses • In-place shelter does not exist, nor does the capability to respond to emergency conditions • Communications and management information systems are inoperative • Utilities are inoperative, with massive gas leaks, sewage spills, fuel ruptures, and HAZMAT spills throughout the site • Sufficient qualified resources are not available to conduct immediate initial damage assessment catastrophic damage results in total recapitalization or abandonment of facility and assets, with long-term discontinuance of business operations until a new facility is constructed • Evacuation of workforce from the site or facility • Extensive external response and recovery is necessary, requiring the relocation of remaining workforce, time-critical and dependency functions, and operations for an extended period of time • Immediate and long-term impact on employees, the community, and the company
Very severe to the business	0.80	VS	• High potential for injury or loss of life • Panic and fear among the workforce is to be expected • Delivery of critical services and products is interrupted • Most communications, management information systems, and utilities are expected to be damaged or destroyed • Severe structural damage with some collapse is anticipated • Crisis management leadership and response capability are severely affected, requiring external assistance • Evacuation of workforce from the site or facility • Requires major effort and expenditure to repair or replace, with long lead time for recovery • Signification loss of revenue is anticipated during the recovery process
Moderately serious to business	0.60	MS	• Medium to moderate potential for injury or loss of life • Employee welfare is affected • Moderate damage to hardened facilities and considerable damage to unhardened facilities is expected • Some communications systems may be available • Organization and leadership element is in-tact • Loss would have a noticeable impact on revenues during recovery • Evacuation of workforce from the site or facility is expected • Damage would result in short-term or limited suspension of operations • Moderate impact on time-critical and dependency functions and activities • No relocation of resources • Managed locally with limited external response • Emergency response capabilities are degraded but partially functional
Slightly serious to business	0.30	SS	• Minor potential for injury or loss of life • Many employees are unaware that an event has even occurred • Slight business disruption is expected • Minor damage sustained by facilities • Damage does not require suspension of operations • Few business operations are physically affected • Requires temporary evacuation of the workforce from the site or facility • Organization and leadership are in-tact • Emergency response capabilities are functional • Loss would generally be covered by normal contingency reserves and insurance coverage
Seriousness to business undetermined	0.00	SU	• Insufficient data are available to determine the impact on business operations

Figure 7.2 Business consequence analysis (C_A).

Source: Sullivant, J., 2007. CFC, CSC, CHS-IV, CPP, RAM-W, Diplomate, ABFET. Strategies for Protecting National Critical Infrastructure Assets: A Focus on Problem-Solving (Exhibit 7.7 Example Worksheet 18-Malevolent Acts & Undesirable Events by Los of Consequences and Probability of Occurrence (P_A) page 151). Wiley & Sons, New Jersey.

- Probability of backup response force is the ability and capability of a backup response force to arrive on the scene and tactically deploy in a timely manner within specified response times, and to assist the response force team leader (or on the scene commander) as directed.[7]
- Probability of event recording is the activation of software protocols to document system transactions and alarms in real time, including archive retrieval capability.
- Probability of backup systems is the activation of backup systems when the primary system fails.
- Probability of emergency power supplies is the activation of emergency power supplies when primary power fails.

Business Consequence Analysis Criteria

I also offer a model for helping you develop a cardinal rank order of consequence loss (Sullivant, 2007, pp. 81–82). Fig. 7.2 may be useful in your decision-making process to allocate adequate resources and funding to protect those resources and assets that need special protection against damage or loss.

The likelihood of a consequence rating (column 1) shows the probable severity of loss inflicted in a descriptive context. The numerical rating (column 2) illustrates the range of loss in quantitative terms, whereas the narrative rating (column 3) shows the ranges in qualitative terms. The consequence analysis (C_A) (column 4) represents the potential magnitude of damage or destruction that could be sustained given specific threat parameters, such as the means[8] usually used to carry out an attack and the site or facility conditions, including population density margins, physical configuration of assets, and the asset's proximity to other hazardous areas, as well as other critical factors. Objective and subjective probability analysis, including expert knowledge, and the measurement cautions discussed under probability of occurrence (P_A) above equally apply to C_A. The following factors play a crucial role in determining the criticality of loss:

- *Human cost:* the physical and psychological harm to employees, customers, clients, and other stakeholders resulting from a loss.
- *Environment impact:* the degradation of the quality of the environment or harm to endangered species.
- *Economic loss:* impacts on the national, regional, and local economy and reduction in the net tax base of the local jurisdiction.
- *Corporate image cost:* loss of reputation and standing in the community and industry, negative press, loss of customer or client base; damage to image, brand, and reputation; loss of confidence among stockholders, customers, clients, stock market, regulators, and the community in corporate leadership's ability to return enterprise to "normal."
- *Asset criticality:* the cardinal rank ordering for business impact that provides the necessary supporting rationale to defend the prioritization of a particular asset loss; looked at singly and collectively, including life-cycle costs, redundant systems, backup units, and the logistical capability to restore or replace a damaged or destroyed asset in a reasonable timely manner.

---

[7] Ibid.
[8] The preferred means of most attacks is the use of explosives, the effect of which is dependent on the amount used, its placement, the quality of control devices, and the expertise of the adversary.

- *Financial cost:* equipment and property repair or replacement and downtime; overtime pay, stock devaluation, loss of sales; reduced cash flow, insurance costs, potential lawsuits, and regulatory fines and/or penalties.

Benefits of Using Risk-based Metrics

Risk-based metrics answer business questions regarding security, which facilitate strategic decision making by the organization's highest level of governance. Key benefits of value to executive and security management are numerous. Metrics show:

- Compliance with legislation, regulations, standards, policies, and procedures. They benchmark specific performance levels and help to guide security decisions by showing when, where, and how security competency moves out of the expected range of performance expectations, and by demonstrating adherence to decisions already made with respect to performance expectations.
- Where the security organization is meeting its performance expectations or where improvement is needed. Metrics allow the organization to adjust its readiness capability while continuing to build upon strengths and correct weak performance. Metrics help to resolve disagreements and nonconformities, or to define when a process or protocol has not achieved the desired results, without pointing fingers at individuals. Metric results make it about correcting the process or practice rather than personality.
- CEOs and governing bodies that they can pilot the security organization like all other organizations in the company and acknowledge its "financial contribution" to the corporation through the protection of critical infrastructure and assets. This means recognizing security activity as a production center rather than a cost center.
- Key business areas that demonstrate signs of high-risk exposure. Metrics offer strategies that show promise for reducing business risk.
- The root causes of security deficiencies, weaknesses, and inadequacies. Metrics identify security trends, both within and outside the organization's control, and guide decision makers in adjusting processes, practices, and protocols, and in allocating reasonable resources and funding to those areas that need greater prevention and protection measures. Metrics can also show the utilization of security resources and expenditures and help develop the security budget.
- Estimate risk exposure associated with various ways of conducting business.
- Uniformity to specified security measures, providing economies of scale and measurably adding to employee well-being.
- The effectiveness of the risk mitigation and regulatory compliance program and how the security organization contributes to the bottom line.
- Operational or human failure costs: cyber threats, theft, fraud, waste and abuse, workplace violence, and other major activity. These costs are immense, and they cannot be adequately planned or budgeted for except under a special contingency budget. Cumbersome and inefficient processes, poor practices, and substandard performance are high-cost areas but are more predictable.
- The productivity of human and technology performance. Metrics allow the organization to monitor performance over time to make midcourse corrections, if necessary.
- C-suite executives why security measures should be implemented to reduce business risk. The direct linkage between identified risk exposure to business goals and operations, and lack of security measures and mitigation solutions makes a compelling case for the need

to reduce business risk. Metrics help to define problematic threats, vulnerabilities, and loss consequences. Metrics speak to the hearts and minds of executives by focusing on areas of business risk that are important to them.

- Executive management the level of business risk so they can understand and make informed decisions on the level of residual security risk exposure they are willing to accept.

Valid and reliable risk-based metrics lead to conclusions that are more accurate and more persuasive communication with senior management. They help to identify the success or failure of existing security measures and proposed security solutions.

Conclusion

A Historical Perspective

Historically, corporate management has viewed security as a cost center rather than a production center and security metrics as merely measuring routine activity, not critical mission tasking that has meaning, value, and usefulness. Under this viewpoint, it is difficult for security professionals to measure security benefits against the service benefits of profit centers. This "old-school thinking" must end. We must make change a high-priority goal to be accomplished. It is not a question of whether this change is necessary, but rather how to persuade executive management that such change is in the best interests of the corporation. Certainly, this is an excellent opportunity for all security professionals to join forces in this crusade.

Useful Metrics Span a Wide Area of Interest

Security metrics measure a wide variety of issues, from human and technology performance to the effectiveness, efficiency, and productivity of processes, practices, and protocols to the ability and capability of an organization to perform its critical tasks. Metrics are not intended to be models of perfection—they cannot be. Rather, they are guidelines that security professionals and executive management should use to help the decision-making process move along. Organizations that use metrics coupled with an analytical process are more likely to make the right decisions. Security metrics allow organizations to hold individuals accountable for specified results and goals. They are a vehicle through which critical security operations and programs can demonstrate their measurable impact on an organization's strategic, organizational, financial, and operational risks and profits. Therefore, it is paramount to advance the understanding of these metrics and knowledge of how to effectively use and communicate metrics, as well as what it takes to make a better metric. Chapter How to Communicate with Executives and Governing Bodies focuses on these important topics.

Balancing Business Innovations and Risk Exposure

The dynamics of the threat environment means that a security director is forced into a state of continuous conflict between the business wanting to drive innovation and the security team needing to rein in risk exposure. Executive decision makers want to know that the business is adequately protected against risk, but they need to weigh the risks of yesterday and today against the opportunities of tomorrow. A win–win situation exists when the senior management team and the security team work hand-in-hand to develop safeguards that allow the chief executive to carry out the corporation's strategic business vision.

Align Security Goals with Company Goals

Metrics should be aligned with the organization's objectives and risks and should measure specific activity, performance or issues that matter to senior management. Presenting metrics that meet measurement standards, are aligned with the organization's objectives and matter to management, and tell a compelling story tailored to the audience; communicating based on risk exposure and over time; using meaningful graphics; keeping presentations short; and presenting metric data at regular intervals will enhance your communication with C-suite executives.

Metric Creditability

Creditable metrics possess scientific validity, organization relevance, reliability, return on investment, and practicality characteristics. At a high level, this strategy can help security practitioners better understand how to effectively communicate metric meaning and value to executives. If a metric is not reliable or valid, then the conclusions drawn from it will be inaccurate. Drawing inaccurate conclusions and communicating misinformation undermines your attempt to describe your point of view, which in turn drives management to further underestimate the importance of security metrics.

Measurement Provides Feedback

Security leaders continue to use metrics mainly to guide budgeting and to make the case for new technology investments. In some cases, they use measurements to help develop strategic priorities for their security organizations. Leaders need to focus on finding the delicate balance between developing a strong, holistic security, and risk management strategy, while implementing more advanced and strategic capabilities to achieve their primary security mission.

Closing Thoughts

In this chapter I have presented an opportunity to advance your capability to measure performance and productivity. The framework is grounded in scientific merit, strategic relevance, and operational reasonableness. This process, in turn, enhances your ability to communicate effectively with upper management in a user-friendly language they understand. Numerous security organizations have successfully measured and evaluated their effectiveness using this approach, and it can work for you and your boss, as well.

Appendix A: Metric Framework and Architecture Platform

Scientific Merit or Value

Reliability

Reliability is the long-term ability of metrics to yield consistent results with little or no variability in reporting in the face of disturbances and that are unaffected by sources of measurement error. There is no over- or under-collecting. Data are collected carefully in real time from actual occurrences, official records, field interviews, and conditions observed while performing security assessments, audits, or inspections, and they are highly reliable and predictable. Repeated measurements using the same method, as well as alternative methods, should achieve the same results.

Validity

Results are based on theory and research that support drawing conclusions from the metric. For example, there is a direct relationship between security intervention and a reduction in business risk exposure. Data are collected from official documents, resources, and observations. Previous uses have validated the metrics.

Generalizability Theory

Conclusions are based on quantitative or qualitative analysis, professional judgment, expertise, and best practices. Conclusions drawn are consistent and applicable across different settings, organizations, or circumstances, including comparisons with similar external organizations.[9]

Strategic Relevance

Organizational Relevance

Metrics gauge the ease or difficulty of operations and provide useful and meaningful information and insight that matter most to C-suite executives, enabling them to carry out their responsibilities better. Metrics are linked to specific organizational missions, objectives, goals, assets, risks, threats, or vulnerabilities. The linkage is strong and of high relevance to the organization.

---

[9] Not all external organizations are willing to share similar data collected, thus attempting to benchmark particular results with many external organizations may not be possible. In those instances, existing security effectiveness may be used as a benchmark to internally measure the improved effectiveness of proposed mitigation actions.

Communication

The combined metrics provide insights into the strengths and weaknesses of security activities. Metrics point out areas that may need strengthening or support areas for continual improvement. Metrics, their purpose, and their results can be communicated easily. Privacy concerns are strictly maintained.

Return on Investment

Return on investment (ROI) can be used to demonstrate cost savings or the consequence of loss in relation to relevant security spending.[10] This involves expressing the following in terms of dollars or some other unit that is relevant to decision makers:

- Cost of security intervention
- Effects of security intervention and unintended consequences related to the intervention
- Investment in security technology that improves effectiveness and productivity

ROI can show the relationship between a security action and practice and the benefit it provides. The relationship between security measures' costs and benefits gained is readily measureable. A sample formula is offered for determining general ROI:

$$ROI = \frac{\text{profit or benefit gain (or losses avoided) due to security measures} - \text{cost of security} \times 100}{\text{Cost of security}}$$

You may use the above sample or one preferred by your own organization—whichever best suits your needs.

ROI considers quantitative factors, such as dollar amounts, and qualitative factors, such as anticipated operational efficiency improvements. ROI should focus on three factors: regulation, revenue, and reputation.

- Regulation refers to being in compliance with relevant laws.
- Revenue references profit.
- Reputation refers to the reactions and beliefs that key stakeholders may form and share with others should security failure occur.

---

[10] Some executives do not consider security risk to be a major component of the overall corporate risk effort, so ROI is not of interest to them. For other CEOs, ROI is a vehicle to justify budgets and can help in examining financial inputs and outputs of selected security activities. I point out that in many instances, the actual financial ROI may be difficult to fully calculate. This is because ROI claims may not be available or able to make the case for greater security investment. This may require extended research, analysis, and independent conclusions to make a persuasive business case. When available, however, ROI can serve as a road map to where a security organization has been, where it presently stands and where it needs to go to achieve mission objectives.

Operational Reasonableness

Manipulation

Data cannot be coached, guessed, or faked by individuals collecting the information.[11] Measurements are based on official records, actual measurements, and practices that are not easy to fake. Quality assurance reviews ensure the authenticity of collected data and maintain the integrity of metrics. Data are highly likely to be correct and current.

Timeliness

Data are gathered in a timely fashion, are up to date, and reflect conditions at the time of collection. Data are collected during a security assessment, audit, or management review. Measurement is straightforward and could be quickly applied by different people over time. It is highly unlikely that any calculations would be out of date. Data derived in this way could be used for drawing conclusions and making real-time decisions.

Cost

There are usually no development costs. Metrics have already been developed and tested, and are ready for use.[12] Administering metrics is a process of management accountability in conducting regular business and is not costly. Little or no training of administrators is required. Obtaining data and calculating results does not offend employees or customers, or disrupt business operations.

---

[11] People could conceivably fake data, but that would mean lying about verifiable facts. Equally important, self-appraisals are not generally objective or reliable because they lack independence of thought and action. They have a tendency to under report or not report on particular areas to "protect" the boss and/or the establishment. Conversely, external security consultants are objective, independent, and free of any conflict of interests and the influences of "work politics." These professionals have no incentive to fake data, or to under or over report or ignore compliance issues, other non-conforming matters or best practices. For these professionals, reporting false or inaccurate data may subject them to criminal prosecution, revocation of certification standing, fines, suspension of business license, or any combination of the above.

[12] Minimal costs may be associated with inserting the description category of topics to be measures in selected metrics.

A User-Friendly Security Assessment Model

The security assessment helps identify security organization strengths and weaknesses, and channels mitigation actions to reduce security vulnerability and increase security resilience.

John Sullivant

Top Takeaways

- Analyze and evaluate performance and behavioral triggers
- Evaluate probability, business risk exposure, and consequence loss
- Conduct a comprehensive security assessment
- Customize an assessment model to fit your particular needs
- Use risk-based metrics to measure and evaluate performance

Overview

In this chapter I present a security assessment model that resonates with executive management because it offers a tool to increase the capability of an enterprise to prevent injury or death to resources, the damage or destruction of assets, or the disruption of business operations. While it is desirable to achieve a perfect and absolutely risk-free environment, the reality is that this goal is unattainable. Therefore a priority for executives, the security director, and stockholders early in the security planning process is to agree on what is or is not acceptable risk so effective security planning can take hold (Sullivant, 2007, pp. 45–49).

Interestingly though, many industries and companies have no regulatory requirement to conduct formal security assessments. But many companies acknowledge the value of doing so as part of prudent business practices, as well as their "duty to care" obligation. These companies know that security assessments take them from where they are to where they need to be. Companies that regularly conduct security assessments are more prepared for crisis and respond to it more effectively, not to mention the likely probability of enjoying lower corporate insurance premiums for implementing and enforcing workable mitigation solutions.

Absent a proven management tool that delivers strategies for synthesizing integrated solutions, or failing to ensure reasonable security solutions are implemented, a corporation has little assurance that its security program is aligned with business goals, is in compliance with regulatory requirements, is capable of addressing the likely threats and hazards it will face or its implementation is effective. Insurance companies have been known to force substantial management and organizational changes on companies with insufficient security measures and programs. There are better ways to improve security—ways that you have total control over—than bureaucratic insurance mandates.

A Reliable Security Assessment Model That Resonates with C-Suite Executives

Fig. 8.1 A user friendly security assessment model, (Sullivant, 2007, pp. 55–84) provides specialized, customized, and tailored research and analysis methodology with laser-like focus by identifying program strengths and weaknesses and developing mitigation analyses to strengthen the security posture and to enhance practices whereby risk and uncertainty can be objectively identified and reduced. The model has applicability in the private, not-for-profit, nongovernmental, and public sectors, and in any size organization.

The model, which is discussed in detail in my book *Strategies for Protecting National Critical Infrastructure Assets*, uses a holistic approach to measurably reduce risk through a combination of threat, vulnerability, and consequence analysis; deliberate mitigation treatments; and prioritization actions that bring value and meaning to C-suite executives. It offers a detailed road map that can help enterprises that are in denial of risk to raise security standards and embrace a new set of strategies to improve security resilience (Sullivant, 2007, pp. 4–5).

At the outset, it is important to note that the model[1] shown is an all-inclusive analytical process. Such a comprehensive analysis may not be suitable for your company at a particular time. In designing the model I made certain that the basic architecture was sufficiently flexible to allow the freedom to define personalized assessment boundaries, and I encourage you to select the dimensions that are most suitable to your immediate needs.

Recognizing the desire to focus on specific problem areas, rather than a general perspective, I created several independent lower tier models that can also be tailored to meet specific needs. I address these models in the following chapters:

- Chapter 9, "Developing a Realistic and Useful Threat Estimate Profile"
- Chapter 10, "Establishing and Maintaining Inseparable Security Competencies"
- Chapter 11, "A User-Friendly Security Technology Model"
- Chapter 12, "Preparing for Emergencies"
- Chapter 13, "A User-Friendly Protocol Development Model"
- Chapter 14, "A Proven Organization and Management Assessment Model"

Why Security Assessments Should Be Important to You

Security assessments are important from both a local and national planning perspective in that they enable authorities at all levels to create building blocks for threat, vulnerability,

---

[1] As of this writing, I have customized and tailored the general Model to fit the Banking & Finance, Food & Agriculture, Energy, including Gas, Oil & Pipeline, Telecommunications, Civil Aviation and Water Sectors. It can also be customized to meet the need of any one of the national critical infrastructure sectors not mentioned, as well as any other unique business operations.

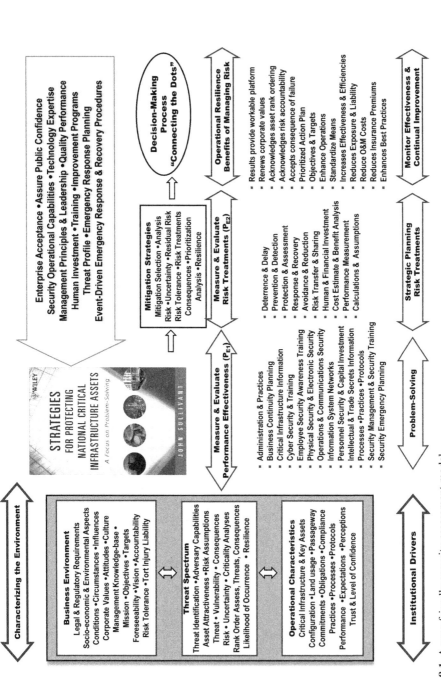

Figure 8.1 A user-friendly security assessment model.

Source: Sullivant, J., CFC, CSC, CHS-IV, CPP, RAM-W, Diplomate, ABFET. 2007. Strategies for Protecting National Critical Infrastructure Assets: A Focus on Problem-Solving. Reprinted with permission from John Wiley & Sons, NJ.

and consequence integration, and allow officials to determine areas and operations of a corporation are at most risk so appropriate investments can be made to protect targeted critical infrastructures, key assets, and resources (Sullivant, 2007, pp. 5).

How to Effectively Use the Model

The model allows chief executives and boards to use a proven framework architecture to develop thresholds for future standards for preemptive or protective actions and to set priorities to build a safe, more secure, and more resilient company through the protection of assets and resources against threats and hazards that could (Sullivant, 2007, pp. 16):

- impair its ability to perform essential services and ensure the public's health and safety
- undermine its capacity to deliver minimum essential services and products
- damage its ability and capability to function
- challenge the public's confidence in its capability to deliver services
- weaken its image, brand and reputation

The model (and all the tailored models) resonates with executives because it is a risk-based measurement and evaluation process that gives specific local meaning to an entity, the goal of which is to systematically (Sullivant, 2007, pp. 61–70):

- characterize the business and operational environment, including critical activities, services, processes, practices, partnerships, dependencies, and stakeholder relationships, and the potential consequences related to a disruptive incident based on realistic risk scenarios
- identify legal, regulatory, and other obligations to which the organization subscribes, and how these commitments influence protecting assets and resources in an all-hazards environment
- develop an operational needs analysis, a compliance analysis or voluntary commitment analysis
- characterize significant threats, hazards, industrial mishaps, natural disasters, and weather-related calamities influencing the workforce and business operations
- reduce threat, vulnerability, and consequence to critical assets through the process of identifying, analyzing, and prioritizing:
  - the likelihood that critical assets may be attractive targets selected for disruption, damage, or destruction based on the intent and capability of an adversary
  - the vulnerability characteristics of assets, processes, functions, and locations that make them susceptible to destruction, incapacitation, or exploitation by mechanical failures, natural hazards, and malicious acts
  - consequences of any disturbance, damage, or destruction to critical assets, taking into account health, economic, psychological, and governance impacts.
- formulate, analyze, and prioritize risk treatments and identify acceptable levels of residual risk exposure
- manage risk through the creation of strategies that mitigate the effects of risk exposure—including preventive and protective capabilities such as deterrence, detection, defense (delay and denial), assessment, reporting, response, and recovery—as well as through continual improvement based on objective measurement and evaluation
- evaluate risks and consequences within the context of changes within the organization or that are made to the organization's operating environment, processes, practices, partnerships, and dependencies

- evaluate the effectiveness of protocols, practices, training and qualifications, security organization, management and leadership, security management knowledge base, and corporate leadership support for security programs
- evaluate the value of security programs, operations, and technology and best practices for effectiveness, efficiency, and productivity
- evaluate the inseparability of physical security, cyber, information, and technology architecture to maximize the effectiveness, efficiency, productivity, and costs of security resilience
- measure and evaluate both the existing performance effectiveness (P_{E1}) and the effectiveness of proposed risk treatments (P_{E2}).

Measuring and Evaluating Performance Effectiveness

Security Analysis Framework

The model provides the framework for conducting specialized, customized research and analysis. It identifies requirements to help an organization develop and implement policies, objectives, and programs, taking into account legal requirements and other commitments to which the organization subscribes, and information about significant threats, hazards, accidents, and weather-related calamities that may have an influence on business operations and the protection of critical assets. It applies to risks (and their consequences) for which an enterprise needs to integrate management, technology, facilities, processes, and people into a resilient security culture. The extent of the application depends on factors such as risk assumptions, risk uncertainty, threat, vulnerability, consequence analysis, and risk tolerance; policy and practices; the nature of activities, products, and services; and the location where, and the conditions in which, it functions.

The model uses metrics (Sullivant, 2007, pp. 73–84) to calculate factors that:

- may cause temporary or permanent loss or degradation of business operations
- measure the effectiveness, efficiency, and productivity of security operations and programs, and the security organization's ability and capability to protect assets and resources against specific threats and crises
- determine security capabilities and abilities to safeguard a corporation against likely threats that may lead to the formulation of strategies and programs to enhance security resilience, objectives, targets, and practices

Theory of Performance Effectiveness

Performance as a theory can be applied to the performance effectiveness (P_E) of critical security activity, security programs, and the actions taken to enhance and improve security resilience. The goal of P_E is to benchmark activity against legal, regulatory, and other commitments that organizations subscribe to and how these standards of conformance and expectations, as well as principles, strategies, processes, and best practices, influence the capability of an organization to perform its prime security mission (Sullivant, 2007, pp. 73–84).

P_E measures the strengths and weaknesses of a security organization. It determines gaps in competency expectations, standards, and requirements, and establishes a starting point for developing mitigation strategies and solutions to correct noted deficiencies, weaknesses, and inadequacies.

The P_E analysis process involves the complete understanding of operations, procedures, methods, techniques, and constraints associated with the security organization and the analytical ability to distinguish between and isolate conditions, circumstances, objects, activities, and relationships that are capable of producing ineffectiveness, inefficiencies, safety conditions, and cost overruns. This includes identifying, examining, and recording data, conditions, circumstances, and events that can contribute to unacceptable outcomes.

To achieve total quality measurement and evaluation, P_E must be reflected as P_{E1} and P_{E2}, which are outlined below.

P_{E1}: Existing Effectiveness

P_{E1} (Sullivant, 2007, pp. 83) is the "before" analysis that measures actual security conditions and the ability and capability of the security organization to perform its mission. P_{E1} answers the question, "How well prepared are you?" P_{E1} represents the effectiveness, efficiency, and productivity of existing protective measures (physical, electronic, cyber, information, personnel, and procedural) and protocols, processes, practices, competencies, management, leadership, and the organization to deliver a reasonable deterrence, delay, denial, prevention, protection, detection, assessment, and response and recovery ability and capability to defend against threats, risk exposure, or vulnerability.

P_{E2}: Proposed Effectiveness

P_{E2} (Sullivant, 2007, pp. 83) represents the effectiveness, efficiency, and productivity of proposed risk mitigation treatments to identified deficiencies, weaknesses, or inadequacies to reduce vulnerability and risk exposure—including the acceptability of residual vulnerability—to enhance overall security resilience. P_{E2} sets priorities for implementing security enhancements and improvements, and helps to establish the budget, milestone schedule, and the allocation of resources to execute operational needs. P_{E2} also offers a road map for monitoring continual improvement actions that may be necessary to achieve security mission goals and objectives. P_{E2} tells you what you have been waiting to hear: how well prepared you should be.

Fig. 8.2 performance effectiveness (P_E) metric and calculation criteria shows how the concept of P_E works. It resonates with chief executives because it focuses on those topics of most interest to them: the security organization's ability and capability to perform its indispensable operational tasks: deterrence, delay, denial, prevention, protection, detection, assessment, response to, and recovery from adverse events in the course of saving lives and protecting assets. No other security mission task is more important than this.

The example illustrates an overall P_{E1} effectiveness rating of 0.41—far below the effectiveness rating of 0.90 preferred within the industry. In this example the strategies and mitigation solutions developed should all focus on correcting the observed deficiencies, weaknesses, and inadequacies rated <0.90, with an overarching goal of achieving an effectiveness rating of at least 0.90. Most certainly, the goal is achievable, but it requires hard work, determination, and executive management's commitment to achieve positive change.

Examples of Critical Areas of Performance Measurement Important to Executive Management	P_{EI} Measurement Rating		
	P_{EI} Level	Numerical	Narrative
Security Policies and Strategies			
Security program policy, processes, protocols	M_E	0.50	Moderate
Strategies & guiding principles	M_E	0.50	Moderate
Roles, responsibilities, & reporting relationships	M_E	0.50	Moderate
Security Organization			
Organization structure & functionality	H_E	0.90	High
Security management & leadership	M_E	0.50	Moderate
Security staff competence, experience, & professionalism	M_E	0.50	Moderate
Use of resources	M_E	0.50	Moderate
Security Operations			
Operational performance capabilities	M_E	0.50	Moderate
Timelines of performance capabilities	L_E	0.10	Low
Planning strategies & risk uncertainty	L_E	0.10	Low
Strategic Security Planning			
Normal security operations	M_E	0.50	Moderate
Security emergency operations	L_E	0.10	Low
Facility requirements, alternate power supplies	L_E	0.10	Low
Restricted Area			
Establishing restricted area	H_E	0.90	High
Boundaries & controls	H_E	0.90	High
Fences, gates, barriers	H_E	0.90	High
Human Resources and Investment			
Background checks	L_E	0.10	Low
Drug-free work environment	L_E	0.10	Low
Security work performance standards for all employees	L_E	0.10	Low
Security awareness training & special security training	M_E	0.50	Moderate

Legend:

P_E Levels	Likelihood Measurement		Performance Measurement
	Numerical	Narrative	
High	0.90	H_E	**Evidence of specific capabilities and performance effectiveness clearly exists.** Operational, regulatory, compliance requirements or other obligations have been fully met. Positive evidence of specific capabilities to address areas examined exist in concept, planning, and execution. Areas given this rating represent a high degree of performance effectiveness. When such actions are integrated with similar activity, high performance effectiveness is anticipated to continue.
Moderate	0.50	M_E	**Evidence of general but not specific capabilities or performance effectiveness exists.** General evidence of performance effectiveness with minimal specific capabilities provides reasonable security measures when employed in conjunction with other related activity. Function requires greater management attention to prevent slippage. Area is a valid candidate for continual monitoring and improvement. Management should flag this activity as a matter of interest. Area requires immediate management attention to correct deficiencies, weaknesses, and inadequacies on a priority basis.
Low	0.10	L_E	**Little or no evidence of capability or performance expectation.** Ineffective or no evidence of capability exist or activities are in noncompliance of regulatory and statutory requirements, fail to meet obligations and commitments, fail to contribute effectively to other related security programs.
Uncertainty	0.01	U_E	**Area not measured.** Status of this activity is in the embryo state or has not sufficiently progressed to a mature development state to determine its overall value to the corporation or security organization. With respect to other more important critical initiatives related below an acceptable bar, this activity registers at the lowest end of the priority list.

Figure 8.2 Performance effectiveness (P_E) metric and calculation criteria.

You would use the identical template to measure and evaluate the proposed mitigation solutions (P_{E2}). The gap between the findings for P_{E1} and P_{E2} provides security analysts an avenue to develop mitigation options, and decision makers with the ability to make the correct choices to improve security resilience.

The Benefits Management Enjoys from Using a Risk-Based Model

The model is important to planners and executive decision makers because it produces a professional, candid, independent, and objective analysis of enterprise security strengths, weaknesses, and vulnerability in order to measure the effectiveness of existing protective measures, evaluate the current status of the security operations and sensitive programs, and identify gaps in the security process (Sullivant, 2007, pp. 47–53).

- The model enables executive management to ask questions before making a decision. It represents a concise, consistent, uniform, and deliberate security management action plan that focuses on enhancing an enterprise's security posture from a systems-level perspective.
- The model provides to the organization and its customers trust and confidence that the organization is able to establish and sustain a safe and secure environment that fulfills organizational and stakeholder requirements.
- The model offers a deliberate means for analysis from a holistic systems-level perspective. It provides a road map to developing resilient strategies to reduce risk through deterrence of, prevention of, detection of, protection against, and mitigation of attempts to damage or destroy infrastructure and assets, incapacitate or exploit human resources and physical, virtual, and tangible and intangible assets; response and recovery planning; security training; and continual improvement.
- The model produces a comprehensive, systematic, and defensible analysis that drives integrated business risk reduction options. It does more than address criminal activities and terrorist threats; by using an all-hazards approach, security assessment activities allow for a more complete suite of integrated business risk-reduction options for various critical business functions.
- The model offers strategies and solutions that can reduce insurance premiums, and these savings often match or exceed the costs of many security upgrades.
- The model teaches what needs to be protected and from whom. It integrates physical measures, processes, practices, information, people, facilities, and equipment, as well as their dependencies and interdependencies with other critical program elements such as safety; ethics; integrity; social and work rules of behavior; human resources capital investment; the security force's experience, expertise, qualifications, training, and certifications; and corporate support of security activities.
- The model helps management rank assets that are most critical to business operations, assets facing imminent threat, and other assets that may be attractive targets so they can gauge corporate priorities for changes to enterprise designs, infrastructure, or policies, processes, and practices.
- The model allows decision makers to channel scarce resources and funding into those areas that need it most. It brings together the right balance of people, information, facilities, operations, processes, and systems to deliver cost-effective solutions, which, when applied and integrated into practice, lead to improved security resilience.
- The model gives management a framework for continual improvement to increase the probability of enhancing and improving security readiness and preparation, response and recovery, and continuity.

Conclusions

The challenges ahead call for the thorough evaluation of security operations and programs. Embracing a process approach to solving security problems allows decision makers to benefit from the relationships between risk, threats, severity analysis, and risk treatment options that address the most critical issues first. The program requires the cooperation and support of management at all levels, working to establish and maintain protective measures, emergency planning, and business continuity initiatives that are appropriate to the needs of a corporation.

Missing this opportunity can lead to bad decisions followed by poor practices. Assessment and threat analysis outcomes bring together:

- concepts and techniques to improve operations
- best practices to overcome inadequate performance
- state-of-the-art technologies to increase system performance and capability

The security assessment process is the road map that brings together information so security planners can "connect the dots" and decision makers can make the right choices. Strategic security planning begins with specialized customized research and analysis to:

- uncover the root causes of operational and technology weaknesses and deficiencies
- identify potential threats, vulnerabilities, and consequences
- uncover archaic, obsolete, and cumbersome protocols, processes, and practices

While identifying strategic deficiencies, programmatic weaknesses, and performance inadequacies is a good philosophy for ensuring conformance to regulatory requirements, industry standards, and best practices, it is only the first step in a series of steps that ultimately lead to successful strategies and security mediation solutions. The measurement and evaluation process continues with delivering a catalog of suggested treatments aimed at reducing threat attractiveness, such as designs that:

- embed hazard resistance and harden critical facilities and assets
- enhance physical, information, personnel, and technology security measures
- build in network resiliency
- resolve system technical performance levels
- converge new technologies and emerging technology measures
- use diverse hot standby and redundant systems
- create policies, processes, practices, procedures, and emergency response plans
- respond to and recover from crisis
- build a culture of security and train employees to act securely and responsibly

Using a proven security assessment model such as the one presented here prevents waste, ensures a thorough analysis, and offers constructive, cost-effective, strategic advice for solving unique security problems. It is a fundamental tool for security practitioners: it bolsters business cases for improving and enhance security resilience—process changes, technology advancements, best practices, additional resources, and adequate funding. Poorly conducted assessments become a waste of time and resources and can lead enterprises to take action that is ineffective, giving the CEO and board a false sense of security.

Developing a Realistic and Useful Threat Estimate Profile

> *Yesterday's threat is history. Tomorrow is where we confront threat head-on. We will never know the truth until after it happens. We can only estimate its being based on analysis and experience. The analyst is therefore concerned about a string of future conditional probabilities.*
>
> **John Sullivant**

Top Takeaways

- Risk exposure and asset protection
- Complexities of the threat environment
- Develop a meaningful and useful threat estimate profile
- Analyze and assess threats, risk exposure, consequences, and probability of occurrence

Overview

You probably think that chief executive officers (CEOs) want to know what threats can harm their company, the consequences of those threats, and what is being done to protect their people and assets. But when it comes to security preparedness, many CEOs are on the "dark side of the planet."

In Chapters The Evolving Threat Environment, and The Cyber Threat Landscape, I introduced the fundamental aspects of the threat environment security professionals face on a daily basis. Here, I draw upon those threat elements to address the importance of formulating a realistic and useful threat estimate profile that has value and meaning to chief executives.

Few would disagree that a corporation requires a comprehensive threat estimate profile if its business is to survive. The risks facing the organization and the way in which threats are profiled and quantified provide a solid foundation for the development of security programs and strategies. This holistic approach involves people, technology, and processes.

Providing Meaningful Strategic Threat Advice to Executive Management Is Essential

As mentioned previously, 60% of upper management believes that security is stronger than it actually is, whereas only 22% of top executives are aware of their company's true security readiness. It is astounding that almost two-thirds of the nation's CEOs say they are in the dark about the true security status of their corporation. This should raise significant concern both in the C-suite boardroom and within the halls of the security organization.

At almost every site visited I found the lack of a prepared threat estimate profile to undermine an enterprise's ability to prioritize deterrence and delay techniques, preventive and protective measures, and the allocation of resources and funding to secure those assets that are most critical to business goals and objectives. Based on my findings, I argue that few corporations invest any effort in developing a threat estimate. In my many years of conducting threat and vulnerability studies, I found little evidence to suggest that corporate-wide security emergency planning—and the development of such plans and response and recovery procedures—was based on a current and meaningful threat estimate profile. In fact, many organizations had not even performed a formal security assessment to identify unit strengths and weaknesses, identify vulnerabilities and risk exposure, and determine the effectiveness of security performance. The few organizations that had a useable and meaningful threat estimate profile seldom kept it up to date, making it too outdated to be useful in updating any of the emergency plans and procedures reviewed. Other organization threat profiles had no local meaning and utility, or served little value in preparing security emergency plans and event-driven response and recovery procedures (more on this topic in Chapter: Preparing for Emergencies).

Only by understanding the range and level of threats, and the potential harm they can cause a company, can C-suit executives make informed judgments to more effectively control security risk. CEOs expect the security director to lead them "out of darkness" and help them not only to make informed risk management decisions in order to increase bottom-line performance, but also to report the true status of the security organization's capability and ability to perform its essential critical mission: deterring criminal and unauthorized activity/intent, preventing easy targets, denying unauthorized access, protecting resources and assets, delaying effort, detecting an act, assessing the threat, responding accordingly to an event, preventing damage, and delaying or stopping an adversary's escape.

In this role, corporate security is both a strategic and operational activity, and the security director must distinguish between these layers. However, research has found that too often the corporate security strategy is not aligned with the corporate business strategy. The consequences of this knowledge gap means that the security organization is likely to be marginalized. Aligning security strategies with business strategies ensures that corporate security programs are in harmony with the company's priorities and places the security director and chief executive on the same page. The threat estimate profile helps achieve this goal.

Threat Planning Relies on the Development of a Useful Threat Estimate Profile

Jack F. Williams Professor of Law, Georgia State University advocates that threat is best understood as the product of an adversary's capability, intent, and authority. He argues threat is also strongly influenced by an adversary's culture and constituencies, and requires a "cultural awareness" of an adversary. Williams advocates that threat analysis is the art of wasting information, that is, the art of peeling away layers of irrelevant information, incorrect information, and disinformation to expose relevant and credible information related to the threat interest of a corporation.

Sources of information that flush out threat include classified, unclassified, and open-source material, as well as expert judgment. It is well accepted and understood among analysts and security professionals that the best sources of information are classified information and hands-on experience, followed far behind any open-source material, much of which contains only bits and pieces of factual information; thus the latter is mostly based on speculation and opinion of the conditions and circumstances reported.

There is no question that solutions to protecting critical infrastructures and assets must be based on a thorough security assessment that accounts for the review and update of an existing threat estimate, or the creation of one where one does not exist. Fig. 9.1 highlights the elements that make up a comprehensive threat estimate profile (Sullivant, 2007, pp. 131–155). A completed threat estimate

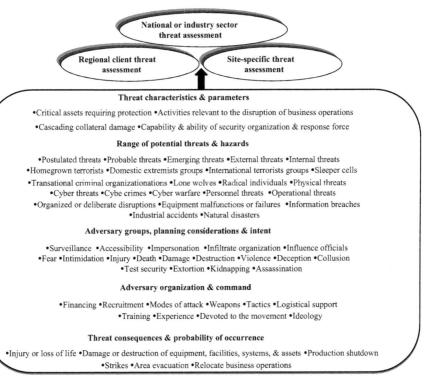

Figure 9.1 Threat estimate profile.
Source: Sullivant, J., 2007 (CFC, CSC, CHS-IV, CPP, RAM-W, DABFET). Strategies for Protecting National Critical Infrastructure Assets: A Focus on Problem-Solving (Exhibit 7.1 Composition of Design-Basis Threat Profile, page 134). Wiley & Sons, New Jersey; 2007.

profile answers these questions – before significant funds and resources are made available:

- What are the consequences of specific attacks on specific assets in terms of business economic impact, health and welfare, damage (including collateral damage), and destruction?
- What points of infrastructure or asset failure (and their location) could have extensive cascading consequences?
- What are the highest-risk areas from a business perspective incorporating consequence, vulnerability, and threat?
- What investment strategies can an enterprise pursue that will have the most effect in reducing overall risk?

As shown above, the threat estimate profile comprises a national threat assessment perspective, a regional or sector-level threat assessment, and a local or site-specific threat assessment, all of which use, to some degree, the elements of the lower-tier platform that brings together numerous inputs from a variety of resources:

- Threat characteristic and parameters
- Range of potential threats and hazards
- Adversary group planning considerations
- Adversary organization and command
- Threat consequences and probability of occurrence

The threat profile offers a systematic forum to judge how well security performance goals are achieved. Strategic security planning therefore begins with:

- conducting a comprehensive security assessment that produces a realistic threat estimate profile so effective, reasonable, and prudent security measures to safeguard business interests, operations, investments, and resources, and to explore gaps in ineffective performance or omission of performance, can be examined
- developing prudent and reasonable security measures, and clear and distinct processes, practices, and protocols—particularly exacting emergency preparedness and continuity planning—to protect against natural and manmade disasters, industrial mishaps, and criminal activity through the development of specific event-driven security response and recovery procedures

Strategic planning continues with:

- examining training needs, identifying competency gaps, and developing training programs
- diligently testing and exercising plans
- improving the capability to respond to crisis
- achieving continual measurement and evaluation of performance

Without proper planning, preparation, and training, employees will lack the guidance and confidence necessary to perform their duties during an emergency, whether a terrorist attack, criminal act, natural disaster, industrial mishap, or other catastrophic event.

Suggested Composition of a Threat Estimate Profile

At the corporate level, there can be three major sections to a threat estimate profile: the national threat assessment, the regional threat assessment, and the local threat assessment, as applicable to a specific industry sector or business.

The National Threat Assessment

At the national level, the national threat assessment is prepared by the U.S. Department of Homeland Security with significant input from the nation's intelligence community and the FBI; the assessment is approved by the president of the United States. This statement focuses on the most critical economic security, national security, and national defense threat considerations affecting America's global interests.

A U.S. corporation with a significant national presence or that is a major government/defense contractor should consider preparing a national threat assessment that addresses its global business interests, including its attractiveness as a target, if appropriate. Four U.S. government policy directives offer broad guidance for preparing national threat statements:

- Presidential Policy Directive 21: *Critical Infrastructure Security and Resilience*
- Presidential Policy Directive 8: *National Preparedness*
- The National Infrastructure Protection Plan (NIPP), which outlines how government and private-sector participants in the critical infrastructure community work together to manage risk and achieve security resilience outcomes
- The National Strategy for Protection of Critical Infrastructure and Key Assets, which identifies a clear set of national goals and objectives that outline the guiding principles that underpin efforts to secure infrastructures and assets vital to national security, governance, public health and safety, the economy, and public confidence. It establishes a foundation for building and fostering a cooperative environment in which government, industry, and private citizens can carry out their respective protection responsibilities

The Regional/Corporate Threat Assessment

Each federal agency, known as a sector-specific agency, leads a collaborative effort for critical security within the 16 national critical infrastructure sectors identified within the NIPP. Each agency develops and implements a sector-specific plan, which details the application of the NIPP to the unique characteristics and conditions of the industry sector. The sector-specific agency, in concert with industry participants through private industry sector coordinating councils, prepares a sector or regional threat statement. This government–industry collaboration helps industry to prioritize protection and preparedness initiatives and investments within and across sectors.

The Local/Site-Specific Threat Assessment

Local or site-specific threat estimate profiles are prepared by a corporate entity and tailored to local circumstances, conditions, and situations. Local threat estimates are the most relevant estimates because they focus directly on unique problems confronting corporations, giving the threat statement local meaning and value to the chief executive. This threat estimate brings together relevant, essential information from multiple sources to help security decision makers set priorities to apply resources where they offer the most benefit for mitigating risk by lowering vulnerabilities, deterring threats, and minimizing the consequences of attacks and other incidences.

A comprehensive threat profile serves as the benchmark for further strategic security policy development and direction, emergency preparedness, and business continuity planning. The threat estimate profile is a "living document" and therefore a crucial element of the overall planning process; its development and upkeep should be a priority initiative for every chief executive.

Without this essential threat estimate, it is difficult to determine what the highest-priority activity should be when planning and coordinating security operations and initiatives. Outputs may be misguided and ineffective, and more than likely mimic a false sense of accomplishment, leading to excessive and counterproductive labor efforts, less-than-satisfactory performance results and expectations, and wasteful expenditures.

Several national strategy programs (which complement the NIPP) offer a wide array of guidance for developing threat parameters and protective measures at the local level:

• Aviation transportation industry	• National defense
• Border controls	• Natural disasters
• Cargo security	• Nuclear power plants
• Chemical manufacturing industry	• Nuclear reactors, materials, and waste
• Chemical, biological, radiological materials	• Pandemic flue
• Commercial and government facilities	• Ports and harbors
• Countering violent extremism	• Rail and truck transportation industry
• Critical manufacturing industry	• Trafficking in human, body parts,
• Dams and energy facilities	weapons, and drugs
• Emergency services	• Telecommunications industry
• Food and agriculture industry	• Water and wastewater treatment plants
• Gas, oil, and pipelines	• Weapons of mass destruction
• Maritime transportation industry	
• Money laundering	

Identifying the Range of Potential Threats and Hazards Is a Critical Planning Process

A valid threat profile contains all potentially postulated, probable, and emerging threats and hazards that could realistically apply to a corporation. The list of threats and hazards can be short or long, depending on factors such as the industry, location, and other considerations. Regardless, it should be sufficiently detailed to provide to security planners the information necessary to formulate effective security measures to guard against such threats.

Fig. 9.2 *Range of Potential Threats and Adversary Characteristics (Appendix A)* is a representative sampling of potential postulated, probable, and emerging threats. The listing is categorized by a series of adversary characteristics, which give security planners and analysts insight into possible adversary planning considerations and intentions to commit particular acts. Adversary planning and execution capabilities are divided into operational, technical, and logistical capabilities and authority (Clark, 2004, pp. 66–173).

- Operational capability focuses on leadership structure, command and control, intelligence, financing, recruitment, experience, expertise, training and education, social outreach, communications, political influence, territory, and infrastructure to operate and provide sanctuary to its members, whether they be terrorist groups, domestic extremist groups, organized crime, transnational criminal groups, or any other criminal element and recognized authority.
- Technical capability focuses on having either internal or external access to the instruments needed to carry out activity.
- Logical capability focuses on having local, regional, or global capability to demonstrate a threat capability.
- Authority refers to internal authority to operate, recruit, and replenish forces, equipment, and supplies and external permission to carry out approved operations.

You can populate the listing by placing a checkmark within the appropriate "bins of capability" as they apply to the specific range of potential threat.

The breakout helps security planners to distinguish which threats and capabilities are more suitable to deterrence, prevention, detection, and protection measures. The analysis also has merit when planning for emergencies because criminal elements and crowd behavior patterns do take advantage of a crisis to commit criminal activity and other unauthorized acts—thus the need for protecting a scene and preserving evidence, as well as the need for law enforcement to safeguard the general community from looters and rioters.

One cannot understand threat without understanding the culture within which an adversary operates. Such factors may include any or all of the following:

- Alliances
- Communications network
- Geography
- Ideology
- Legality
- Legitimacy of a higher authority to grant permission to act and to discipline
- Philosophy
- Political infiltration
- Relationship with other criminal or terrorist groups
- Religion
- Social values
- Sociopolitical and religious attributes, including universe of operation and influence

Failing to recognize the culture space within which an adversary lives, operates, and retains authority can lead to analytical drift, subconscious projection, and superficial threat analysis. Analysts need to pay attention to performance signs for clues about potential targets and attack means.

"Bins" of capability, intent, and authority help to evaluate credibility, reliability, relevance, inferential force, and an adversary's purpose. From an analyst's perspective, credibility is the measure of belief and authenticity, reliability is the measure of consistency and coherence, relevance is the measure of fit, inferential force is the measure of weight, and adversary purpose is the measure of intent. Both the list of threats and adversary characteristics can easily be customized to fit your unique planning parameters, giving utility and meaning to your senior management.

Consequence Analysis and Probability of Occurrence for Threats and Hazards

Fig. 9.3 *Consequence Analysis (C_A) and Probability of Occurrence (P_A) of Threats and Hazards (Appendix B)* takes the data presented to the next level of threat analysis. It brings together the results of consequence analysis (C_A) and probability of occurrence (P_A) for each threat and hazard and puts them into perspective relative to organization characteristics. This involves establishing a linkage between C_A and P_A in the legend of Figure 9.3 to analyze the relationship between threat and hazard conditions and the vulnerability of each critical asset to determine mitigation selection and evaluation, with the understanding that not all risks can be addressed and not all assets can be protected because of limitations of resources and funding, and practicality. Accordingly, security risk characterization forms the basis for deciding which actions are best suited to mitigate security risk.

Using the legend C_A criteria presented in Figure 9.3, each listed threat and hazard is given a consequence severity rating based on the narrative that describes the potential harm that could develop should an event occur. For illustrative purposes, the narrative is presented in general terms, offering a wide range of application to various infrastructures and assets. To achieve better utility and local meaning, threats, hazards, and the narrative can easily be modified to fit the particular configuration and structural makeup of specific critical assets and other site conditions.

Once you have assigned a C_A rating from the legend in Figure 9.3—F, VS, MS, SS, or SU—to each threat and hazard, you can determine the realistic P_A, taking into consideration factors that would influence your decision making. Use the legend P_A presented in Figure 9.3 to complete this analysis by assigning each threat and hazard a P_A rating of H, M, L, or I.

Once you have completed the C_A and P_A analysis, you are ready to start the next steps in the strategic planning process: validating mitigation risks, selecting mitigation actions, and evaluating the potential of residual risk exposure. Together, these data provide decision makers with sufficient crucial information to prioritize risk, consequences, and probability to ensure that resources and funds are used where they are most needed. Because some threats are less likely to occur than others, ranking or prioritizing each threat according to the likelihood of occurrence against the criticality of a particular asset, and against the consequence of asset loss should an event actually happen, is essential to sustaining critical business operations (Sullivant, 2007, pp. 109–129).

Benefits of Having a Threat Estimate Profile

When the elements of threat, vulnerability, and consequence are combined, they form the risk associated with critical infrastructures and assets. The result is a comprehensive systematic and defensible analysis of an asset's criticality that drives integrated risk reduction activities. The threat estimate profile allows decision makers to:

- define the level and range of a natural disaster, weather-related calamity, industrial mishap, criminal activity, or other major catastrophic event
- determine the probability and consequences of threat occurrence
- understand an adversary's capabilities, operations, tactics, and support mechanisms
- provide insight into strategic, tactical, and operational planning; countermeasures development; program implementation; and staffing needs by reducing threat attractiveness, vulnerability, and the ensuing consequences of loss
- formulate strategies to protect assets against and mitigate the effects of threats, vulnerabilities, and consequences
- channel scarce resources and funding into those areas that need it most by bringing together the right balance of people, information, facilities, operations, processes, and systems to deliver cost-effective solutions, which, when applied and integrated into practice, lead to improved awareness, preparedness, prevention, response, and recovery from events—whether manmade crisis, accidents, or natural disasters.

Conclusions

Too often, corporate security strategies are not aligned with corporate business strategies. Aligning security strategies with business strategies can ensure that corporate security programs are in harmony with company priorities and can place the security director and chief executive on the same page. A valid threat estimate profile helps to achieve this goal. A threat estimate profile helps planners and decision makers to:

- define the level and range of natural disaster, weather-related calamity, industrial mishap, criminal activity, or other major or catastrophic event
- determine the probability and consequences of threat occurrence and understand an adversary's capabilities, operations, tactics, and support mechanisms
- provide insight into strategic, tactical, and operational planning; countermeasures development; and program implementation
- determine staffing needs

The information that makes up the threat profile is never static. The threat profile is a "living document" that requires constant review and updating as the threat environment changes. It should always be used as a backdrop to developing corporate security strategies, planning, and direction.

Not having a reliable, useful, and meaningful threat profile makes it difficult to determine what the highest-priority activity should be when planning and coordinating security operations and initiatives. Any analytical effort would certainly be misguided and ineffective, and more than likely mimic a false sense of accomplishment, leading to excessive and counterproductive labor efforts, less-than-satisfactory performance expectations, and wasteful expenditures.

Appendix A

Range of Potential Threats	Adversary Characteristics				
	Adversary Type	Operational Capability	Technical Capability	Logistics Capability	Authority
Arson					
Assassination, murder					
Assault, battery, assault with deadly weapon					
Backpack bomb					
Biological attack					
Bomb threat					
Breaking & entering					
Bribery					
Burglary					
Chemical attack					
Civil disobedience					
Corruption					
Cyber terrorism, crime, warfare					
Damage or destruction to critical infrastructure, systems, & assets					
Data entry error by employee					
Stock fraud					
Denial of services					
Disruption of courier or delivery services					
Economic espionage					
Embezzlement					
Extortion					
Financial scams					
Forced entry					
Forcible rape					
Forging criminal alliances					
Fraud, waste, & abuse					
Graft					
Ground assault					
Harassment					
Hostile termination					
Impersonation					
Insult & emotional trauma					
Intrusion (trespassing)					
Intimidation					
Investment manipulation					
Kidnapping					
Loss, damage, destruction of:					
HVAC units					
Cable infrastructure					
Communications capability					
Drainage removal capability					
Environmental controls					
Fuel/water supply					
IT systems, office systems					
Primary/backup power					
Records or data					
Manipulate, economic trade, currency value, market stability					
Misuse, damage of security, SCADA, & other control systems					
Money laundering					
Penetrating organizations					
Pilferage					

Figure 9.2 Range of potential threats and adversary characteristics.

Piracy					
Possessing, brandishing or exhibiting weapon					
Public transportation disruption					
Radiological bomb					
Rape					
Release of poisonous gases					
Robbery					
Security violation					
Small aircraft with explosives					
Smuggling					
Subversive activity					
Subversive political action					
Suicide bomber					
Surreptitious entry					
Tampering with critical systems & assets					
Terrorism					
Theft of property: personal, stockroom, inventory					
Theft of service					
Threats to personnel safety					
Trafficking in humans, body parts, endangered species					
Trafficking in drugs, weapons, nuclear materials					
Train bomb					
Treason					
Unauthorized release of information					
Use of power to further crimes					
Vandalism & sabotage					
Vehicle bomb					
Verbal & written threats					
Violation of restraining order					
Water assault					
Workplace violence, demonstrations, strikes					
Wrongfully influencing government/corporation officials					

Figure 9.2   Continued.

Appendix B

Modes of Attack (Threats & Hazards)	Consequence Analysis (C_A) of Event Occurrence	C_A	P_A
Air, ground, & water assault	Could cause injury or loss of life and damage or destruction of infrastructure, assets, and other property. Could have a devastating affect on entity operations and a catastrophic affect on community services, including collateral damage to surrounding areas.		
Arson; Earthquake; Electrical storm; Fire; Flood; Hurricane; Snowstorm; Tornado; and Tsunami	Could cause massive injury or loss of life and widespread damage or destruction of critical operations such as production operations, computer systems, utilities, electrical equipment, power and communication lines, and disruption of gas, water, sewage, and other services. High potential for collateral damage to surrounding areas. May hinder rescue efforts. Recovery may have a long-term affect on business operations and services.		
Assassination; Murder	Loss of life causing fear, business disruption, or temporary shutdown of services or evacuation of area or workplace.		
Assault; Battery; Assault with a Deadly Weapon; Threats to Personal Safety; Verbal & Written Threats	Could cause injury or loss of life, damage to property, or business disruption.		
Biological attack	Can cause casualties and fatalities or deny the long-term use of an area or building.		
Bomb threats: vehicle, backpack, train airplane	Could create uncertainty and fear, and serve to destabilize the work environment. Could stop operations or cause an evacuation of the area or the shutdown of services. Could cause severe injury or death, or destruction on a large scale, destroy power and communications lines, or disrupt fuel and water services. Significant damage to buildings, including total structural collapse, may occur. Could have a devastating affect on entity operations and services. Loss of public confidence in the organization to provide a safe and secure environment may also occur.		
Breaking & entering	Minor disruption and damage.		
Bribery; Corruption; Defraud; Embezzlement; Extortion; Financial scams; Forging criminal alliances; Fraud, waste, & abuse; Graft; Investment manipulation; Manipulaion of economic trade, currency value, market stability; Money laundering; Penetrating organizations; Smuggling; Wrongfully influencing officials	Could cause financial loss or disrupt business; could taint brand, image, reputation, and business relationships.		
Burglary; Robbery	Minor disruption, uncertainty, and fear. Short-term impact.		
Chemical attack	Could cause casualties and fatalities, and deny the long-term use of the work environment.		
Civil disobedience	Could stop work and cause evacuation of the workplace		
Cyber terrorism, crime, warfare	Could have a devastating affect on entity operations.		
Damage or destruction of:			
Critical infrastructure and assets	Could hamper critical dependency functions such as firefighting, police, and medical response, and could tax other emergency responders.		
Monitoring units	Could affect the proper working order of processes. Could cause the immediate interruption of services and operations.		
Pumps & motors	Could disrupt the flow process and cause segments of the piping system to rupture or collapse. Loss would limit or deny some services.		
Pipelines	Loss of pressure would limit or deny some services.		
Data entry error by employee	Could have an affect on normal business processes or cause a subsequent delay in business transactions, with minimum financial loss.		
Denial of services	Could delay or prevent the continuation of operations. Minor work disruption.		
Disruption of courier or delivery services	Could affect time-critical and time-sensitive activities including financial loss cause and disruption of water operations.		
Economic espionage	Could significantly affect business operations, trade secrets, and financial loss.		
Epidemic	Could occur when a contagious illness affects a large number of people within the surrounding area. Could have a devastating short-term impact on business through a large number of people being absent from work. Certain illnesses could have a longer effect on the business operations, with long-term illness or death resulting.		

Figure 9.3 Consequence analysis (C_A) and probability of occurrence (P_A) of threats and hazards.

Source: Sullivant, J., 2007 (CFC, CSC, CHS-IV, CPP, RAM-W, DABFET). Strategies for Protecting National Critical Infrastructure Assets: A Focus on Problem-Solving (Exhibit 7.7 Example Worksheet 18-Malevolent Acts & Undesirable Events by Loss of Consequences and Probability of Occurrence (P_A) page 151). Wiley & Sons, New Jersey.

Modes of Attack (Threats & Hazards)	Consequence Analysis (C_A) of Event Occurrence	C_A	P_A
Forced entry	Minor disruption and damage. Short-term business impact.		
Forcible rape	Major concern for personal safety and adequate safe work environment. Could affect business operations for an unspecified period. Local community may loose confidence in organization protecting workforce or visitors.		
Harassment; Stalking	Could cause fear, indecision, or business disruption.		
Heat	Excessive heat may cause considerable loss and human suffering. May affect computer rooms and security monitoring centers that depend on controlled environmental conditions for equipment to operate.		
Hostile termination; Insult & emotional trauma	Could cause business disruption or injury. Short-term business impact.		
Industrial contamination	Results from polluted air, polluted water, chemicals, radiation, asbestos, smoke, dampness and mildew, toxic waste, and oil pollution. Conditions could disrupt business operations processes by mandated evacuation for long periods; in addition, could cause sickness or loss of life.		
Impersonation	Could place the workforce and business operations in jeopardy. Could result in unauthorized access to critical assets and operations, and damage or destruction of critical infrastructure or assets.		
Intrusion (trespassing)	Disruption of routine business.		
Intimidation	Could cause fear, indecision, or business disruption.		
Kidnapping	Could cause injury or loss of life. May disrupt business for the duration of the event.		
Legal problems	Discrimination, sexual harassment, contract disputes, copyright disputes, or violations of health and safety regulations could result in financial loss or business disruptions, as well as the loss of public confidence in the organization to conduct ethical business operations.		
Loss, damage, destruction of:			
HVAC units	Could have consequences for operations where AC units are needed to protect sensitive equipment, perishable goods, or patients. Could cause the shutdown or movement of operations.		
Cable infrastructure	Damage to main cable paths could have a long-term affect on business operations.		
Communications capability	Disruption could result in the shutdown of critical business processes.		
Drainage removal capability	Most likely to cause a health issue. Possible shutdown of operations and evacuation of workforce during recovery period.		
Environmental controls	Could affect facility life support systems and cause residual damage to independent systems. May cause a shutdown or the movement of operations.		
Fuel/water supply	Impact could affect the ability to provide heat or operate equipment and vehicles. Could cause a shutdown.		
IT systems, office systems	Could have consequences for water processes and the capability to maintain services where hardware failure, cable damage, water leaks, fires, AC system failures, network failures, and telecommunications equipment failures exist.		
Primary/backup power	Could affect AC lights, telephones, communications, and computers. Could cause a shutdown, affecting business operations.		
Records or data	Could be disruptive where poor back-up and recovery procedures result in the need to re-input and recompile records. Could be embarrassing to the organizational image where information is totally lost and not available.		
Misuse, damage of:			
Security, SCADA, and other systems	Could interfere with the capability to detect, assess, and respond to alarms; interfere with critical operations; or cause a portion of or the entire system to shut down. Misuse could result in the corruption of information or false information. Loss of public confidence in the organization to provide a safe and secure environment may also occur.		
Negative publicity	Unfavorable press comments, release of inaccurate or unreliable information, or information leaked to the press from disgruntled employees or others could distract from business operations.		
Neighborhood hazard	Seepage of hazardous waste or escape of toxic gases or sewage can cause injury or death to employees and the community.		
Pilferage	Disruption of routine business operations; property and financial loss.		
Piracy	Could have a devastating affect on entity operations and services.		
Public transportation disruption	Major effect on business because of the inability of employees to get to work. Disruption could cause major accidents, equipment failures, and damage or destruction of public services.		
Radiological bomb	Could cause casualties and fatalities, and deny the long-term use of the work environment.		
Release of poisonous gases	A significant amount of released chlorine could create the potential for a serious threat to life.		
Security violation	Could cause unauthorized access to critical assets or information, or damage or destruction to critical infrastructure or assets.		

Figure 9.3 Continued.

Modes of Attack (Threats & Hazards)	Consequence Analysis (C$_A$) of Event Occurrence	C$_A$	P$_A$
Small aircraft with explosives	Could have a devastating affect on entity operations.		
Subsidence and landslides	Could cause massive fatalities and widespread destruction of infrastructure and disruption of services.		
Subversive activity; Subversive political action	Could cause significant harm to business operations, financial loss, or could taint brand, image, and reputation. Business partners and community may loose confidence in the organization's business ethics and ability to provide services.		
Suicide bomber	Could have a devastating affect on entity operations.		
Surreptitious entry	Could cause unauthorized access to sensitive areas or information, resulting in harm to business operations and potentially financial loss.		
Tamper with systems & assets	Could cause surreptitious access to critical systems, assets, and information.		
Theft of property: personal, stockroom, inventory; Theft of service	Disruption of routine business operations; property and financial loss.		
Trafficking in humans, body parts, endangered species, drugs, weapons, and nuclear materials	Could cause a major disruption in business operations and services, affecting significant financial loss, criminal prosecution, damage to brand, image, and reputation, loss of industry and community respect and confidence to continue conducting business. Could create significant ethical and integrity concerns, including loss of business license.		
Treason	Could cause significant business disruption and damage to brand, image, and reputation, including ethical and integrity concerns.		
Unauthorized release of information	Loss of trade secrets, copyright, sensitive, priority, or classified information. Could result in embarrassment and possibly significant financial loss.		
Use of power to further crimes	Could cause significant business disruption and damage to brand, image, and reputation, including ethical and integrity concerns.		
Vandalism & sabotage	Could cause injury or loss of life, damage to property, business disruption.		
Workplace violence, demonstrations, strikes	Could affect morale and absenteeism, create fear and uncertainty, and increase the turnover rate of employees. Could affect productivity and result in claims for workers compensation, harassment claims, and a need for increased security measures.		

Legend:

Business Consequence Analysis (C$_A$) Criteria

Severity of Consequence	Likelihood Rating		Consequence Analysis [C$_A$]
	Numerical	Narrative	
Fatal To The Business	0.90	F	•High potential for the effects of life and health, injury or loss of life, or economic and social damage. •Alarm expected among leadership and workforce. •In-place sheltering and response capability non-existent. •Communication systems and utilities inoperative with gas leaks, sewage spillage, fuel ruptures, and HAZMAT spills throughout the site. •Catastrophic damage or abandonment of facility until new facility is constructed. •Extensive external response and recovery necessary, requiring the relocation of remaining workforce, time-critical functions and operations for extended time. •Immediate and long term impact on employees, community, and company.
Very Severe To The Business	0.80	VS	•High potential for injury or loss of life. •Delivery of critical services and products interrupted. •Most communications systems and utilities damaged. •Severe structural damage with some collapse anticipated with additional utilities being damaged. •Crisis management leadership and response capability severely affected. •Evacuation of workforce from the site or facility •Requires major effort and expenditure to repair or replace with long-lead time recovery. •Significant loss of revenues anticipated during the recovery process.
Moderately Serious To The Business	0.60	MS	•Medium to moderate potential for injury or loss of life. •Employee welfare affected. •Some communications systems may be available. •Organization and leadership element in tact. •Loss would have a noticeable impact on revenues during recovery. •Threat to workforce and company. •Evacuation of workforce from the site or facility •Damage would result in short-term or limited suspension of operations. •Minor facility damage, no relocation of resources. •Emergency response capabilities degraded but partially functional.
Slightly Serious To The Business	0.30	SS	•Minor potential for injury or loss of life. •Many employees unaware of emergency. •Slight business disruption. •Minor damage to facilities. •May require temporary evacuation of workforce. •Organization and leadership in tact. •Emergency response capabilities functional.
Seriousness To Business Undetermined	0.00	SU	•Insufficient data available to determine impact on business operations.

Figure 9.3   Continued.

Probability of Occurrence [P$_A$] Criteria

Severity of Occurrence	Likelihood Rating		Occurrence Measurement
	Numerical Rating	Narrative Rating	
High	0.90	H	Risk exposure is high
Moderate	0.60	M	Risk exposure is moderate
Low	0.30	L	Risk is low.
Uncertain	0.00	I	Insufficient data available to evaluate circumstances and conditions

Figure 9.3   Continued.

Establishing and Maintaining Inseparable Security Competencies

Deterrence, delay, prevention, protection and detection are meaningless capabilities unless you have the ability to assess, respond to and recover from a major threat event.

John Sullivant

Top Takeaways

- Importance of executing ability and capability
- Criticality of detect, prevent, protect, assess, response and recovery
- Integrating the principles of timely security reactions
- Reality of dealing with potential failure
- Importance multitasking and multidisciplinary competencies

Overview

The concept of "inseparable security competencies" is characteristically embedded in any security organization, regardless of size, whether public or private. Few chief executives I interviewed, however, expressed any understanding of the true value and meaning these concepts have in supporting their business goals and objectives. The capabilities concept contains two major segments that permeate every aspect of an enterprise. The first element entails the strategic vision and tactical insight to effectively plan and develop strategies to deter, delay (or deny), prevent, protect, detect, assess, respond to, and recover from any attempt to disrupt, damage, or destroy an entity's resources, critical infrastructure, and key assets as well as classified, sensitive, and propriety information. The second element involves the timely strategic and tactical integration of human and technology performance to direct and carry out those actions necessary to contain, neutralize, or defeat a wide array of threats. Here, I emphasize the importance of establishing, distinguishing, and maintaining these competencies.

Are Your Security Competencies a Top Priority?

It is noteworthy to report once again that a security organization has only one primary security mission: to deter, delay, prevent, protect, detect, assess, respond to, and recover from any significant security or security-related event that affects the operation or the survivability of the corporation. Any other activity performed by a security organization is secondary (Sullivant, 2007, pp. 165–169).

These indispensable competencies call for a security organization to have the necessary strategic and tactical planning vision and insight to preserve life and safeguard assets, prevent unauthorized access to critical areas and information, achieve agreed upon involvement and commitment, and ensure the ability and capability to perform to regulatory requirements, industry standards, best practices, or management expectations. Moreover, it calls for the creation of integrated processes, policies, and protocols, and to obtain and sustain the necessary resources, facilities, operations, and technologies to achieve overall security resilience.

Unless and until you commit to establishing and maintaining the necessary degree of care and diligence expected (or required), achieving the ability and capability to perform your primary mission is doubtful. Therefore it is essential that you understand and recognize the significance of these abilities and capabilities because this knowledge directly influences how seriously you take the task of measuring and evaluating these critical security competencies, and accepting their performance outcomes (Sullivant, 2007, pp. 169).

Fig. 10.1 *Eight Inseparable Security Competencies* illustrates the relationship, interdependency, and suitability of these capabilities in a highly reactionary industry in both planning and execution.

The processes of deterrence, delay, prevention, protection, detection, assessment, response, and recovery are by default time-sensitive and time-dependent functions that vary from one situation and set of circumstances to another and under varying threat

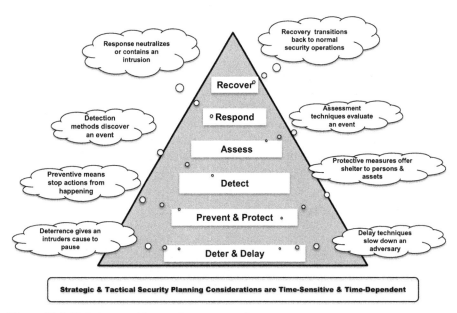

Figure 10.1 Eight inseparable security competencies.

conditions. The operational significance of this chain reaction relationship is that to be effective, the ability of the security organization to detect, assess, and respond to a given event is measured not in hours or minutes, but in almost real time, spanning only 5–8 s under the greatest-severity threat conditions. Any hesitation on the part of a security organization to react outside this window could be catastrophic for the enterprise. Understanding the integrated role these competencies play in strategic security planning is essential to carrying out your prime security mission. These security techniques, means, and methods—when planned, designed, and applied properly—create a formidable prevention and protection strategy that can serve an organization well in reducing risk exposure, while improving and enhancing organizational and security resilience. I discuss each strategy in the subsections below.

Deterrence Is Mostly an Intangible Strategy

Deterrence is a by-product of the various security strategies embraced by a security organization. Deterrence may encompass administrative processes, protocols, practices, and security awareness, as well as physical and technological measures and techniques aimed at protecting critical infrastructure and key assets from an array of threatening conditions.

- Administrative measures may involve the redesign of suitable security systems, changes in protocols and practices, more emphasis on employee security awareness, and an increase in intelligence-gathering activities.
- Physical measures may be natural or manmade barriers or facility architectural design.
- Technology measures may include alternative materials and processes, interoperable communications and information networks, and advanced and emerging security technologies.

The goal of deterrence is to create conditions that make it more difficult for an adversary to carry out a threatening activity, thus presenting an unacceptable risk to the adversary in inflicting harm, injury, or death to resources or in damaging or destroying critical assets and other properties. When an adversary perceives an unacceptable risk, the effectiveness of deterrence can influence the adversary to adjust or change the mode of penetration, attack, tactic, and weapons used, as well as increase the time it takes the adversary to complete a particular mission. Deterrence aids delay, prevention, protection, detection, assessment, response, and recovery, and it provides to employees, governing authorities, and the community a level of confidence that a safe and secure work environment exists.

Delay Channels the Population

Physical barriers are used to restrict, channel, deny, delay, or prevent an adversary from gaining access to a protected area and reaching an intended target. Barriers can be natural, such as mountains, deserts, water obstacles and rivers, cliffs, ditches and canyons, seas, or other natural features that are difficult to traverse; they can also be structural, such as fences, floors, walls, vaults, barricades, fences and gates, grills, roofs, bars, barbed wire, and other structures or vast open space and distances of travel. Delay is also designed to slow down the adversary in reaching a vulnerable point or asset until a response force capable of defeating the adversary can arrive at the scene. For example, conditions that determine how long it would take an adversary to reach an objective is dictated by such factors as:

- perceived strength and capability of the security organization and its response elements
- configuration of the area
- site or facility hardness and standoff distances
- types and quantity of physical barriers to be crossed
- distance to targeted area
- expertise and tactical skill sets
- types of tools, weapons, and equipment the adversary must use
- a safe escape route and time required to depart the area

Penetration resistance time is measured from the moment of detection, typically at the boundary of the property or restricted area housing critical assets, to the moment the adversary reaches a targeted asset. Ideally, the time it takes a response force to reach or connect with the adversary should not exceed the time an adversary, once detected, would need to reach a targeted asset. Few security organizations incorporate this time-sensitive response capability into their emergency planning or practice sessions. Even fewer exhibit a willingness to expend resources and funding to acquire this capability.

Much of the regulated security industry, however, mandates some degree of delay/penetration and response time requirements. Some industry standards address volunteer delay/penetration and response times as well.

- The facility delay/penetration criterion can vary based on the characteristics of particular infrastructures and assets, their mission, regulatory mandates or industry standards, and whether national, regional, or local security interests are at stake.
- Some operational security requirements call for a 5-min delay/penetration time to be built into the security design. Under this architectural standard, the in-place security response force is expected to maintain the ability and capability to respond and engage an adversary within that 5-min window—preferably before the adversary reaches a targeted asset and has time to cause harm, injury, damage, or destruction.
- Other criteria can range from 15- to 30-min delay/penetration resistance times for high-value assets such as commercial nuclear power stations, power generation plants and dams, water treatment and waste plants, and other critical infrastructures, such as defense manufacturing and research, development, test, and evaluation centers.
- For Department of Defense and other national critical assets, stringent delay/penetration resistance time may exist for such assets as high explosives, ammunitions, and weapons.
- Military strategic and tactical weapons systems and personnel on alert also have stringent delay/penetration resistance requirements, as do national intelligence facilities, telecommunications systems, space satellite systems, and National or Military Command, Communications and Control C^3 facilities.
- The protection of nuclear weapons and the assurance that they remain continuously within the custody of the U.S. government, whether deployed on land, on sea, or in the air, have special security measures and delay/penetration timelines.

Notwithstanding the various delay/penetration and response times evoked throughout the private and public sectors, one thing is clear. The more critical a particular asset is to the interests of U.S. national security or the economic survivability of a corporation, the greater the delay/penetration time—and the more security resources with greater abilities and increased capabilities need to be allocated to protect the asset. This results in a higher capital investment and higher operational and training costs to secure these special assets.

Typically, within the private sector, such abilities and capabilities are rare. The authority, responsibility, and accountability to protect the most critical assets and operations affecting national security or corporate survivability within the content of national defense RDT&E or production are generally assigned to special security organizations that possess the necessary skill sets, knowledge base, expertise, training and qualifications, logistics, and resources to engage in such special mission assignments under industry and government special agreements. Delay/penetration resistance techniques help the deterrence, prevention, protection, detection, assessment, and response processes, giving the security organization time to assemble and react to a given threat condition in a timely manner.

Prevention

Prevention has various collective meanings, all aimed at achieving the same outcome. I define prevention as:

- specific operations aimed at deterring, preempting, interdicting, or disrupting illegal activity
- protecting lives and providing for the general well-being of the workforce
- assessing and analyzing conditions to determine the full nature and source of the threat to reduce risk exposure
- means and techniques to avoid, preclude, or limit the impact of a disruption; eliminate, deter, or prevent the likelihood of a disruptive incident and its consequences; remove human or physical assets or their lockdown location; or help stop something from happening or arising, thus significantly reducing risk exposure.
- increasing security operations, heightening inspections, and improving surveillance operations
- applying intelligence and other information to a range of activities and sharing information, warning, and alert notices with others

  Prevention helps the deterrence, delay, protection, detection, and assessment processes.

Protection

Protection involves those capabilities necessary to shield, preserve, and secure resources and assets, keeping resources safe from injury or death and assets safe from damage or destruction.

- Protective measures can include the integration of resources, processes, practices, protocols, and facility designs to guard against malevolent attacks such as terrorism and sabotage, criminal activity, disasters, and loss of services or injury from system or equipment failures.
- Protective measures may include the removal of hazardous materials, relocation of operations and resources, or the total lockdown of a facility or site, and providing increased security patrols and fixed posts, as well as implementing special security compensatory measures.

- Standoff distances are also a means of shielding that helps to reduce or minimize the effects of an explosive charge placed at or near the boundary of an area or facility, or collateral damage sustained from a nearby asset or facility under attack.

Protection helps the deterrence, delay, prevention, and detection processes.

Detection

Detection measures are designed to expose the presence of intruders, unauthorized weapons, explosives, and other contraband; criminal behavior; and any compromises in security system integrity. Detection monitors the validity of access controls, circulation controls, and behavior patterns, and communicates an alarm. Ideally, detection should take place as far away as possible from the critical assets requiring protection.

Detection techniques help the prevention, delay, protection, assessment, and response processes.

Assessment

Assessment is the evaluation of unusual events such as security breaches, criminal behavior, or unauthorized activity. Humans, technology, or a combination of both can perform assessment. Assessment may require the strategic deployment and use of area patrols and fixed posts complimented by security technology such as CCTV cameras that activate in conjunction with sensors in alarm status. Other means can also contribute to the assessment process:

- Employee security awareness and reporting of incidents
- Procedural checks and balances such as passwords and code words
- The "buddy system," or "two-person" rule
- Verification and authentication systems
- Environmental control systems
- Management information systems
- Supervisory control and data acquisition systems
- Supervisory oversight of any combination of the above

With all these techniques in the "security toolbox," a security organization—in concert with other business units—can maintain a reasonable ability and capability to perform detection and assessment through direct human observation; enforcement of protocols, processes, and practices and security awareness, assisted by technology.

The use of technologies also enhances the safety and effectiveness of first responders and reduces the need for expensive use of patrols and fixed posts to perform the assessment function. Security lighting and advanced infrared technology also enhance surveillance and assessment capabilities.

The use of remotely dispersed intrusion detection and surveillance devices creates the need for a security organization to be aware of the validity, severity, and nature of an event that triggers an alarm. Beyond the technical capability to visually announce an alarm and to use video to surveil areas, the responsibility to assess and analyze developing situations and conditions rests solely with the expertise and experience of the system operator, as well as the leadership and experience of the security management team. This team must direct and carry out a response capable of containing, neutralizing, or stopping an undesirable event. For security incidents, the window of this initial assessment is extremely time-critical and time-sensitive.

Response

The security response addresses the short-term, direct effects of an incident. Response activities may include:

- operations aimed at preempting, interdicting, or disrupting illegal or unauthorized activity
- prioritizing assignments for normal posts and patrols
- increasing or expanding security operations and continuing investigations into the nature and source of the threatening incident
- applying intelligence and other information and actions to lessen the effects or consequences of an incident
- providing area and perimeter security and strict access control during a widespread pandemic that may involve the isolation or quarantine of personnel pending transportation to medical facilities

Recovery

Once response actions are complete, recovery addresses those actions that are required to get the security force and corporation back to normal business operations:

- Maintaining the security of the area affected, preserving evidence and controlling access to the scene during the initial stages of rescue operations and investigation
- Maintaining the security of the area during construction to repair and/or replace lost facilities, infrastructure, and assets based on the criticality of business operations
- Determining what short-term and long-term compensatory measures will be required and the resources, facilities, and equipment needed to sustain such operations
- Providing assistance to return the affected area back to normal business operations by shifting security priorities while still maintaining a high state of alert
- Planning the reestablishment of normal security operations for the affected area(s) while supporting other areas of the corporation on an extended work schedule
- Adjusting the corporate threat alert notification system based on the severity of the threat event and corporate vulnerability exposure to circumstances, conditions, and situations created by the initial threat condition
- Evaluating security conditions during and after the event to determine the need to reduce or expand security operations, to determine additional resources and logistical support needed to continue security operations, and to identify lessons learned.

Timely Interdependencies of Security Capabilities

There can be no doubt that the principle of timeliness is crucial to effective security operations (Sullivant, 2007, pp. 169–172). In the realm of security operations, deterrence, delay, prevention, protection, detection, assessment, and response are critical time-sensitive and time-dependent capabilities that cannot be ignored unless executive management takes on the awesome responsibility of accepting the consequences of residual risk exposure without approving the continuation of reasonable security compensatory measures. I discuss each of these principles below.

Principle of Timely Security Deterrence Should Focus on "Curb Appeal"

The principle of timely deterrence refers to attractiveness as a target (or, in real-estate terms, its "curb appeal") the enterprise demonstrates to its customer or client base, community and governing bodies, as well as adversaries. The architecture of the corporation should display strength, confidence, and leadership. Its configuration and layout should give an adversary cause to pause and assess the probability of a successful breach or, conversely, the consequences of failing to successfully complete an attack. The goal of timely deterrence is to lead the adversary to the conclusion to "shop elsewhere."

Principle of Timely Security Delay

The principle of timely delay introduces a series of strategic obstacles and nuisances into the path of an adversary; these are aimed at increasing the time it takes the adversary to reach a protected asset or activity, thereby increasing the risk of unnecessary exposure while permitting time for an adequate response to develop and take hold. Overcoming obstacles and processes to achieve an objective requires the adversary to have more resources, logistical support, communications and equipment, and an equal amount of assistance to ensure an escape route and find a safe heaven immediately afterward. If the technical delay mechanisms used are ineffective, an aggressor could trip one or more lines of detection, open or bypass one or more portals to gain access to an area, or circumvent several protocols to complete the assignment and leave the area before the response force arrives. Or an aggressor could seal off a series of alarms in the system and still take the time needed to complete the mission, knowing that the response will be inadequate.

Principle of Timely Security Prevention

The principle of timely prevention is the continuing link of security measures in progress. Its aim is to introduce integrated safeguards and physical barriers, processes, administrative procedures, and building architecture and layout designs that reduce an adversary's attraction to critical infrastructures and key assets.

Principle of Timely Security Protection

The principle of timely protection takes into consideration built-in architectural design safeguards such as explosive and penetration resistance technologies; heating, ventilation, and air-conditioning protection screens and filters; physical barriers and safe havens and other means and mechanisms to minimize injury or safe life, or damage or destroy property until a response force capable of engaging and neutralizing an adversary arrives on the scene.

Principle of Timely Security Detection

The principle of timely detection requires that the penetration of a protected area or asset be detected as far as possible from the facility, system, or function and before the adversary reaches the intended target. A security program's detection capability is only as good as the security force, employee security awareness, and the properly deployed and integrated security systems that perform to expectations or standards.

Principle of Timely Security Assessment

Real-time assessment includes the immediate actions taken to react to security and security-related events in real time. Real-time assessment involves the processing of critical information and potentially harmful conditions in sufficient time to be useful in the formulation of a timely response. The goal of timely assessment is to provide the security organization with a real-time assessment capability to observe and evaluate situations and conditions, to track the aggressor(s), and to provide the necessary direction to the response force to control, contain, or neutralize the threat in almost real time. An effective assessment capability has two elements: event identification and event tracking.

Event Identification

Assessment must be able to distinguish between normal acceptable activity and behaviors and any deviation from these norms. Human assessment can accomplish this (in part) through a motivated and dedicated workforce, security awareness training, security patrols and fixed posts, and the reporting of unusual activity or behavior. But the critical aspect of human assessment mostly rests with the security system operator and supervisor within the security monitoring station. When human assessment is complemented by video technology, the application of cameras must provide for near-real-time activation of a detected event to distinguish clearly the severity of the threat (including, if possible, the identity of the perpetrator(s)) to determine a proper response. Where integrated security systems are deployed, a tripped alarm should announce and display at a remote monitoring station in 1 s or less. Where CCTV components are integrated into the detection system, camera activation and display of the alarmed zone at the monitoring station should occur in 1.5 s or less. This combined transmission time accounts for a 2.5-s lapse before the system operator can even interact with the system to perform a "human assessment" of the conditions, circumstances, and situations that caused the alarm. In most instances a qualified and certified security system operator can digest the scene and recognize what is happening in 3 s. It can take the operator an additional 3 s to notify and dispatch an in-house response force to the scene. This brings the total time lapse up to this point to at least 8.5 s—more than enough time (a skilled aggressor needs 5 s)[1] for a skilled adversary to clear an 8-foot chain link fence or other barrier, move out of the footprint of a camera, and blend in with the surrounding environment.

Tracking the Adversary and Activity

For the safety of the response force and standby observers, it is crucial that the security force know the exact status of conditions at the scene as well as the capability and activity of the aggressor(s) if it is to effectively contain, neutralize, or defeat the adversary. This can be accomplished only through proper human assessment. To achieve this goal, the security system must have the capability to track the sequence of events and the movements of the perpetrator(s). Once the aggressor(s) is out of a camera's view, the system operator must expend additional time and energy searching for and tracking the intruder(s) before he or she can guide the response team toward the aggressor(s) by reporting the intruder's activity, and in determining the severity of the penetration, if possible.

The Muddied Water

The situation becomes more complicated when the security organization must rely on receiving information from employees and others; from operations, communications, and other centers that monitor activities; or by communicating with one or more local law enforcement agency. Under these circumstances and conditions People get caught up in the moments surrounding excitement, uncertainty, and often fear. Some people loose their thoughts, others speculate what they actually heard or saw. Others want to feel important and either exaggerate or lie about the events that happened. Here are some examples:

- First reports and information received from employees and others could take several minutes after an occurrence. Experience reveals that such initial reports are always fragmented, incomplete, and even contradictory. This often delays the initial assessment process and the response team from getting to the scene in a timely manner. It may also limit the usefulness of the response team once the team arrives on the scene.
- Making contact with law enforcement agencies and explaining the threat situation could take several minutes, usually followed by an undetermined amount of time for them to arrive on the scene. Although many police departments (and other law enforcement agencies) have an exceptional record of responding to incidents within the private and public sectors Fox News recently reported that the average national response time for law enforcement is 11 minutes. I have tested many law enforcement agencies and have clocked their response time between 5 to 10 minutes, although some agencies can take up to 30 min or more to show up, depending on available patrols, distances and traffic conditions, and other public service priorities. Additional time is usually expended after law enforcement units arrive at the scene because they often require a briefing of the circumstances and conditions that caused the call for assistance, as well as safety issues that could impede their response. Being escorted by corporate security personnel to where the adversary(s) is or was last sighted can also delay the law enforcement response.

[1] Sandia Laboratory has completed reliable and validated penetration tests of 6-foot, 7-foot, and 8-foot fences and other barrier systems under various weather conditions. Fences and barriers were cleared in 3–5 s on successive successful tests.

Principle of Timely Security Response

The principle of timely response involves the immediate actions that prevent loss of life or property and provide emergency assistance to others. For security it involves the ability to demonstrate a timely, gradual, and flexible response that is sufficient to prevent, control, contain, or neutralize the event that justified the call and that can react to more than one event-driven threat scenario simultaneously. The makeup of the response force is not important—what is important is the ability and capability of the response force to react under the time constraints imposed upon it. The response may involve the ability and capability to:

- carry out its function of saving lives and protecting assets
- neutralize or contain a threat
- establish and secure the perimeter of an area
- preserve the integrity of an area and control access
- assist in the evacuation of an area or building
- guide and assist external first responders such as police, firefighters, and medical personnel to the scene
- report conditions, circumstances, and situations to management

Principle of Timely Recovery

In times of crisis and danger a security organization must possess the ability and capability to:

- expand and contract its shifting resources and changing priorities, and to disperse and work individually and as a group
- coordinate and work with affected internal business units and with external emergency service agencies, law enforcement officials, and other governing agencies, as the situation calls for
- continue protecting the scene, control access, perverse evidence and help remove injured personnel
- recall off-duty personnel, brief them on conditions, and make assignments
- manage on-duty personnel and shift their mind-set from normal security operations to one or more emergency crisis while potentially transitioning into a 12-h shift
- remove from duty and replace security personnel who may have been injured or lost in the line of duty; replace others who would need to be relieved to eat, rest, and sleep, and then return for another extended shift
- transition the staff back to normal security operations while maintaining an emergency security posture for as long as necessary to support enterprise recovery operations
- gradually withdraw the expanded security force from the area when corporate restoration operations are completed

Conclusions

Inseparable security operational competencies are an characteristic inherent in any security organization, regardless of size. Equally important is the effective planning and deployment, and timely execution of these crucial capabilities. Without them, a security organization cannot perform its prime mission.

Deterrence

The principle of timely deterrence aims at giving an intruder cause to pause. It is the visual evidence that a security program and commitment by management will induce some perpetrators to look to attack other facilities where exposure would be less risky for them.

Delay

Delay slows an adversary in his or her attempt to reach a targeted asset so a response force capable of containing, neutralizing, or defeating the adversary can interrupt the intrusion.

Prevention

Prevention methods are used to avoid, preclude, or limit the impact of a disruption; eliminate, deter, or prevent the likelihood of a disruptive incident and its consequences; remove human or physical assets to their lockdown locations; and help to stop something from happening or arising.

Protection

Protection shields, preserves, and keeps resources from injury or death and assets from damage or destruction.

Assessment

Security technology plays a vital support role when systems are programmed to respond to specific hazardous stimuli. For instance, when a harmful contaminant is released within a research laboratory, the monitoring system may be programmed to sound an alarm when the agent is detected. The response may include sealing the portals and utility openings and releasing neutralizing agents to sanitize the area through a secondary and protective ventilation system, followed by a human response to remove personnel from the affected area when it is safe to enter. As such, the overall technical solution to a security response must assist—never hinder—the security organization when executing a human response to an incident.

Response

Deterrence, delay, detection and assessment are meaningless unless the security organization has the ability and capability to respond to the scene and to neutralize or contain an adversary. The capability to response is operationally dependent on a human function, as is visual assessment and surveillance. A security organization must maintain the capability to intercept, contain, and neutralize an aggressor before he or she can reach the intended target.

Recovery

Recovery is the ability of the security organization to operate well enough to meet its obligations to protect the life/safety of employees, and protecting property in any given emergency while transitioning back to normal security operations is essential while business units concentrate on restoring business and revenue capacity. More attention needs to be given to security recovery operations to effectively support corporate recovery efforts, to prevent security force "burnout" from working extended shifts for prolonged periods, and to avoid staff shortages.

Closing Thoughts

A security organization must maintain the capability to detect, assess, and track the sequence of events and the movements of a perpetrator(s) from the start of the engagement through the conclusion of the incident. Security organizations that fail in detecting, assessing, and tracking security events and in initiating an appropriate response within 5–8 s are substandard performers. These security organizations cannot adequately perform their prime security mission. A technical audit or assessment of a security system is an excellent risk management tool to measure and evaluate the performance parameters of a security system, to determine mitigation solutions that are necessary to bring an existing system up to par with industry standards, or to determine to replace it with state-of-the art technology.

A User-Friendly Security Technology Model

Security technology was never intended to replace or reduce the security force, but to make it easier for them to focus human attention on assessment, analysis, decision making, and accountability. The application and configuration of security technology, therefore, must always complement security operations and never hinder, hamper, or slow down the security organization from carrying our its critical security mission.

John Sullivant

Top Takeaways

- Create a technical security strategy
- Interdependencies of the technical security planning and security design planning processes
- Significance of technology application and system configuration considerations
- Criticality of system quality performance parameters
- Quality maintenance and logistics support capability
- System failures and the need for compensatory measures
- Inspection and testing of security systems
- Selected case histories

Overview

Security operations are becoming increasingly computerized and rely more and more on the finite performance standard of electronic capabilities to improve the effectiveness and efficiency of the security organization. When security technology is properly pulled together and correctly applied to protect critical assets and processes, the result is a functionally integrated security system that offers capabilities that are unmatched and unachieved by a human attempting to perform the same functions.

This demands we know how well security systems perform and what actions we must take to correct deficiencies, weaknesses, and nonconformities to performance expectations or specification standards. The application of system availability, readiness, reliability, maintainability, supportability, and survivability, as well as technology application and human factors engineering, are crucial elements that significantly contribute to achieving security mission requirements.

A Dire Need Exists to Embrace a Technical Security Strategy

The execution of a sound technical security strategy requires extensive research, thorough planning, comprehensive understanding of the critical issues and risks inherent in any security system upgrade or new procurement undertaking, and exhaustive teamwork between the security organization, the engineering unit, executive management, the procurement division, and other business units.

The demand for developing a technical security strategy stems from poor technology performance and the lack of a strategic vision to correct the problem, and a lack of understanding the fundamental mission of security technology. *Appendix A - Selected Security Technology Deficiencies and Weaknesses* graphically illustrate selected histories that tell a compelling story about the widespread security technology conditions and circumstances that exist throughout the industry. One approach to developing a technical security strategy is to pool enterprise resources with technology designers and system integrators to help advance an overall understanding of technology performance, system capabilities and limitations, application theory, and life cycle care. The security director must assuredly orchestrate this umbrella strategy, lead the nurturing of team-building skills, and embrace the use of advanced techniques that ensure timely detection of, assessment of, and response to security events.

The Technical Security Planning Process Is Often Misunderstood and Underestimated

As can be seen in Fig. 11.1 - An integrated technical security planning process: a unifying umbrella strategy, An integrated technical security planning process: a unifying umbrella strategy, functional areas of responsibility are divided yet interwoven

Security Planning	Security Design & Engineering Planning
Pool expertise: • Design & engineering • Systems integrator • Technology developer • Security consultant Perform technical security analysis Characterize: • System mission & configuration • Performance parameters • Human engineering factors • Time-sensitive/time-dependent factors • Quality factors & safety issues • Maintenance & logistics concept • System failures & compensatory measures • Inspection & testing requirements • Training qualifications • Continual improvement program Cochair design reviews	Participate in technical analysis Translate operational needs into technical performance capabilities, standards, and quality factors: • Readiness & dependability • Suitability & availability • Reliability & supportability • Maintenance accessibility & logistics • Recovery & survivability • Warranties & guarantees • Develop design plans & drawings Cochair design reviews

Figure 11.1 An integrated technical security planning process: a unifying umbrella strategy.

between the security organization and the design and engineering unit. The figure illustrates in the most general terms the exchange of management and engineering excellence necessary to carry out the overall technical planning process.

At its highest level, the division of planning activities is convenient for the purposes of this discussion. In its simplest form, security planning and security design planning merge to become a management and engineering analysis process. The former falls within the realm of security operational competencies, whereas the latter draws on architecture and engineering aptitudes to support operational needs. To successfully deliver a functional security system, the security organization and the engineering unit must work hand in hand. Early technical decisions have a profound effect on the delivery of a functional system with matching performance expectations. Appendix A: Security Technology Deficiencies and Weaknesses Case Histories clearly bring this point to the forefront.

The Technical Security Analysis Provides a Road Map to Decision Making

The first step in the technical planning process is to characterize the configuration and performance capability of an installed security system, if one exists. The security director, in concert with the engineering department, is responsible for conducting this technical analysis or ensuring that a qualified security consultant performs one. Fig. 11.2 - Security system technical analysis methodology, a security system technology analysis model, illustrates the investigative process from a systems-level perspective (Sullivant, 2007, pp. 179, 273). The model is flexible and can be customized to fit the unique needs of any security organization, large or small.

Purpose of the Technical Analysis

The technical analysis measures the strengths and weaknesses of in-place security technologies, identifies limitations and gaps in application and performance, and evaluates the consequences of system ineffectiveness. The security technology analysis aims to:

- characterize system objectives, technology application, performance parameters, and mission
- characterize quality factors and system capabilities
- characterize human factor engineering dependencies between man–machine interfaces
- determine time-sensitive and time-dependent characteristics
- identify gaps in system performance and protective features
- analyze system deficiencies, vulnerabilities, weaknesses, and consequences
- determine the system's life expectancy
- increase system performance and capability in an all-hazards environment
- build in network resiliency
- introduce improvements to strengthen performance, safety, integrity, and survivability
- evaluate the system operator's knowledge base and competency
- identify gaps between existing training and training needs

The process emphasizes a total quality systems approach to problem solving that contributes to determining mitigation solutions that are acceptable to executive management.

Figure 11.2 Security system technical analysis methodology.

Benefits Derived from the Technical Analysis

Decision makers can benefit from the analysis because it helps them understand:

- how systems can best be deployed, how integration increases the performance capabilities of the security organization, and their relationship with and dependency on other security program activities
- system vulnerabilities and weaknesses and the technology's effectiveness, efficiency, and productivity for detecting, deterring, assessing, and responding to security-related events in near real-time
- the consequences of their decisions about system usage and performance, how to steer long-term planning needs for facility and space use, and how to channel scarce resources and funding into those areas that need it most
- what remedies work best to strengthen system performance and enhance the integrity of system operations and survivability
- how effective use and careful handling of the equipment and its proper maintenance as called for by the manufacture protects the warranty and extends the life cycle of the entire system

The Role of Security Technology Planning

The security director assimilates the technical analysis and feeds the findings into the overarching technical security planning process. In this role, the director collaborates with scientists, technology developers, system integrators, unit engineers, and others to:

- solve system technical issues using a systematic approach and develop mitigation actions from a business and management perspective
- ensure regulatory compliance
- train the organization to achieve its inherent operational effectiveness

Embracing The Challenges of New Technology Advancements

When no system exists, the director has the option of starting a technical analysis review process by researching and analyzing data, and performing a competitive analysis of the initial platform to develop a preliminary design document that characterizes system performance, maintenance, logistics, training, and other important characteristics. Or, the director may opt to a unit engineer, or have a security consultant perform this task. Regardless of the party performing the analysis, it is crucial that the design document serves to communicate system performance expectations to the engineering group responsible for creating the engineering drawings and delivering a functional and acceptable system to the security director. Preparing a design is a complex task and includes, but is not necessarily limited to, the following substrategies. The design document or system specification must define:

- The goals and objectives of the security system.
- Critical system operational capabilities and abilities that must be performed and by whom.
- Critical processes and best practices, including system self-healing features.
- Realistic event-driven response and recovery scenarios.

- Critical time-sensitive and time-dependent activities that are important to the design.
- System fail-safe and integrity features.
- Quality performance standards, safety and human factors engineering.
- Life cycle logistics, maintenance, and depot support needs.
- Failures that would call for implementing security compensatory measures.
- Inspection and testing requirements.
- Training and certification requirements.

In the design document or specification it is crucial to describe clearly, in unambiguous terms, all critical system performance characteristics, requirements, and standards that must be met, including any acceptable design alternatives and constraints or limitations that may influence the design.

The Role of Security Design and Design Engineering

The lead engineer is responsible for developing an acceptable technical design and is responsible to the security director for delivering a functional and workable design and associated integrated plans. Security design planning begins early in the security planning stages, starting with the results of the technical analysis and a preliminary design concept. As the design matures, and with guidance furnished by the director, engineers resolve technical and human interface considerations, perform trade-off analyses, assist in verifying performance expectations, and capabilities, and perform a series of design reviews with stakeholders. Typically, three design reviews are called for: the preliminary design, the detailed design, and the installation design.

A significant goal of design planning is to ensure time-sensitive and time-dependent security operational needs and performance standards specified by regulations, industry best practices, and local operational requirements are met. Another design goal is to ensure system configuration and performance complement security operations, and never hinder, hamper, or slow down, the security organization in carrying out its ability and capability to perform its critical mission: deter, delay, prevent, protect, detect, assess, respond to and recover from one or more security events or other emergencies in near-real time.

Also, the application of security technology is not intended to replace or reduce the security force, but to make it easier for them to focus on incidents, events and threats, and exchanges with other persons. Under this concept, security technology helps realign the security force so human skills can be applied to critical decision-making tasks such as reporting conditions, assessing circumstances, investigating incidents, and determining the type of responses. Proper security response requires strategic and tactical planning, agreed-upon involvement, and capability to perform to expectations. Throughout the design process, engineers must work hand in hand with the security director and security staff to:

- identify the characteristics of hardware, software, facilities, data, personnel, and training
- translate operational needs into technical performance characteristics
- define system technical performance capabilities, including system integrity features
- integrate technical compatibility of physical, functional, and program interfaces
- integrate quality factors into the engineering process to meet operational objectives
- clarify complex technical interdependencies, synergies, and trade-offs

Quality Factors and Safety Features

Experience has repeatedly demonstrated that emphasis on quality factors (readiness, suitability, availability, reliability, maintainability, supportability, and survivability) and safety concerns must start during the earliest planning activities to ensure the characteristics of the system are dealt with and established at the front end of the security planning and system engineering and design cycles.

Retrofitting quality factors and safety features after the design is complete and the procurement process has begun can be a costly "mistake" and often cost prohibitive to correct, forcing the security director to accept a poor design, weak system performance, and accept substandard performance from the security workforce. Retrofitting security into the design after the fact can increase costs anywhere from 30% to over 300% from the original cost estimate. I cannot emphasize enough the importance of you not falling into this trap. You will never be able to recover from engineering flaw.

What Does Integration Mean to the Security Professional?

System integration is the bringing together of a set of component subsystems into one arching system and ensuring that all components function together as an integrated whole throughout the system's life cycle. This means that design management and engineering analysis for system performance and technology enhancement is a work in progress always measured against the changing mission requirements.

As security integrators, we must have a deep understanding of the prime security mission and its capabilities, and we cannot be ambiguous about what that is. Security organizations operate under a tremendous amount of scrutiny—always under the microscope of politicians, special interest groups, regulators, government agencies, and the public.

That opens up a lot of visibility about how a security organization operates and how it responds to security threats, which is just one area that it needs to react to. These threats come in all shapes and forms, ranging from intentional threats from misguided youth, trespassers, insider threats, hardened criminals, domestic and international threats, transnational organized crime, illness and disease, including threats from natural and manmade disasters, industrial accidents, and weather-related calamities.

Technology Application Has High-Visibility Challenges

Security systems can be deployed in almost any area, serving multipurpose objectives. The security director also has the awesome responsibility of establishing quality factors and safety and performance parameters to ensure systems are designed to perform under various conditions and circumstances.

Importance of a Quality System Maintenance Program

Maintenance Concept

A good security maintenance program meets three objectives: reduce equipment downtime caused by equipment failure or malfunction, ensure the equipment operates on a continual and uninterrupted basis, and extend the service life of equipment to a reasonable level.

A sound maintenance program includes a clear maintenance concept; the type and level of maintenance necessary to support the system; categories of equipment to be serviced, when, and the type of service; maintenance and logistics needs; organizational responsibilities; support equipment, tools, consumables, and spares; and the records and reports used in implementing maintenance.

The maintenance concept must be clear and describe the broad planned approach to sustaining a simplistic maintenance program for the life of the system. Areas to consider include:

- the level of maintenance necessary to sustain levels of readiness, suitability, availability, reliability, maintainability, human factors, safety, supportability, and survivability requirements
- the concept of "pull and replace" and exceptions thereto. This means system components must be readably accessible for inspection and servicing without major disassembly or reassembly, and without disconnecting primary and secondary power sources.

Within the commercial marketplace there are typically three levels of maintenance: preventive maintenance, corrective maintenance, and depot support.

Preventive Maintenance

Preventive maintenance keeps a security system in top shape and performing to expectations. It calls for scheduled maintenance checks and services (usually on a quarterly basis) to offset the effects of the environment and normal equipment wear, and to preclude the premature malfunction or failure of equipment.

Preventative maintenance is typically performed on equipment while the system is online and generally without the need to disassemble/reassemble equipment or disconnect power. For those rare instances when it may be necessary to shut down a portion of the security system for safety reasons, it may also be necessary to plan for the extent and type of security compensatory measures that may need to be implemented to maintain a level of security comparable to that provided by the failed component or that part of the system power has been shut down. More on this topic in a moment.

Corrective Maintenance

Corrective maintenance includes all actions performed to restore failed equipment to its specified condition. At the unit level, system availability can best be achieved when failed equipment is simply removed from service and replaced by a new or refurbished spare part. The "pull and replace" concept minimizes system downtime as well as costly security compensatory measures. Under this concept:

- failed equipment is replaced online and may require the brief disconnection of power
- failed equipment is returned to the depot for analysis and the determination to repair or replace the failed unit

The exception to a pull and replace policy applies to such components as vehicle gate tracking systems, gate operators, automated vehicle drop-arms, vehicle crash barriers, fences and gates, and lighting, to name a few. These components are usually repaired on site and may require disassembly and reassembly, including shutting off the power source(s) at some time during the repair process.

A good practice for the maintenance group to embrace before they begin performing any type of corrective maintenance is to notify the security organization so the unit can plan for necessary security compensatory measures and put them in place before maintenance begins. The security organization must also be notified when corrective maintenance is completed so the system can be tested before maintenance crews are released, and security compensatory measures can be terminated in an orderly and timely fashion and security resources reallocated to other activities.

Depot Support

The depot augments on-site maintenance capabilities on an on-demand basis. Depot support may include product and service warranty, hardware and software troubleshooting, consultation and diagnostics support, logistical support and spare replacements, and on-site technical assistance and training. Maintenance agreements generally spell out service and support requirements.

Embracing Inspections and Tests Extends the System Life Cycle

Inspection and testing programs have significant long-term value because these activities validate that the system continuously performs as designed and intended throughout its life cycle. They also provide a vehicle for reporting to design teams, through the development of fact-based test reports, any unusual difficulties, deficiencies, or questionable conditions for further review and potential action, as necessary.

Once the system is operational and ownership has transferred from the installation contractor to the end user, it is in the best interests of the security organization to embrace a continuing program of self-inspection and operational tests for the life cycle of the system. These inspections and tests ensure system integrity against tampering, damage, or destruction and continual reliable performance and minimize system downtime. This activity includes physical inspections, system diagnostic tests, operational tests, and performance tests.

Always Conduct Physical Inspections at the Start of Each Shift Change

- Walk down the fence line of restricted areas to inspect the fence fabric for cuts, other damage, or signs of tampering on gate locks.

- Examine electrical panels and other hardware such as sensors, cameras, barriers, and gates for damage or signs of tampering.
- Check doors, windows, and other openings to ensure they are secured and/or locked and for signs of forced entry.
- Check general areas for suspicious persons and packages.

Always Conduct System Diagnostic Tests at the Start of Each Shift Change

Whenever system operators change shifts, conduct a system self-diagnostic test to verify the integrity of system features, circuit continuity, and the activation and working order of all alarm points. System diagnostic testing may also be programmed to automatically run during specific times, including after a power loss.

Always Conduct Weekly Operational Tests

Once a week test:

- fence sensors by tapping the fence fabric
- area sensors by walking, running, jumping, and crawling through the detection zone
- doors and windows that are alarmed by opening and closing them
- tamper-switch alarms by opening and closing circuitry panel doors
- automated vehicle barrier systems and vehicle gates for operability
- the camera footprint to verify whether any shift in the camera field of view has occurred. Walk the outer edges of the camera zone, validating results against preset plots or recordings of previous walk tests performed. Conduct this test both during daylight hours and in darkness.

Tests need not be completed in one sweep. Rather, you can schedule them throughout the week by assigning designated zones to the various shifts.

Shift leaders are the ideal supervisors to schedule operational tests and to ensure the results are captured within the retrieval system or entered into the system transaction/activity log. The off-going shift leader briefs the incoming shift leader of inspection and test deficiencies, as well as the status of any maintenance issues and the tests completed during the shift, including any maintenance and tests pending or scheduled to be performed.

Maintenance Performance Tests

It is crucial to test the security system after corrective maintenance is performed, after each inoperative state,[1] and when necessary—such as during severe weather conditions or a major industrial accident that affects system operations. Only those functions directly affected by maintenance activities need to be tested.

During maintenance, it may be necessary to place some portions of the system in the ACCESS mode. In the ACCESS mode, a single sensor or group of sensors or

[1] An inoperative state exists when power is disconnected to perform maintenance or for any other reasons, when both primary and backup power sources fail to provide power, or when power applied to equipment has failed to kick-in.

access control devices, vehicle gates, and barriers may be shunted, which would preclude the announcement of an alarm or advisory notice.[2]

Seasonal Performance Tests

Perform these tests on a quarterly basis to measure the variance in system performance resulting from seasonal temperatures and changes in weather conditions. Moreover, a thorough performance test should be conducted at least 30 days before the system or any equipment warranty expires to take advantage of any warranty services and products that may be necessary.

Test Plans and Test Procedures

Test plans and test procedures guide and control test activity. Test plans outline roles and responsibilities, performance standards, safety precautions, and test limitations and constraints, as well as the records and reports required to be maintained.

Test procedures provide systematic instructions to verify system performance and protective features. Procedures identify the specific test trials to be performed; the pass/fail criteria to be applied; the test population, methodology, and equipment used; safety considerations for each test trial; and the test logs to be used to record test results.

Collection and Composition of Test Data and Test Logs

One method of computing data and examples of test logs are offered in *Appendix B - Sample Test Logs*. You may use these test logs as designed or modify them to meet your particular testing and reporting requirements.

System Failure Modes and Compensatory Measures

It is essential the security director develop contingency event-driven response and recovery procedures that addresses specific implementing security compensatory measures for the lost capability of failed equipment or system failure.

Whenever system performance is degraded or lost, it is prudent to implement security compensatory measures that are comparable to the affected performance lost in order to overcome any security vulnerability created by such failure. When spare parts are not stocked on site, implementing compensatory measures becomes a crucial consideration, particularly in instances when such measures may need to remain in place for extended periods until spare parts can be ordered, received, and installed and performance testing be satisfactorily completed. Fig. 11.3, security system failure modes and compensatory measures illustrates the three potential system failure modes important to security operations: catastrophic, major, and minor. The matrix is not all

---

[2] Placing the system in the ACCESS modes does not constitute an inoperative state unless accompanied by or followed by any of the stated conditions.

Potential System Failure Modes	Definition	Suggested Minimum Security Compensatory Measures
Catastrophic failures	Exists when the entire system or any portion of its subsystems becomes inoperative, including the: ▪ Annunciation and display subsystem ▪ Intrusion detection subsystem ▪ Access control subsystem ▪ CCTV system ▪ Communication subsystem ▪ Power subsystem ▪ Lighting subsystem	Implement compensatory measures immediately (no later than 15 min after the detected failure). ▪ Increase staffing of the security operations center. ▪ Activate the security crisis management center. ▪ Implement a unit recall. ▪ Mobilize maintenance crews. ▪ Notify executive management. ▪ Increase supervision, posts, and patrols to cover for lost capability. ▪ Provide portable security systems and lighting, where feasible. ▪ Increase up-channel reporting requirements, as necessary. ▪ Plan for and schedule extended work shifts, as necessary.
Major failures	A major failure exists when the system loses: ▪ Its ability to detect an intruder attempting to penetrate at least one line of detection ▪ CCTV cameras within an entire detection zone ▪ One or more sensor zones, two or more gate operations, two or more access control zones ▪ Tamper and line supervision protection ▪ Area or perimeter lighting ▪ Redundant or backup capability	Implement compensatory measures within 30 min. ▪ Increase staffing of the security operations center. ▪ Activate the security crisis management center. ▪ Implement post priority options. ▪ Initiate a unit recall. ▪ Mobile maintenance crews. ▪ Notify executive management. ▪ Increase supervision, posts, and patrols to cover for lost capability. ▪ Provide portable security systems and lighting, where feasible. ▪ Maintain up-channel reporting requirements, as necessary. ▪ Plan for and schedule extended work shifts, as necessary.
Minor failures	A minor failure exists when the system loses: ▪ Its ability to detect an intruder crossing one line of detection, where two lines are used ▪ One gateoperator or vehicle barrier ▪ One or two card readers ▪ One camera within the same zone	Implement compensatory measures within 1 h. ▪ Increase staffing of the security operations center. ▪ Increase supervision, posts, and patrols to cover for lost capability. ▪ Implement post priority options, if necessary. ▪ Notify executive management if conditions worsen. ▪ Provide portable security systems and lighting, where feasible. ▪ Maintain up-channel reporting requirements, as necessary.

Figure 11.3 Security system failure modes and compensatory measures.

inclusive but only represents a sampling of the most common system failures and outlines a suggested decision-making process to implement security measures.

Conclusion

When stand-along security equipment or disparate systems prevail, they provide little or no security protection and often provide a false sense of security to executive management, governing authorities, and the workforce.

This perception is quickly dispelled when security equipment is configured into meaningful interoperable segments that can create the potential for total system integration. However, quality hardware and software integration greatly depends on the reliability, dependability, and quality expertise of the modified and dedicated people who are responsible for operating and maintaining the system. Only then can there be true system integration.

Appendix A: Selected Security Technology Deficiencies and Weaknesses

Background Information

This information reviews relevant case histories. This information is shared to provide a better understanding of the scope of problems security directors face on a daily basis and for further research for the interested reader. The information represents eye-witness accounts and personal observations noted and reported as I performed security assessments, audits, and inspections, and as I participated in one-on-one interview sessions with numerous chief executive officers, chief operating officers, and other corporate senior officials; directors of security and their respective staff members; and other company employees.

Overview of Selected Case Histories

- At almost every site I visited within the private sector (except for regulated locations) I found the total absence of a formal test, inspection, and maintenance program for installed security systems. Management at these locations could not produce convincing evidence these activities were being accomplished, or whether these systems were performing to acceptable industry levels. (*Poor planning and supervision, lack of a system maintenance program*)
- When testing security systems, many had a probability of detection (Pd) ratio below 0.80[3] and no better than just an opportunity to detect or witness an event by chance. Security organizations that are saddled with such weak system performance could not demonstrate their ability and capability to detect intrusions and assess penetrations, thereby being unable to demonstrate an adequate response to security events. (*Poor or no maintenance program, lack of understanding of system performance characteristics*)
- In most locations (including some regulated sites) exterior CCTV cameras were not deployed to provide maximum utilization or adequate coverage. Other cameras were not synchronized for call-up when sensors or access control devices were activated, lacking the capability for immediate real-time assessment and response to security alarms. Several cameras were not always monitored, and I found monitors and cameras that were turned off. Site officials could not provide an adequate explanation of the intent and purpose of specific cameras or why some monitors and cameras had been turned off. Neither could system operators or security managers provide any reasonable explanation for the noted conditions. (*Poor planning and understanding of system applications*)
- In most instances, I found that the design development and installation of security systems had started without defining formal system parameters, requirements, performance standards, or operations, maintenance, logistical, and training considerations. (*Poor leadership planning, coordination, and decision making*)

---

[3] While no universal mandate for commercial security systems exists, most corporations pursue a probability of detection (Pd) of 0.90 or greater (Sullivant, 2007, pp. 194). A good design, quality selection of components and subsystems, and quality installation by an experienced system integrator can easily achieve this detection ratio.

- Many security systems lacked their own independent and dedicated uninterruptable power supply. Existing backup power supplies were insufficient to support most system operations. (*Poor security design planning*)
- At one location, batteries for most card readers were outside specification standards. These batteries were corroded and leaking acid. The shelf life of these batteries had expired 5 years earlier, and site officials could not determine when the batteries were procured. A review of the system database revealed that backup power systems had never been tested. The first recorded transition of the system was February 9, 1998, suggesting that the system (including the batteries) were procured and installed around that time. During our visit in 2008, no other record of inspection or testing of batteries could be found, and site maintenance officials could not recall every serving the batteries during the 10-year period in question. (*Poor system integration planning, installation management, and maintenance program*)
- For many corporations, outsourcing of the design and installation of security systems is difficult to pursue, particularly when a unionized labor force of engineers, electricians, maintenance workers, and other disciplines were available and potential layoffs were looming. Even when not influenced by the union, many corporations adopted a "go-it-alone" mentality despite the lack of expertise or experience in strategic security planning, security engineering, or the installation of complex security systems. Under this concept of operation, several procurements reduced system parameters under the guide of cost savings; installation attempts had resulted in poor workmanship and deployment gaps; misguided attempts at system integration; and erroneous programming of software parameters that in effect, degraded system performance from the start. This vulnerability was predicable and both executive and security management should of known it. (*Failure to understand and recognize limitations of in-house capability and expertise in security design planning, procurement, and installation; poor engineering leadership decision-making capability*)
- Security design recommendations implemented in a piecemeal or indiscriminate fashion, rather than in a systematic and logical manner, led to the continuing deterioration of program effectiveness, producing significant cost overruns from original project estimates and eventually becoming counterproductive to achieving security strategies, goals, and objectives. (*Inexperience, limited knowledge of technology performance and application*)
- Legacy systems abide across the security industry in both the public and private sectors. Most of these systems cannot be upgraded in a cost-effective manner and require complete replacement with state-of-the-art systems to support today's security needs. Moreover, most systems were not really "systems" at all. Rather, they consisted of individual stand-alone components operating independently of each other. For instance, access control devices, sensors, and CCTV cameras were not configured into an integrated system, nor did they provide for the operational capability for real-time detection of, assessment of, and response to security alarms. At many locations components were not fully programmed, making detection and assessment extremely difficult and in some instances even impossible to perform. Inadequate communications often contributed to the ineffectiveness of the security response force. (*No system integration, poor planning, and poor budget forecasting*)

Generally, not having a clear and distinct design document or functional system specification that spelled out the mission of the system, its performance characteristics and expectations, its technical interfaces, and its measurement and evaluation tools led to poor security design planning, system configuration, and technology deployment as well as weak emergency planning at all the sites visited. This fallacy was predicable, and both executive and security management at each independent location should have known it.

Appendix B: Sample Test Logs

General Information

The test logs listed below are offered for informational purposes only in helping you document the performance testing of your security system (Figs. 11.4–11.13).

In each test log, "P" indicates pass and "F" indicates failure. The measurement emphasizes a "GO" "NO-GO" result, meaning that equipment either works or it doesn't. This type of testing does not recognize a range of failure. While only a single line item for each test sample is shown, it is recommended you perform at least 10 test trials for each alarm point or device tested.

Enter "N/A" in any area that does not apply to a particular test log entry.

Location:			Date:	Start Time:		Finish Time:		Weather Conditions:			
Alarm Point:	Climb	Tap	Lift	Tamper	Line Supervision	Power Loss		Alarm Display & Annunciation		
								Graphics & Audio	CCTV	Printer
1.	P F	P F	P F	P F	P F	P F		P F	P F	P F

NOTE: Perform the following tests for each fence mounted sensor zone in the system.

Climb Calculations	Tests	Pd Rate	Tap Calculation	Tests	Pd Rate
Number of successful tests		=	Number of successful tests		=
Number of attempted tests	10		Number of attempted tests	10	

Tamper Calculations	Tests	Pd Rate	Lift Calculations	Tests	Pd Rate
Number of successful tests		=	Number of successful tests		=
Number of attempted tests	10		Number of attempted tests	10	

Line Supervision Calculations	Tests	Pc Rate	Power Loss Calculations	Tests	Pc Rate
Number of successful tests		=	Number of successful tests		=
Number of attempted tests	10		Number of attempted tests	10	

Graphic Display Calculations	Tests	Pc Rate	Audio Activation Calculations	Tests	Pc Rate
Number of successful tests		=	Number of successful tests		=
Number of attempted tests	10		Number of attempted tests	90	

CCTV Activation Calculations	Tests	Pc Rate	Printer Calculations	Tests	Pc Rate
Number of successful tests		=	Number of successful tests		=
Number of attempted tests	10		Number of attempted tests	90	

NOTE: Pd = probability of detection

Pc = probability of communication

Test Certification
Data Collector:
Test Director:
Observer:

Figure 11.4 Fence-mounted sensor test log.

Location:		Date:		Start Time:		Finish Time:		Weather Conditions:			
Alarm Point:	Walk	Run	Crawl	Jump	Tamper	Line Supervision	Power Loss	Alarm Display & Annunciation			
								Graphics & Audio	CCTV	Printer	
1.	P F	P F	P F	P F	P F	P F	P F	P F	P F	P F	

NOTE: Perform the following tests for each exterior microwave sensor zone in the system.

Walk Calculations	Tests	Pd Rate	Run Calculation	Tests	Pd Rate
Number of successful tests		=	Number of successful tests		=
Number of attempted tests	10		Number of attempted tests	10	

Crawl Calculation	Tests	Pd Rate	Jump Calculation	Tests	Pd Rate
Number of successful tests		=	Number of successful tests		=
Number of attempted tests	10		Number of attempted tests	10	

Tamper Calculations	Tests	Pd Rate	Line Supervision	Tests	Pd Rate
Number of successful tests		=	Number of successful tests		=
Number of attempted tests	10		Number of attempted tests	10	

Power Loss	Tests	Pc Rate	Graphic Display Calculations	Tests	Pc Rate
Number of successful tests		=	Number of successful tests		=
Number of attempted tests	10		Number of attempted tests	10	

CCTV Activation Calculations	Tests	Pc Rate	Printer Calculations	Tests	Pc Rate
Number of successful tests		=	Number of successful tests		=
Number of attempted tests	10		Number of attempted tests	90	

NOTE: Pd = Probability of detection
          Pc = Probability of communication

Test Certification	
Data Collector:	
Test Director:	
Observer: (Print Name, Signature & Date):	

NOTE: (1) Perform this test three times: Morning, Afternoon and Evening
           (2) In addition to the test log above, use the microwave plot on the next page to pinpoint the exact location of any test failures.

Note: Perform the following sensor plot for each exterior microwave sensor zone established around a restricted area.

Exterior Microwave Sensor Plot

Outer Fence

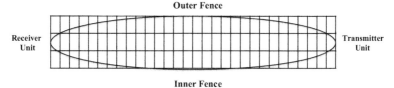

Inner Fence

Use the above diagram to plot the exact location of any microwave test failures. The diagram is not to scale but is representative of a typical perimeter microwave sensor zone with a receiver and transmitter.

Identify each test failure by numerical designation, starting with number 1. List the first failure as 1, the second failure as 2, and so on. Estimate the distance of the failure from either the outer fence or the inner fence, which ever distance is the shortest to the center of the isolation zone, as applicable to the width and length of the zone.

Record the distance in measurements of feet to correspond to the numerical number assigned (for example: 1 – 10 feet from outer fence; 15 feet from start/end of zone). Each grid square on the diagram represents 10-square feet. For sample purposes, the length of the zone depicted is 300 feet in length and 30 feet in width.

You may have to customize this plot diagram to match the exact measurements of each of your zones. Use one plot per zone tested.

Figure 11.5 Exterior microwave sensor test log with zone plot.

Location:		Date:		Start Time:		Finish Time:		Weather Conditions:				
Alarm Point:		**Intrusion**	**Tamper**	**Line Supervision**		**Power Loss**		**Alarm Display & Annunciation**				
								Graphics & Audio		**CCTV**		**Printer**
1.		P | F	P | F	P | F		P | F		P | F		P | F		P | F

NOTE: Perform the following tests for each door, window or portal that has a contact sensor installed.

Intrusion Calculations	**Tests**	**Pd Rate**	**Tamper Calculations**	**Tests**	**Pd Rate**
Number of successful tests		=	Number of successful tests		=
Number of attempted tests	10		Number of attempted tests	10	

Line Supervision Calculations	**Tests**	**Pd Rate**	**Power Calculations**	**Tests**	**Pd Rate**
Number of successful tests		=	Number of successful tests		=
Number of attempted tests	10		Number of attempted tests	10	

Graphic Display Calculations	**Tests**	**Pc Rate**	**CCTV Activation Calculations**	**Tests**	**Pc Rate**
Number of successful tests		=	Number of successful tests		=
Number of attempted tests	10		Number of attempted tests	10	

Printer Calculations	**Tests**	**Pc Rate**
Number of successful tests		=
Number of attempted tests	60	

NOTE: Pd = Probability of detection
       Pc = Probability of communication

Test Certification
Data Collector:
Test Direct:
Observer:

Figure 11.6 Door contact sensor test log.

Location:		Date:		Start Time:		Finish Time:		Weather Conditions:					
Card Reader #:	**Access Granted Validate Card – Keypad #**	**Access Denied Invalidate Card - Keypad**	**Exit Release**	**Tamper**	**Line Supervision**	**Power Loss**	**Alarm Display & Annunciation Test Trials**						
							Graphics & Audio		**CCTV**		**Printer**		
1.	P | F	P | F	P | F	P | F	P | F	P | F	P | F		P | F		P | F		

NOTE: Perform the following tests for each card reader/key pad within the system.

Measure of System Consistency Calculations for Card Reader/Key Pad	**Tests**	**Pd Rate**	**Measure of Separability Calculations for Card Reader/Key Pad**	**Tests**	**Pd Rate**
Number of authorized successes		=	Number of unauthorized successes		=
Number of authorized attempts	10		Number of unauthorized attempts	10	

Exit ReleaseConsistency Calculation	**Tests**	**Pd Rate**	**Tamper Calculations**	**Tests**	**Pd Rate**
Number of successful tests		=	Number of successful tests		=
Number of attempted tests	10		Number of attempted tests	10	

Line Supervision Calculations	**Tests**	**Pc Rate**	**Power Loss Calculations**	**Tests**	**Pc Rate**
Number of successful tests		=	Number of successful tests		=
Number of attempted tests	10		Number of attempted tests	10	

Graphic Display Calculations	**Tests**	**Pc Rate**	**CCTV Activation Calculations**	**Tests**	**Pc Rate**
Number of successful tests		=	Number of successful tests		=
Number of attempted tests	10		Number of attempted tests	10	

Printer Calculations	**Tests**	**Pc Rate**
Number of successful tests		=
Number of attempted tests	80	

NOTE: Pd = Probability of detection
       Pc = Probability of communication

Test Certification
Data Collector:
Test Director:
Observer:

Figure 11.7 Card reader/keypad test log.

Location:		Date:		Start Time:		Finish Time:		Weather Conditions:	
Equipment Number or Portal Location		**X-Ray Machine**			**Metal Detector**		**Hand-Held Detector**	**Mobile X-Ray Machine**	
		Picture Quality						**Picture Quality**	
1.		P	F	P	F	P	F	P	F

NOTE: Perform the following tests for each portal that contains contraband detection equipment within the system.

X-Ray Machine Calculations	**Tests**	**Pd Rate**	**X-Ray Machine Picture Quality Calculations**	**Tests**	**Pd Rate**
Number of successful tests		=	Number of successful tests		=
Number of attempted tests	10		Number of attempted tests	10	

Metal Detector Calculations	**Tests**	**Pd Rate**	**Hand-Held Detector Calculations**	**Tests**	**Pd Rate**
Number of successful tests		=	Number of successful tests		=
Number of attempted tests	10		Number of attempted tests	10	

Mobile X-Ray Machine Calculations	**Tests**	**Pd Rate**	**Mobile X-Ray Machine Picture Quality Calculations**	**Tests**	**Pd Rate**
Number of successful tests		=	Number of successful tests		=
Number of attempted tests	10		Number of attempted tests	10	

NOTE: Use suitable approved training devices to detect weapons and other contraband

Pd = Probability of detection

Test Certification
Data Collector:
Test Director:
Observer:

Figure 11.8 Contraband detection equipment test log.

Location:		Date:			Start Time:			Finish Time:			Weather Conditions:				
Alarm Point:	**Walk**	**Run**		**Crawl**	**Jump**		**Tamper**	**Line Supervision**	**Power Loss**	**Alarm Display & Annunciation**					
										Graphics & Audio	**CCTV**	**Printer**			
1.	P F	P F	P	F	P F	P F	P	F	P F	P F	P F	P F	P F			

NOTE: Perform the following tests for each interior motion sensor within the system.

Walk Calculations	**Tests**	**Pd Rate**	**Run Calculations**	**Tests**	**Pd Rate**
Number of successful tests		=	Number of successful tests		=
Number of attempted tests	10		Number of attempted tests	10	

Crawl Calculations	**Tests**	**Pd Rate**	**Jump Calculations**	**Tests**	**Pd Rate**
Number of successful tests		=	Number of successful tests		=
Number of attempted tests	10		Number of attempted tests	10	

Tamper Calculations	**Tests**	**Pc Rate**	**Line Supervision Calculations**	**Tests**	**Pc Rate**
Number of successful tests		=	Number of successful tests		=
Number of attempted tests	10		Number of attempted tests	10	

Power Low Calculations	**Tests**	**Pc Rate**	**Graphics & Audio Calculations**	**Tests**	**Pc Rate**
Number of successful tests		=	Number of successful tests		=
Number of attempted tests	10		Number of attempted tests	10	

CCTV Activation Calculations	**Tests**	**Pc Rate**	**Printer Calculations**	**Tests**	**Pc Rate**
Number of successful tests		=	Number of successful tests		=
Number of attempted tests	10		Number of attempted tests	90	

NOTE: Pd = Probability of detection

Pc = Probability of communication

Test Certification
Data Collector:
Test Director:
Observer:

Figure 11.9 Interior motion sensor test log.

Location:	Date:	Start Time:	Finish Time:		Weather Conditions:				
Equipment Enclosure #:	Intrusion	Tamper Distance	Line Supervision	Power Loss	Alarm Display & Annunciation Test Trials				
					Graphics & Audio		CCTV		Printer
1.	P | F	P | F	P | F	P | F	P | F		P | F		P | F

NOTE: Perform the following tests for each equipment enclosure, control box or panel within the system.

Intrusion Calculations	Tests	Pd Rate	Tamper Calculations	Tests	Pd Rate
Number of successful tests		=	Number of successful tests		=
Number of attempted tests	10		Number of attempted tests	10	

Line Supervision Calculations	Tests	Pd Rate	Power Calculations	Tests	Pd Rate
Number of successful tests		=	Number of successful tests		=
Number of attempted tests	10		Number of attempted tests	10	

Graphic Display Calculations	Tests	Pc Rate	Audio Activation Calculations	Tests	Pc Rate
Number of successful tests		=	Number of successful tests		=
Number of attempted tests	10		Number of attempted tests	10	

CCTV Activation Calculations	Tests	Pc Rate	Printer Calculations	Tests	Pc Rate
Number of successful tests		=	Number of successful tests		=
Number of attempted tests	10		Number of attempted tests	70	

NOTE: Pd = Probability of detection
Pc = Probability of communication

Test Certification
Data Collector:
Test Director:
Observer:

Figure 11.10 Equipment enclosure test log.

Location:	Date:		Start Time:		Finish Time:		Weather Conditions:		
PTZ Camera	Up	Down	Left	Right	Zoom In	Zoom Out	Focus	Picture Quality	IR Lite
1.	P | F	P | F	P | F	P | F	P | F	P | F	P | F	P | F	P | F

NOTE: Perform the following tests for each Pan-Tilt CCTV camera in the system. You can develop a separate test log for testing each fixed CCTV camera in the system.

Up Calculations	Tests	Pd Rate	Down Calculations	Tests	Pd Rate
Number of successful tests		=	Number of successful tests		=
Number of attempted tests	10		Number of attempted tests	10	

Left Calculations	Tests	Pd Rate	Right Calculations	Tests	Pd Rate
Number of successful tests		=	Number of successful tests		=
Number of attempted tests	10		Number of attempted tests	10	

Zoom In Calculations	Tests	Pc Rate	Zoom Out Calculations	Tests	Pc Rate
Number of successful tests		=	Number of successful tests		=
Number of attempted tests	10		Number of attempted tests	10	

Focus Quality Calculations	Tests	Pc Rate	Picture Quality Calculations	Tests	Pc Rate
Number of successful tests		=	Number of successful tests		=
Number of attempted tests			Number of attempted tests		

IR Lite Calculations	Tests	Pc Rate
Number of successful tests		=
Number of attempted tests	10	

NOTE: Pd = Probability of detection
Pc = Probability of communication

Test Certification
Data Collector:
Test Director:
Observer:

Figure 11.11 Closed-circuit TV controls test log.

Location		Date:	Start Time:	Finish Time:	Weather Conditions:		
UPS Alarm Point:	Remove AC Power	Record Time & Voltage-level	90-minutes into the Test, Measure Voltage-level	At end of 4-hours, Measure Voltage-level	Restore AC Power – Measure Voltage level after 12-hours	Alarm Display & Annunciation	
						Graphics & Audio	Printer

NOTE: Perform the following tests for each UPS within the system.

UPS Calculation at Start of Test	
Remove AC Power and record time.	Time
Record voltage-level. The first voltage reading is not a PASS/FAIL reading. The UPS must support system operations without any degradation to all system functions.	Voltage

UPS Calculation 90-minutes into the Test	
Record time	Time
Record voltage-level 90-minutes after removal of AC Power. This reading should not fall below 87.5 of normal, or no lower than 10.5Vdc. The UPS must support system operations without any degradation to the system functions.	Voltage

UPS Calculation 4-Hours into the Test	
Record time	Time
Record voltage-level 4-hours into the test. This reading is not a PASS/FAIL reading but serves to establish a known mean during specified times (i.e. normal/adverse operational conditions). The UPS must support system operations without any degradation to the system functions	Voltage

UPS Calculation 12-Hours into the Test	
Restore ACP Power, record time and let it charge for 12-hours	Time
Record voltage 12-hours after AC Power has been restored. The minimum acceptable voltage reading at this time should be 11.5 Vdc.	Voltage

Alarm Display & Annunciation	Tests	Pc Rate
Number of successful audio activation tests		
Number of attempted audio activation tests	4	=

Printer Calculations	Tests	Pc Rate
Number of successful audio activation tests		
Number of attempted audio activation tests	4	=

NOTE: Pc = Probability of communication

Test Certification
Data Collector:
Test Director:
Observer:

Figure 11.12 Uninterruptible power supply (ups) test log.

The test director (usually a security supervisor) oversees and manages test team members and authorizes the retest of any alarm point that registers below the accept/reject criterion of 0.90% probability of detection or 0.90% probability of performance. A rating of <0.90% in any test trial category constitutes a failure of the item tested, which must be scheduled for retesting at the earliest possible opportunity.

Location:		Date:	Start Time:	Finish Time:	Weather Conditions:		
Battery Alarm Points	Remove AC Power	Record Time & Voltage-level	90-minutes into the Test, Measure Voltage-level	At end of 4-hours, Measure Voltage-level	Restore AC Power – Measure Voltage level after 12-hours	Alarm Display & Annunciation	
						Graphics & Audio	Printer

NOTE: Perform the following tests as indicated per backup battery within the system.

Battery Calculation at Start of Test	
Remove AC Power and record time.	Time
Record voltage-level. The first voltage reading is not a PASS/FAIL reading. The battery must support device operations without any degradation to all functions.	Voltage

Battery Calculation 90-minutes into the Test	
Record time	Time
Record voltage-level 90-minutes after removal of AC Power. This reading should not fall below 87.5 of normal, or no lower than 10.5Vdc. The battery must support device operations without any degradation to all functions.	Voltage

Battery Calculation 4-Hours into the Test	
Record time	Time
Record voltage-level 4-hours into the test. This reading is not a PASS/FAIL reading but serves to establish a known mean during specified times (i.e. normal/adverse operational conditions). The battery must support device operations without any degradation to all functions	Voltage

Battery Calculation 12-Hours into the Test	
Restore ACP Power, record time and let it charge for 12-hours	Time
Record voltage 12-hours after AC Power has been restored. The minimum acceptable voltage reading at this time should be 11.5 Vdc.	Voltage

Visual Display & Annunciation	Tests	Pc Rate
Number of successful audio activation tests		=
Number of attempted audio activation tests	4	

Printer Calculations	Tests	Pc Rate
Number of successful audio activation tests		=
Number of attempted audio activation tests	4	

NOTE: Pc = Probability of communication

Test Certification
Data Collector:
Test Director:
Observer:

Figure 11.13 Backup battery test log.

Safety Information

Only *qualified security or maintenance personnel* should conduct test trials on intrusion detection sensors, contraband detection equipment, access control devices, and console and CCTV controls. Only qualified maintenance personnel should conduct test trials on equipment enclosure tampers, UPS and backup batteries, line supervision, power loss, and voltage reading test trials.

Only *qualified system operators* monitor the announcement and display of alarms, collect data, and document test trial results on test logs. One observer should witnesses the conduct of each test trial performed in the field to verify that testing was conducted in accordance with the approved test procedure. A second observer should witnesses the alarm data reporting process, visual display of test trials, the functioning of CCTV controls, as well as the reactions of the system operator when responding to test trial events.

Preparing for Emergencies

12

We always jump at the idea of protecting ourselves from industrial accidents and weather-related calamities. But many leaders take a step back when it comes to terrorism, criminal activity and other incidents initiated by those who wish to do us harm, particularly psychopaths, the mentality ill, hate groups, or disgruntled persons, content to have local law enforcement address these issues. At the highest level of strategic planning we ignore our duty to care principal—and we are responsible and accountable for the consequences.

John Sullivant

Top Takeaways

- Leadership and communications
- Security emergency operations
- Creating a security emergency response plan
- Creating event-driven security response and recovery procedures

Overview

In this chapter I talk about the ambitious goal of bridging the gap between how prepared we are and how prepared we need to be, as well as how to prioritize efforts to narrow this gap? The answer to these and more questions lies somewhere between a completed security assessment that includes the preparation of a vulnerability analysis and the development of a realistic threat estimate profile. Throughout the pages of this book I have persistently mentioned that early detection and identification of security problems at the source is not the strong suit of many executives or security professionals, or, at the very least, it does not seem to be a priority that is high on their agenda.

What I reveal here and elsewhere relative to security emergency planning and response and recovery capabilities is that too many executives and security professionals seem to be "asleep at the switch." Too many security professionals demonstrate their inexperience when it comes to developing comprehensive and useful security response plans and response and recovery protocols. I have witnessed too many instances of vague and ambiguous statements of intent rather than commitment, and when tested (as I have done on numerous occasions) the results support my conviction that many security organizations simply fail when it comes to responding to and recovering from a crisis. I have found that little or no thought is given to strategic planning vision, as evidenced by poor performance in carrying out emergency security operations. When executives disengage from the security planning process, they must equally share in the responsibility and accountability for dismal security performance.

Here I continue the chronicle of business risk exposure to individuals who wish to do us harm or to accidental or natural destructive events, and their potential affects on the welfare of a corporation, its resources, and its assets.

Security Emergency Planning Is Critical to Organizational Survival

Security emergency planning is subject to a wide range of social, economic, and technical factors. In his book "Emergency Response Planning for Corporate and Municipal Managers", Paul A. Erickson, PhD (2006, pp. 13), advocates that we should collaboratively and holistically embrace the process of security emergency planning, coordination, development, and implementation. This calls for chief executive officers to step up and take responsibility for the safety and security of the workforce and the corporation against the potential risks that their operations face. Meeting this executive responsibility requires the execution and testing of security response plans that detail:

- strategic planning and the prioritization of assets, resources, funding, and training to build required competencies
- specific steps to be taken to prevent or respond to an emergency
- necessary corporate coordination and liaison with competent local, state, or even national authorities

Planning for Prevention, Protection, Response, and Recovery

While many executives and corporations have a good record of accomplishment in planning for and responding to natural disasters and industrial accidents, they are less accomplished in preparing for other crisis. With so much attention on crisis planning, response, and recovery, one might suspect that corporate America is as prepared as it can be, but unfortunately this is not the case.

Security Survey Looks at Capability Through Plan Development and Training

Steelhenge Consulting of London, England conducted an international survey of companies in 2014 in the U.S., Canada, Central and South America, Africa, Middle East, Australia, New Zealand, Asia, Europe, and the U.K. All economic sectors were represented as were all parts of the world, with the exception of Russia. Significant highlights of the survey[1] reveal that:

- 76% of companies surveyed lack a basis crisis management plan. 45% felt having one was not important or necessary.
- 56% of companies surveyed have not conducted crisis drills, tests, or exercises.
- 50% of the companies surveyed have ineffective or incomplete security emergency response plans or no plans at all that address manmade crisis and incidents. 28% of these companies waited for a brutal experience of a crisis to occur before creating a plan.
- 50% of the companies surveyed who out source security responsibilities have little confidence in the provider's ability to provide adequate protection or delivered promised services.
- 50% of the crisis management plans are based on operational need and senior management direction. Very few are prepared to meet regulatory compliance.
- 81% of the companies that had plans, did not define roles and responsibilities; 24% lacked effective communications support; 50% reviewed or audited their plans after an exercise,crisis, or "near-miss", but 40% had no program to review or conduct training, or exercises; and 13% had done no preparation at all.

Highlights of Industry Standing From a Global Perspective

Survey summary results include:

- 47% of the companies were very well prepared and had a structured program for crisis management and emergency response plan review, staff training and exercises, with a good staff awareness.
- 40% of the companies were prepared and had a crisis management or emergency response plan but no regular program of reviews, training, exercises, and little staff awareness.
- 8% of the companies were not well prepared. They were aware of the potential impacts of a crisis but no formal plan or program in place for training and exercising, and very little staff awareness.
- 4% of the companies were ill prepared. They had no resources committed to crisis management or emergency planning and minimal or no staff awareness.

Prevention and protection strategies are pre-event work in progress planning activities that take place in a highly dynamic and evolving (threat and work) environment and are performed before an event occurs. Prevention and protection actions include strategic planning activities that help to reduce risks:

- Assessment and vulnerability analysis
- Likelihood of event occurrence
- Mitigation processes and procedures
- Infrastructure and facility protective measures
- Prioritizing actions, resources, and funding
- Training

[1] Preparing for Crisis - Crisis Management Survey 2014 Report (distributed Internationally in February and March 2014). Steehenge Consulting, 16 St Martin's Le Grand, London ECIA 4EN.

Deterrence against threats and hazards is also work in progress and begins with properly planning and implementing effective security measures to minimize risk exposure. The process continues with appropriate training of people, the diligent exercise of plans, and the capability and leadership to resolve actual crisis. Without determination and proper planning, preparation, and training, employees will lack the guidance and confidence necessary to perform their duties during any emergency, whether a terrorist attack, criminal activity, a natural disaster, a weather-related calamity, or other catastrophic event.

Response and recovery strategies are work in progress actions implemented after an event. Response activities are done immediately following an event to save lives and minimize damage or loss of assets. Recovery involves those actions that are necessary, once response functions are completed, to begin restoration and rebuilding business and security operations, and to get people and the corporation back to their pre-incident situation as soon as possible.

Alert Notification Systems Serve as Triggering Mechanisms to Carry Out Security Planning Considerations

Another disturbing issue is that not all U.S. companies subscribe to an alert notification system. Security planners associated with companies that do embrace an alert notification system are more likely to have sufficient advanced warning to review security strategies and agree on timely, reasonable, and prudent response actions. Companies that fail to subscribe to an alert notification system are more likely to make uninformed decisions, wrong decisions, or decisions that lead to chaotic results.

Fig 12.1, illustrates a few examples of potential crises that could qualify as triggers to increase a change in the corporate security posture. I offer these tips because they may be helpful in your security planning endeavors.

A corporate alert notification system, such as the one illustrated, offers a means to analyze and prioritize information regarding the potential risk exposure to the corporation based on verifiable and reliable intelligence. By using such a system, in conjunction with implementing corporate security response plans, decision makers have the options available to increase the protection of known targeted assets in order to make it more difficult for an adversary to harm or damage those assets. Therefore, it is important for an enterprise to clearly define what it can and must do in the event of an incident or event and to coordinate capabilities and activities with partner organizations in order to carry out necessary response actions. The system also uses any error in timing or coordination that could occur during an adversary's attempt to carry out an attack. A significant security incident at one location or apparently unrelated incidents at several locations could be rapidly communicated up or down channels, across the industry, or internally within the corporation to determine an appropriate security response or series of integrated responses.

An alert notification system can also help security decision makers deliberately plan for the increased security of other critical assets because of an imminent threat or actual attack against a particular asset. Such actions could be based on predetermined

Threat Alert Level	Risk of Attack	Level	Potential Triggering Incidents
Low	Low	1	• Normal security posture and conduct of business operations
Guarded	General	2	• Heightened-awareness advisory notices issued by local, state, or federal officials
Elevated	Significant	3	• Uncorroborated threats identified by federal, state, or local authorities • Threat hoaxes occurring in the city that may affect corporate operations and business • Threat alert advisory notices received by federal, state, or local authorities • Threat information received by corporate resources
High	High	4	• Confirmed, significant event against local community or business • Confirmed, credible threat against corporate assets or other business enterprises • Confirmed, credible threat or political destabilizing action against the city • Confirmed, credible threat against the industry region • Confirmed, credible threat against a commercial enterprise within the United States • Confirmed, credible threat against the U.S. government
Severe	Severe	5	• Actual terrorist attack against the corporation or another nearby enterprise(s) • Actual terrorist attack in the city • Actual terrorist attack within the industry region • Actual terrorist attack against a commercial enterprise(s) within the United States • Actual terrorist attack against the U.S. government

Figure 12.1 Corporate alert notification system and potential triggering incidents that may affect a corporate threat level.

event-driven response procedures designed to minimize disruptive consequences that may themselves interact in ways that could create additional vulnerabilities. For instance, efforts to develop and implement compensatory measures to include equipment, additional security personnel, and special actions necessary to ensure that the effectiveness of electronic security systems are not affected by power failure or infrastructure damage or destruction. Virtually all threat alert notifications have the potential to cause the security organization either to increase its security posture in anticipation of an event occurring or to provide immediate response to cope with a specific event for an indefinite period of time.

C-suite executives, directors and managers of business operating units, and the director of security can then agree on the prioritization of response actions such as those highlighted in Fig. 12.2. This figure takes the alert notification triggering metric to the next logical planning and decision-making level: What do we do? When do we do it? Who does what? Fig. 12.2 depicts a proposed top-level sequence of activity by level of threat condition and by specific event-driven tasks by those responsible for carrying out assigned actions. It represents a top-level guideline of roles, responsibilities, authority, and accountability to protect the corporation, its resources and assets, and its critical business interests. Together, Figs. 12.1 and 12.2 are a formidable

Event-Driven Tasks	Threat Level Condition					Agency of Primary Responsibility
	1	2	3	4	5	
Detect	Stay attuned to employee attitudes, modes, social habits Execute responsible actions					Security organization
	Employ day-to-day security measures	Increase vigilance	Exercise partial recall Increase status reporting	Exercise full recall Extend monitoring capability Augment operational centers	Exercise mutual response agreements Increase security posture Expand surveillance capability Expand response capability	
	Brief executive management					
Prepare	Advance management's involvement and prepare for general readiness & execute responsible actions					
	Review operating procedures	Review emergency response plans and procedures Raise awareness		Extend work week	Alert crisis management team	All management levels
				Exercise selected response options		
	Activate security crisis management center Increase intelligence gathering					Security organization & other agencies
				Alert support agencies		All management levels
				Increase awareness		
	Brief executive management					
Prevent	Inspect & test for readiness – carry out necessary actions					End users
	Maintain vigilance	Alert population			Closed to public	All agencies
	Control access	Inspect protective equipment and gear				All agencies
	Patrol areas	Exercise selected emergency response options				All management levels
	Assess & respond	Brief executive management				All management levels
Protect	Full range of response emergency actions – establish response & recovery capability					
	Maintain vigilance	Increase security at designated faculties				Security organization
		Screen all vehicles, persons, materials				Security organization
		Increase workforce supervision				All management levels
		Plan for the evacuation of all non-essential employees				All management levels
		Increase frequency and types of water tests and airborne contamination tests				Designated responders

Figure 12.2 Emergency planning considerations in preparing respective event-driven response and recovery procedures.

management toolbox for planning and executing specific event-driven response and recovery operations discussed next.

Planning for Security Event-Driven Response and Recovery Operations

The enormity and complexity of the security mission and the uncertain nature of events make the effective implementation of security response and recovery efforts a great challenge. The concept of security response and recovery stems from an irreversible commitment to possess the ability and capability to protect corporate resources and assets under uncertain conditions, with exceptional performance outcomes. The concept implicitly advances the notion that a security organization must maintain the flexibility to transition from normal security operations to uncertain emergency security operations without jeopardizing critical business operations, while concurrently responding to varying and specific undesirable events. Fig 12.3 graphically displays this revolving process. It also merges the projected corporate alert notification system and its integral event-driven response and recovery options into actionable decision-making activities.

Normal Security Post Instructions and Procedures

Security post instructions and procedures provide day-to-day guidance for carrying out security activities. Deviations from these instructions generally require the approval of security supervision or management.

Event-Driven Security Response Procedures

Event-driven security response procedures contain techniques, tactics, methods, and practices to use when confronting threatening situations. These are general guidelines that are subject to modification and adjustment because of uncertainty, an adversary's actions, and other conditions and circumstances. These actions are internal to the security organization. All security response and recovery procedures contain sensitive

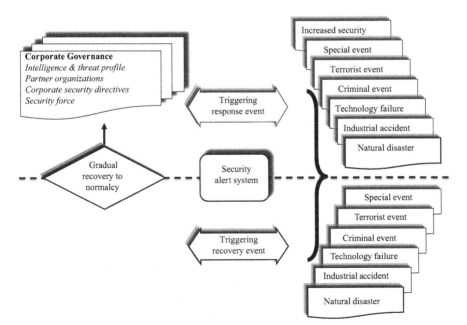

Figure 12.3 Event-driven security emergency response and recovery matrix.

security information, which must be published and maintained separate from other corporate emergency plans and guidance.

Event-driven response procedures outline actions that are required to cope with possible threat scenarios and prescribe uniform measures to be taken to address the range and level of threat conditions. Here are some additional helpful tips to use when developing security response procedures:

- Prepare a response procedure for each event that is likely to occur, as stipulated in the company-approved corporate threat estimate profile. I discussed this strategy in Chapter Developing a Realistic and Useful Threat Estimate Profile.
- Make sure each response procedure is a self-contained stand-alone event-driven guidance.

Some examples of event-driven security response procedures that may be useful to your organization include, but are not necessarily limited, to the following:

• Account for security personnel	• Hostage situation
• Airborne, Chemical, biological, radiological contamination or attack	• Hurricanes and Tornados
	• Implement mutual assistance packs
• Assault	• Implement positive identification measures
• Assist disturbed persons	
• Assist handicapped persons	• Increase general security posture
• Augment operational centers	• Increase patrols
• Lockdown buildings or entire campus	• Increase security at designed areas
• Bomb explosion—conventional	• Inspect personal protective equipment
• Bomb explosion—dirty bombs	• Intruder—breaking and entering
• Bomb explosion—nuclear	• Intruder—robbery in progress
• Bomb threat caller	• Intruder—trespassing
• Bomb threat search and evacuation	• Intruder—vandalism
• Child care center protection	• Kidnapping and extortion
• Communications failure	• Lightening storm
• Civil disturbance and demonstration	• Malicious destruction of property
• Clear gathering areas	• Medical help for injury and illness
• Duress alarm activation	• Officer down alert
• Earthquake—building damage	• Power failure
• Earthquake—area damage	• Protect deployed crews from sniper fire
• Emergency security staff relief	• Recall off-duty security personnel
• Emergency safe haven	• Sabotage of critical assets
• Equipment shutdown	• Search persons, vehicles, materials
• Evacuate area/building	• Search and clear areas
• Executive protection	• Shooter incident
• Explosion or fire	• Substance abuse and alcohol use
• Extended monitoring and surveillance	• Tampering with systems
• Find missing persons	• Test security systems
• Form additional response teams	• Termination of employee for cause
• Floods & heavy rains	• Threatening communications
• Frontal attack on area or facility	• Use of supporting forces
• Hazardous material incidents	• Workplace violence
• Help evacuate injured persons	

Event-Driven Security Recovery Procedures

It has been my experience that security recovery from any event is the most over-looked factor in security planning. Eyewitness accounts and studies confirm that few executives and security planners pay attention to security recovery during the planning stage. Those I have personally interviewed and surveyed say there are too many unknown variables to effectively plan recovery. I totally reject this notion and I am disappointed at the lack of strategic vision exhibited by so many of my colleagues.

Make this mistake no more! Recovery is a crucial planning consideration for any response before an incident occurs. Simply put, recovery is nothing more than an "exit strategy." How can you charge head-on into uncertainty, without investing in a parachute that works? It only makes sense that you understand what you are doing, what you can expect, and when and how you plan to withdraw or regroup from a given situation. Surely you must understand the lives of your people and others are at stake. When do you plan for scheduling, relief, rest, and looking after the troops? When do you plan for logistics? In the course of responding to any crisis, how do you maintain the security of corporate business operations? How, when, and by whom are these resources, equipment, supplies, and other needs put in place? Surely, planning for recovery is not something you would after you commit an entire organization to a particular crisis. If you are of this mind-set, my advise is to get out of the security business because not only you are a danger to yourself, but to your organization, the entire corporation, and the rest of the profession—who I am certain are not eager to make your acquaintance or share the same foxhole with you.

As a responsible security professional in a leadership role, security recovery must receive your explicit attention. Get rid of the notion that you can take care of logistics and other matters after you engage a crisis. When you realize you are in trouble, it is too late. Without an exist strategy you cannot operate well enough to protect the lives and safety of the workforce or property in any given crisis as executive management expects. When General Dwight D. Eisenhower was the Supreme Allied Commander of Europe during WWII, he told his multi-national staff that once the battle begins, all plans far apart, but planning for the battle is everything. I believe this wisdom is still valid today.

Security recovery operations involve two basic multitrack tasking assignments: First, it calls for the immediate intervention by the security organization to help the corporation minimize further losses brought about by an event so executive management can begin the process of corporate recovery, including activities and programs designed to reassemble the workforce and restore critical business functions to an acceptable condition as soon as possible. In addition to normal security operations that must be maintained, special security operations required to protect corporate assets during the recovery process are in themselves works in progress that cannot be ignored. Second, it requires the exercise of flexibility because the security organization is required to reorganize, adjust, shrink, or expand as necessary to meet concurrent threats without jeopardizing the security and safety of the corporation, as well as the remaining business activities unaffected by events, including security activity at remote domestic and international corporate sites. This is also a concurrent security work in progress.

At the corporate level, recovery activities include damage and impact assessments, prioritization of critical processes to be resumed and return to normal operations, and reconstitution of operations to a new condition and standard. Steps may include any or all of the following:

- plans and processes to bring the enterprise out of the crisis that resulted in an interruption of business operations
- those actions necessary to rebuild interim and long-term infrastructure, including security systems, supervisory control and data acquisition systems, data management systems, and management information systems
- activities, resources, and priorities to support the reconstitution of business operations and services to an acceptable level
- implement measures for social, political, environmental, and economic restoration
- incorporate mitigation measures and techniques, as feasible
- evaluate the crisis to identify lessons learned
- report after the incident
- develop initiatives to mitigate the effects of future incidents

At the security organization level, recovery involves short- and long-term activities: the short term activity is to provide the business side of the entity security protection to achieve the above goals, while protecting normal on-going business activity, the long term activity involves transiting the security organization from its current state of emergency operations back to its normal operating posture without jeopardizing the integrity of the corporate recovery effort while performing services to support both business recovery operations and transitional activities. Security recovery actions to support corporate recovery efforts may take months or even years to complete, and cannot even begin until the business side of the enterprise has healed from its wounds, and has recovered to normal operations.

By the very nature of its mission, security recovery operations involve assessing injury or loss of any members of the security staff and any damage or destruction sustained to security facilities, equipment, and communications resulting from a particular crisis. As a security planner you must consider the following in assessing your security organization's recovery capability:

- A security organization would probably experience casualties and the damage or destruction of security facilities, equipment, and communications during a direct attack by an adversary or a major disaster.
- A direct attack or disaster will certainly impair the reporting to duty of a significant portion of the security staff, or prevent those on duty from receiving relief or being able to go home to their families.
- Collateral damage can conceivably be brought about by a nearby attack involving conventional explosives against other high-risk corporate entities in the near vicinity that could impair a security organization's capability to function. The partial or total destruction of security and other facilities, the shutdown of operations, the disruption of vehicular traffic and mass transportation, the demand on lost utilities, the unavailability of emergency services, the closure of streets, and the establishment of security corridors around a large area could directly affect security and business operations for an indefinite period. Never lose sight of the emergency response and recovery lessons learned from the 9/11 attacks. Recovery of the World Trade Center and surrounding affected areas has taken more than 14 years. Some reconstruction efforts are still on-going at this writing.

Strategies for Integrating and Prioritizing Security Response and Recovery Operations

A common error committed by security professionals is the failure to embrace security emergency preparedness and planning as a holistic discipline (Erickson, 2006, pp. 29–61). For security to succeed, it must not loose site of its purpose, that is, to perverse life and limit the loss of life and personal injury; to protect resources, assets, facilities, and information; to limit damage and destruction of property in the support of business goals and objectives; and to continue supporting business units while concurrently responding to a crisis. All these factors must work together and must be interconnected to provide maximum benefit.

Fig 12.4 graphically illustrates how security response and recovery priorities must match the priorities of the corporate business services. The figure outlines a basic water and power utility and demonstrates the multitasking responsibilities it would undertake, including the direct and indirect support role the security organization would be expected to maintain and sustain, not only during normal security operations but also during a crisis. The only reason security exists is to support the enterprise's business goals, objectives, and productivity, even during times of crisis. Enterprise recovery is important to a security organization because it cannot even plan to transition from a recovery mode back to normal security operations until all business operations affected by the crisis have first returned to normal.

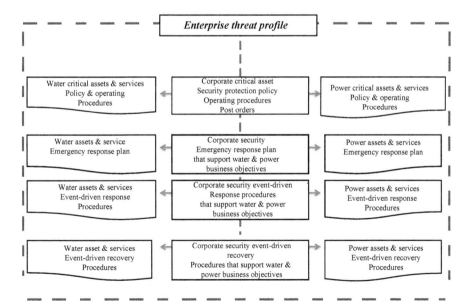

Figure 12.4 Corporate strategy for prioritizing security response and recovery during a crisis.

During uncertainties, it is imperative that security management maximizes the use of available security officers, irrespective of rank or seniority, to perform critical life-saving tasks. Under such circumstances and conditions, union agreements (where they exist with respect to seniority or bid assignment) should be suspended during the crisis until such time that sufficient security staff members are able to report to duty and the situation permits the orderly realignment of the security work force to a more stable schedule. The suspension of any union agreements should remain in effect only as long as necessary; in no event should it last beyond the completion of the security recovery transition period for the declared emergency. A good management/labor relationship effort is crucial to carrying out this emergency workforce policy.

Security Emergency Response Plan

The security response plan provides the framework and authority to plan, coordinate, develop, and carry out necessary security actions. Sharing security responsibilities and delegating authority to act are key components of the successful implementation of any security response (Erickson, 2006, pp. 65–91).

The Wavering Complexities of Security Emergency Planning

Effective security emergency planning emphasizes protecting corporate resources and assets from the full range of plausible threats, not just those that are most frequently reported or considered to be the most likely to occur. To achieve this it is necessary to develop, monitor, and maintain threat level information and to combine the results of threat analysis into the elements of security and emergency preparedness into a cohesive program in which all elements are compatible and operational ability is maintained across business unit boundaries. This drives the need to develop proactive event-driven response and recovery procedures for specific undesirable events on a continuous basis as business operations adjust, modify, or change approaches to achieving business goals.

In addition, the response plan details hazards that are relevant to the direct impacts, disruptions, and cascading effects of natural disasters and industrial mishaps. Moreover, it calls for strategies, plans, policies, and procedures to prepare for, mitigate, respond to, and recover from a variety of undesirable events in an all-hazards context. This focus includes:

- a user-friendly and meaningful comprehensive corporate threat estimate profile that identifies the range and levels of threats and modes of attacks, and determines the criticality of assets, consequences of loss, and the probability of occurrence, as well as natural disasters and industrial mishaps
- a security organization and coordinating structure to enable effective partnerships across the corporation and between and among governing agencies and community responders
- an integrated approach to enhancing protection of the physical, cyber, and human elements in which individual protective measures complement one another
- the development and use of tools to help from effective risk-mitigation solutions in an all-hazards context

Not doing so is irresponsible. The emphasis is on preparing levels of capabilities to address a wide range of realistic threats and hazards. Risk can be managed through developing readiness priorities of capabilities to address a range of scenarios, analyzing intelligence information, understanding capabilities, and effectively using resources.

Critical Elements of a Security Response Plan

At a minimum, a security emergency response plan should address the following critical elements:

- Security mission, security emergency organization and staffing, crisis management and leadership, and continuity of command. Security is a reactionary business that requires exhaustive research and coordination, continuous strategic planning and development and the commitment to respond to security emergencies. To effectively achieve this posture those individuals with security responsibilities use the same organization, technology, resources, and basic skill sets for both normal security operations and emergency response situations. There can be no proper security planning or response without the existence of strong leadership and an on-site chain of command. Equally important is the assignment of security responsibilities to all organizations and individuals for carrying out specific actions at projected times and places during an emergency; these often exceed the routine responsibility of any one business unit and set forth lines of authority, accountability, and organizational relationships during an emergency.
- Intelligence, rumor control, and communications control. Coordinating with intelligence sources and liaising with the media distills misinformation, incomplete information, or distorted information. Communication plays a vital role in both the prevention of a security emergency and the emergency itself.
- Ability and capability to carryout event-driven response and recovery activities.
- Maintain internal and external dependencies, including mutual agreements and reenforcement capabilities and support. The plan must identify steps to address mitigation concerns during security response and recovery activities.
- Ability and capability to transition from normal security to an emergency security posture. Both normal and emergency security operations call for the exercise of strong leadership over physical security, electronics security, cyber security, information security, personnel security, and corporate-wide security emergency planning that gains the continual confidence and support of the CEO and other C-suite executives. Transitioning from a day-to-day security posture to an emergency security configuration must happen as smoothly, efficiently, and effectively as possible because such a shift in momentum directly affects the entire enterprise. This includes executing post and patrol priorities; determining extended work hours and relief capabilities; prioritizing asset protection and implementing security compensatory measurements; maintaining the security of the perimeter and area; controlling access to the scene; preserving evidence; and providing security escorts and executive protection, as necessary. The plan must show how all actions will be coordinated and describe how people and property will be protected during emergencies, disasters, and accidents.
- Planning for and providing logistical support: transportation, mobilization, and mobility (air, sea, and land); evacuation logistics and security; medical assistance and evacuation; reliable backup communications; food service, lodging, maintenance; and security facilities and equipment, including prepositioned emergency supplies, materials, and equipment. The plan must also identify personnel, equipment, facilities, supplies, and other resources that are available for use during security response and recovery operations
- Providing for the well-being of the security workforce: personal affairs and counseling; family assistance, comfort, and counseling; and financial assistance

- Emergency budget and capability to procure emergency supplies, materials, equipment, and security consulting services
- Security training and exercises. A security response plan is only as good as the training given to the personnel who must implement the plan. Practice drills are essential for refining individual and group skill sets and for updating the security response plan and procedures.

Security Planning Constraints and Limitations

To be sure, there are inherent planning constraints and limitations that must be recognized at the outset. As mentioned previously, it is not practical or feasible to protect all resources, assets, systems, networks, functions, and information against every possible threat nor are. All are all assets uniformly "critical" in nature; therefore, a risk-based security strategy enhanced by intelligence and information analysis and reporting provides the basis for an effective security response strategy. While complete protection against all potential threats is not possible (particularly the threat of explosion and those dangers imposed by chemical, biological, and radiological attacks), applying best practices can reduce vulnerability and consequences. For example, emergency response planning actions must consider the following security priorities:

- *Priority 1:* Respond to prevent further injury or loss of life.
- *Priority 2:* Respond to those assets, systems, networks, and functions designated as most critical to the mission and other business interests.
- *Priority 3:* Respond to those assets, systems, networks, and functions that face a specific, imminent threat
- *Priority 4:* Respond to other assets that may become potential targets to terrorists or criminal elements over time. Advance warning of potentially vulnerable assets, systems, networks, and functions is crucial. This fosters a proactive approach to enhance decision-making processes and response to the various levels of threat.

The security challenge goes beyond most corporate-level emergency response plans. Today's threats call for an ongoing, dynamic, and interactive process that ensures the continuation of a security organization's core activities before, during, and—most important—after a major crisis. Proactive planning and preparation by the security organization for potential security- and safety-related incidents and disruptions diminish both the impact and duration of the disruption and help to avoid or minimize the suspension of critical security activities, thereby allowing a return to normal security operations as rapidly as possible (Sullivant, 2007, pp. 157–176).

Conclusions

The attacks on September 11, 2001, thrust disaster planning into the spotlight, and subsequent crises—hurricane Katrina, outbreaks of infectious disease, the earthquake in Japan, and the devastating tsunami, as well as piracy, kidnapping, assassinations, beheadings, bombings, and other attacks—are tragic reminders that extraordinary events that affect businesses and our daily lives are all to ordinary.

The fact that a number of large organizations do not have crisis management/emergency plans, and the majority do not run a program to develop response capabilities is frightening to say the least. Any readers that are still doubters as to the value of crisis management and emergency planning and preparation only have to speak to organizations who have suffered a crisis.

New organizational community threats are beginning to escalate in probability, breadth, and severity. By recognizing these emerging patterns, astute security professionals can be in a position to begin preparedness measures in the early stages of threat development. But identifying those new risks is only half the equation.

In performing my work, I frequently observed how personnel and bureaucratic rivalries among senior officials had taken precedence over effective security emergency planning and response to emergencies. Before any serious discussions of correcting security emergency planning and response begin, management needs to accept responsibility for the damaged relationships among the staff and start repairing interpersonal communications, build a team/clientele, and focus on the critical need to improve and enhance security emergency planning response capabilities when such an intense atmosphere prevails.

While complete protection against all potential threats and hazards is not possible, we can apply a series of integrated security strategies, protocols, and prevention and protection measures to reduce risk exposure to an acceptable level. Security response and recovery protocols that are not predicated on or guided by the results of a threat assessment and vulnerability analysis and mitigation strategies are at best guesswork and usually incomplete, ultimately off target, and produce no results when they are needed most.

Make no mistake about it: the threat is real, and it consists of more than mere terrorism. It will continue to increase in frequency, severity, and lethality. It can take many forms and affect anyone at any time and at any location. Most security consultants, including myself, agree that our greatest threat and weakness lie within: the insider threat. Security precautions and preparations to minimize risk exposure must turn inward; we must take a closer in-house look at the people who are charged with planning, developing, coordinating, approving, directing, and carryout security policies, plans, protocols, and measures and enforcing guidelines, standards, and specifications, least we bread a new "Walker family, NSA contractor Edward Snowden, FBI agent Robert Hansen, MIT professor Daniel Elllsberg, and PFC Bradley Manning."

Appendix A: Case Histories: Security Emergency Planning Fallacies

Background Information

This information is a review of relevant case histories. The information is shared for a better understanding of the scope of problems security directors face on a daily basis and for further research for the interested reader.

Source: The information represents eyewitness accounts and personal observations that I noted and reported in the course of performing security assessments, audits, and inspections, and during one-on-one interview sessions with numerous chief executive officers, chief operating officers, and other corporate senior officials, directors of security and their respective staff members, and other company employees.

Security Emergency Planning Lacks Strategic Insight and Determination: Selected Case Histories

Significant shortcomings in the development of functional security response plans, including event-driven response and recovery procedures, exist throughout the industry. Most plans lack organization and clear presentation of critical information (*poor planning, management, and communications skills*).

I found little evidence to suggest security emergency planning, or to suggest that the development of such plans and response and recovery procedures was based on a validate threat estimate profile or any other threat assessment tool. The few organizations that had threat profiles of file seldom kept them up to date. The majority of these threat profiles were too outdated to be useful in updating any of the plans reviewed (*poor planning*).

- Few security response plans exist. When they do, most are weak in identifying security responsibilities and actions.[2] Time-critical, time-sensitive, and time-dependent security actions lacked specificity. Procedures failed to identify particular security event-driven actions, including dependency support (*poor planning and experience*).
- We found no visible evidence of a Command, Control and Communications C^3 structure in security plans to demonstrate that key leadership exists to direct security emergency operations. Many corporate emergency response plans were written in generic terms with respect to roles, responsibilities, and authority (*poor planning and leadership*).

---

[2] Security operations and response actions to security events and other emergencies are normally considered "sensitive security information". In some instances, such operations and response actions are even classi-fied. Generally, corporate-wide emergency response plans are shared with local governing authorities and emergency response entities. Generally, they are not exempt from public disclosure. Some states mandate by law that such plans be public documents and must be available to the public on demand. To protect the integrity of security operations and specific security response actions, it is in the best interest of the corpo-ration not to include security responsibilities and actions in the corporate-wide response plan, but only give reference to its existence as a separate document. The contents of such security response plans and proce-dures are protected under state and federal laws, and other regulations. Their content and access to such plans and procedures is based on a right and need to have access to the information for the official duties.

- No security event–driven response procedures or checklists existed at most locations to address system malfunctions or catastrophic failures, including actions to take in the event of power or communications failures or degradation of system performance. Commensurate security compensatory measures are almost nonexistent across the entire industry (*poor planning and management*).
- There were no security event–driven response procedures or checklists in many Command, Control and Communications C³ centers describing what actions to take when an emergency occurs (*poor management*).
- The lack of professional security leadership at several sites underscores the immaturity and weakness of published corporate and security response plans. Immature policies, standards, and procedures often confuse and distort information rather than provide effective guidance. These security organizations could have prevented many predictable security events (or at least minimized their effect) by developing clear event-driven response and recovery protocols, conducting appropriate security training, and performing adequate management oversight of activities.
- Many enterprises failed to demonstrate adequate capabilities to respond to a crisis at nearly every level of security emergency preparedness.
- One organization failed utterly in preparing for and responding to a disaster that was long predicted and imminent for days. I wonder how much more profound the failure would have been if a disaster—such as a gas/oil/chemical explosion and the subsequent fires, collateral damage, and loss of life and injuries—was to take them totally by surprise.
- None of the security organizations I visited had planned for security recovery operations or had any functional and user-friendly recovery procedures (*poor planning*).

A User-Friendly Protocol Development Model

Shortfalls in the development of protocols exist throughout all industry sectors and within most security organizations.

John Sullivant

Top Takeaways

- Protocols that are right on target
- Value of written communications in passing on critical information
- Management becomes easier with clear and distinct guidance
- Measure and evaluate the effectiveness, efficiency, and productivity of protocols
- Gain insight from protocol case histories

Overview

Nobody likes regulations. In our business, however, everyone recognizes that some uniform guidance is necessary and essential for a security organization to provide consistency and clarity to security policy, protocols, and practices. Equally important is to remove and dismiss regulations that are outdated, duplicative, or even counterproductive. Unnecessary or poorly targeted regulations do not help employees or improve security, but they do cost entities time and money. They also obstruct the innovation and connections needed to make security programs more resilient.

The challenge is to build a security culture that can effectively eliminate outdated rules and regulations and ensure that new ones are properly coordinated to develop practicable and workable guidance, and instructions that are meaningful, clear, necessary and enforceable. Most security organizations work hard to provide quality service and make good use of scarce resources. Management needs to work equally hard to produce reasonable and manageable protocols. Any protocol that fails to meet this simple test should never be written.

Adopting a Protocol Strategy Is Crucial to Quality Performance

Since every document you write is a reflection of your organization and your people, you must acquire communication skills that produce professional results, perfect content and clarity, and appropriate organization, grammar, usage, punctuation, and sentence structure in your writing.

A protocol strategy has meaning and purpose only if it focuses on desirable characteristics that are common to all technical and professional publications, in which the goal is to communicate instructions, guidelines, standards, specification requirements, and direction and where noncompliance or failure to follow the protocol, or omission and vague context, could result in serious consequences. Consequences could be such activities as safety and security violations, activities that may lead to personal injury or loss, damage or destruction to equipment and assets, or financial loss resulting from inattentiveness or careless work habits, including the potential loss of proprietary or classified information (Sullivant, 2007, pp. 165, 169).

Protocols communicate rules, directions, and guidelines that control behaviors and outcomes that are agreeable to the leaders who are involved in carrying out their intent and purpose. Within the realm of security activity a representative sampling of protocols consist of:

• Policies, regulations, and directives	• Engineering drawings and plans
• Business unit security instructions	• Security threat profile
• Security reports	• Facility evacuation and fire plans
• Alert notification notices	• Post orders and special orders
• Security system O&M instructions	• Security contracts and statements of work
• Inter/intra agency correspondence	• Security mutual assistance agreements
• Security management plans	• Shutdown and startup procedures
• Security operations plans	• Training materials
• Standard operating procedures	• Security emergency plans
• Crime prevention literature	• Event-driven recovery and recovery
• Security system design specifications	procedures

Jeffrey Hunker[1] (2009, pp. 15–17) of Carnegie Mellon University argues that there is value in looking at instances in which protocol strategy evolves to provide an ongoing and sustaining framework for better security execution, such as matching protocol needs with the opportunity to improve processes, practices, and work habits. According to Hunker, Some themes for improving protocol development include:

• Threats should prioritize policy	• Implementation matters
• Managing tension	• Leveraging lessons learned
• Better measurement tools	• Delegating authority, responsibility, and accountability

---

[1] Hunker was the founding director of the Critical Infrastructure Assurance Office (which was later merged within the Department of Homeland Security), a member of the National Security Council, Senior Director for Critical Infrastructure, a member of the Council of Foreign Relations, and dean of the Heinz College at Carnegie Mellon University.

Threats Should Prioritize Security Policy

I previously brought to light the consequences of not developing a useful and meaningful corporate threat estimate profile that could be used in making security decisions, including the development of sound protocols. Without a valid threat estimate profile, policy development is hindered by the inability to fully identify and understand the threats that surround the business environment. This uncertainty has three significant consequences (Hunker, 2009, pp. 15–17; Sullivant, 2007, pp. 92–96):

- At its highest level, security policy defines the investment interests of a corporation. Lower-tier instructions relate to more immediate actions, and without clarity and understanding of threats and policy, lower-tier protocols become blurred and overall policy implementation suffers.
- With multiple and indiscriminate threats not clearly defined, various business units within a corporation are prone to form their own perception of security, rather than address or follow corporate strategic security needs.
- The prioritization of policy goals is impeded. The lack of clearly linking threats to business goals and operations weakens your ability to channel resources and expenditures to the activity of greatest importance.

Unless you embrace these issues and address their resolution, you will not able be to create a sound platform for better security protocols, practices and processes.

Managing Tension

As an element of good protocol development, management needs to control tension between excessive controls, omission, and gaps, and between contradicting guidance and conflicts of interest within the policy framework.

Better Measurement Tools

Most security professionals are unaware that metrics do not always have to measure direct impacts; they can also serve to address dependencies and interdependences within multiple functional areas. In some instances they can be proxies for specific outputs that are inherently difficult to identify and measure. For example, maintaining a secure and safe workplace is not only a laudable goal in itself, it drives major performance and productivity improvements. It reduces fraud, waste and abuse, and other criminal activity; creates an awareness of health and safety concerns that focus on reducing injuries to the general workforce; and can lower insurance rates and workman's compensation expenses (Sullivant, 2007, pp. 104, 106).

Implementation Matters

While management defines the basis for action, the execution of policy depends on the actions of those who are responsible for developing the plans, procedures, and other protocols necessary to implement the policy, including management oversight and monitoring for continual improvement in the areas of effectiveness, efficiency, and productivity.

Leveraging Lessons Learned

As the theme of this book explicitly suggests, our greatest, predictable failing is that we consistently and repeatedly duplicate the same mistakes. Condoning or accepting the theory of "vulnerability creep-in," as described in Chapter The Many Faces of Vulnerability Creep-in, reinforces this behavior.

Delegating Authority, Responsibility, and Accountability

As a student who has studied the art of protocol creation, I am troubled by some of the observations I have witnessed and reported over the years (see Appendix A for highlights of selected case histories). For instance, all too often it remains unclear who knows what to do during a crisis, who manages or drives the security agenda, and who is responsible and accountable for decision making and carrying out orders. To remove the cloud of doubt, chief executives and other leaders need to establish exacting lines of delegated authority, responsibility, and accountability, and to permit the respective staffs and business unit managers to consistently enforce protocols and remain within those boundaries. This is particularly an important management tool for the security organization (Sullivant, 2007 pp. 207–212).

Need for Protocols

At the highest level, policy creation sets the direction for achieving security goals and objectives. Policy then becomes the acceptable norm adopted by an organization. For example, when policy states that "employees will adhere to security performance standards," the general goal or behavior pattern will not change over time. Policy does not state what the security performance standards or behaviors are, or how management will enforce such standards. Rather, lower-tier publications such as regulations, directives, plans, and procedures are used to carry out the intent of formal policy which can easily be modified and updated as necessary, without having to adjust the original policy statement. Policy decision makers should also ensure that policies and lower-tier protocols do not contain conflicting requirements, guidance, or behavior. When such conflicts exist, management must take prompt action to resolve any conflict or contradiction in carrying out the protocol. Without a strong connection between a policy statement and its respective implementation protocol, it is very likely that there may be a mismatch between the intent of the policy and the interpretation of carrying out its strategy.

Purpose of Protocol Reviews

A critical review of security protocols offers management the essential information it needs to (Sullivant, 2007, pp. 92–94, 104–212):

- Establish reliable direction and guidance that fosters organizational resilience that are consistent with the standards a corporation subscribes to, in accordance with the organization's

overall business goals and objectives. In many instances these commitments are indispensable to the boundaries of the security organization, its mission, and it goals, obligations, legal responsibilities, and other requirements that are consistent with its commitment to protect and preserve human life and property, support corporate business goals, and protect its brand, image, reputation, integrity, and relationships with stakeholders and the community.
• Identify inconsistencies, omissions, and other discrepancies that may lead to the revision of existing protocols or the creation of new guidance that replaces outdated or unworkable instruction, bringing the security organization into alignment with management's expectations, regulatory requirements, legal requirements, and industry best practices.

A protocol strategy that addresses the full range of measures at its disposal protects the enterprise and its workforce, assets, and facilities. Such a strategy must be embraced and enforced by all divisions of the company. When fully integrated into a comprehensive security program, protocols enhance the effectiveness and efficiency of security resilience through the joint efforts of all corporate division chiefs and subordinate branch managers by using the combined technical, professional, and management resources available across the entire corporation.

Quality Review Process for Essential Security Protocols

A major administrative goal of management is to deliver a specific collection of protocols that help to guide security organizations to carry out security activity in a uniform and efficient manner. Fig. 13.1 Publication Quality Assurance Review Methodology illustrates a user-friendly metric scale that gauges the organization, presentation, and content of documents that warrant measurement and evaluation. Seven measurement indicators are used: management, planning, coordination, operations, logistics, administration, and finance.

These indicators play a key role in the protocol development process. They are desirable quality assurance characteristics common to all technical and professional publications in which the goal is to communicate instructions, guidance, standards, specifications, and direction where noncompliance or failure to follow protocol could result in serious consequences such as injury or loss of life, damage or destruction of equipment or property, or financial losses.

Three rating levels, ranging from "meets evaluation criteria" (GREEN) to "addresses most or some evaluation criteria" (YELLOW) to "fails to address regulatory competency requirements or acceptable industry standard" (RED), are used to evaluate the acceptability of a publication. These indicators are important because they show a clear and distinct separation between:

• a document that satisfies *all* the stated evaluation criteria and requires no rework
• one that addresses *some* of the evaluation criteria but needs redesign and revision to meet acceptable best practices
• one that *fails* to meet standards and requires major rework to make it compliant with industry practices

I use a top-down, bottom-up evaluation technique to examine the scope, purpose, content, and organization of publications. The process allows for a better understanding of the vertical and horizontal interfaces between publications, as well as

Name and Date of Publication under review: (Enter information in this section)		Metric scale
MANAGEMENT	Does the document reflect:	
	▪ a stragetic, tactical or operational vision?	
	▪ the scope and mission goals and objective?	
	▪ a visible decision-making process?	
PLANNING	Does the document reflect:	
	▪ a set of principles and priorities?	
	▪ definitions of authority, responsibility and accountability?	
	▪ how the strategy relates to other goals and objectives?	
	▪ means of continual improvement?	
COORDINATION	Does the document reflect:	
	▪ the use of a quality assurance review process (see Figure 6-8A)?	
	▪ coordination of the document with appropriate stakeholders?	
	▪ a legal review, when necessary?	
	▪ an avenue for continual improvement?	
	▪ executive or senior management approval?	
OPERATIONS	Does the execution of the strategy:	
	▪ set priorities, milestones, and performance measurement?	
	▪ satisfy regulatory requirements, commitments, or obligations?	
	▪ foster team-building skills?	
	▪ obtain ideas from employees and gain their ownership for change?	
LOGISTICS	Does the document reflect:	
	▪ enterprise resource identification, management, and monitoring?	
	▪ a communication strategy to create shared expectations?	
	▪ clear and distinct language that is user-friendly and understandable?	
ADMINISTRATION	Does the document address:	
	▪ policies, procedures, & resources to achieve the stated strategy or goal?	
	▪ record-keeping procedures?	
	▪ reporting progress?	
	▪ best practices across all activity?	
FINANCE	Is budget allocation visible that addresses:	
	▪ what the strategy will cost?	
	▪ types of resources and investments needed?	
	▪ where resources and investments should be targeted?	
	▪ developed based on the threat profile?	
	▪ risk reduction based on the mission?	

Legend

Green	The publication satisfies the minimum regulatory requirements, industry standards, or best practices for issuance. It only requires annual review and updating as conditions and circumstances change.
Yellow	The publication satisfies most or some of the regulatory requirements, industry standards, or best practices but contains information that is incomplete, unclear, or administrative inconsistencies. Document needs revision to bring it into compliance with missing requirements. Document may remain in service while being revised. The document should be revised at the earliest possible time.
Red	The publication fails to meet regulatory requirements or acceptable industry standards in both format and content, affecting critical security and safety related processes and practices. It requires revision to bring it into compliance with requirements, industry standards, or best practices. The document should be removed from service, if practical, while it is being revised. If it is not feasible to remove the document from service, an alert notice should be issued to users to implement the protocol with causation or identify specific portions of the directive to be suspended pending its modification. The document should be updated immediately.

Figure 13.1 Publication quality assurance review methodology.

information dependencies between internal business units and external organizations, that may affect business operations, security activities, and their contributions to performance effectiveness.

The review process also identifies whether the absence of specific information within a particular protocol could lead to deviations from compliance and the application, safety, security awareness, user-friendliness, and usability of the guidance.

Benefits Derived from Protocol Analysis

The goal is to revise or remove guidance that does not contribute to the wellness, effectiveness, efficiency, and productivity of the organization. Specifically, the analysis must:

- ensure compliance exists with security measures
- determine which security measures need to be revised, and those that should be removed from service because they are archaic, obsolete, and cumbersome practices
- identify existing instruction that requires updating or correction, or create new rules of behavior that reduce costs and improve overall workforce effectiveness, efficiency, and productivity for consistency as a new generation of employees joins the company

Such guidance is a good management tool that helps effective practices outlast the person who developed them.

Conclusions

Well-developed protocols provide distinct value and meaning to those affected by their creation.

- They delineate authority, responsibility, accountability, and succession of leadership.
- They establish a command structure with effective leadership.
- They offer a set of actions predicated on goals and objectives guided by the threat profile.
- They set the standard for interfaces, dependencies, reporting relationships, and communications.
- They identify and allocate resources, facilities, and equipment to accomplish the mission.
- They establish evaluation and measurement tools to benchmark performance.
- They define training requirements and qualifications.
- They provide a quality assurance feedback loop to correct program deficiencies.

Protocols must always be designed to enhance overall security activity and to reduce exposure consistent with the threat. Improving policies, procedures, and other directives also contributes significantly to the protection of resources, assets, facilities, systems, functions, and products that are vital for many reasons—most of which are based on economic considerations and industry best practices. Having this clear and distinct exchange of communications is important to any business enterprise because:

- Resources require a large capital investment to acquire, train, maintain, and retain.
- Assets, facilities, systems, and products are expensive to acquire, install, and maintain.

- Intellectual property and other confidential and sensitive data directly affect the corporation's competitive edge and are vital to the efficiency and effectiveness of business operations.
- Finally, laws and best practices call for the safeguarding of resources, assets, facilities, systems, and functions so that if they are compromised, disrupted, injured, damaged, or destroyed, there is potential for criminal consequences and civil liability.

Another important aspect of formal protocols is that decision makers, planners, and writers must be cognizant of is the use of the terms "shall," "should," "may," and "will"—all of which have specific legal meaning as well as liability considerations.

While the commitment to rules, processes, and procedures is not to be overlooked, initiative, discretion, training, and experience need to prevail in situations that are not covered by formal instruction and when a situation accelerates out of control and scope of performance expectations involving the perception of danger, decision making, or inaction beyond operational and procedural tolerances.

Appendix A

Protocol Case Histories

Background Information

This information is a review of relevant case histories. The information is shared for a better understanding of the scope of problems security directors face on a daily basis, and for further research for the interested reader.

Source: The information represents eyewitness accounts and personal observations I have noted and reported in the course of performing security assessments, audits and inspections, and one-on-one interview sessions with numerous chief executive officers (CEOs), chief operating officers, and other corporate senior officials, directors of security and their respective staff members, and other company employees.

Overview of Selected Case Histories

The mission, responsibilities, authority, and accountability of many security monitoring stations or security communications, command, and control (C^3) centers is not described in any of the documents reviewed (*poor planning and management*).

Security procedures, post instructions, and operating orders for special events require significant revisions to provide clear, user-friendly guidance (*poor written communication skills*).

During entry briefings, several CEOs acknowledged that most security policies were issued by executive decree because not all group leaders would sign off on the policy. During the interview process, it was evident that this unilateral action created friction between the staff and the security organization, notwithstanding that the decree was issued by the CEO without security advice and consent (*ineffective team-building skills*).

The purpose of many procedures, including roles and responsibilities, reporting relationships, and accountability, were not clearly delineated. These sections are written in such general terms that they lack specificity, particularly where internal and external dependencies, community interfaces and jurisdiction, and mutual assistance played a significant role in the response. In the protocols I reviewed it was difficult to determine who or what department is accountable for implementing or supporting many of the procedures (*poor planning and management skills*).

The clarity and presentation of important ideas and the message were confusing and difficult to grasp. In many instances the guidance was ambiguous and vague (*Poor communication skills*).

Clear and distinct security protocols are lacking at many locations, even though these deficiencies were identified and reported to those organizations on numerous previous visits (*poor management and leadership skills*).

Distinguishing between policy statements and mission statements, and the details associated with the execution of procedures that describe the systematic actions to take, was and remains a challenge. In many instances, "applicability" and "responsibilities" were scattered throughout the body of the protocols, making for difficult reading and understanding of purpose (*poor communication skills*).

At most locations visited, security plans required significant clarity to address and integrate key program elements influencing the capability and ability to deter, delay, prevent, protect, detect, assess, and respond to criminal activity and other events (*poor communication skills*).

Many facility access and circulation control protocols were loosely implemented. On several occasions, I noticed that established security practices were being completely ignored (*poor planning, ineffective enforcement*).

At most locations, the human resources division did not address a security work standard within the employee manual to measure employees' conformity to security rules, practices, and behavior (*poor planning and work habits*).

Continuing research suggests that most corporations have little insight into their security protocols, making them more complacent about threats and more easily targeted. Burying one's head in the sand may be a good security strategy for ostriches. However, there can be no arguing that it is *not* for security organizations.

A Proven Organization and Management Assessment Model

14

A security organization that fails to focus on total quality management, fails in everything it does.

John Sullivant

Top Takeaways

- use a management assessment model to audit organization competency
- complexities of organization and management reviews
- use risk-based metrics to measure and evaluate performance
- chief executive officer's perspective

Overview

It is a grave mistake to presume to understand executive management better than they understand themselves unless you have walked in their shoes. Perhaps the best advice this old soldier can give you is to understand them as people who, by their own account, carry the corporation on their shoulders, while you carry only the burden of proof to exercise security change. There is no doubt that internal debate about the merits of change will frequently surface between C-suite executives, the senior staff, and the security organization. But such debate may evolve into healthy constructive discussion, with each side giving in a little; thus such differences could be a good thing, giving rise to positive resolution.

This chapter speaks to maintaining a functional and viable security organization that is capable of performing its critical mission: deterrence, detection, prevention, protection, assessment, response, and recovery. I also emphasize the importance of effective security management and strong leadership to create and implement security strategies, and to provide oversight of security activities that resonate with C-suite executives.

In my view, the goal and objective of a security organization is to establish and maintain a family of corporate-wide security strategies that are acceptable to the chief executive. Such an organization provides the necessary framework for the coordination of prevention and protection efforts at all levels of management and across all aspects of corporate business operations. Lest we forget: security is a shared responsibility, and executive management and the senior staff are a key ingredient in the successful implementation of an overall corporate security program.

Security, however, is a reactionary function that requires exhaustive research, coordination, continuous strategic planning and development, and the commitment to respond to security uncertainty. To effectively achieve this posture, those individuals with security responsibilities use the same organization, technology, resources, and basic skill sets for both normal security operations and emergency response situations. As such, transitioning from a day-to-day security posture to an emergency security configuration must happen smoothly, efficiently, and effectively, because such a shift in momentum directly affects the entire enterprise.

Both normal and emergency security operations call for the exercise of strong leadership over such areas as physical security, electronics security, cyber security, information security, personnel security, and corporate-wide security emergency planning that gains the continual confidence and support of the chief executive officer (CEO), other C-suite executives, and the senior staff.

Embracing the Mission of the Security Organization

In accomplishing the security mission, a security director faces complex challenges in a diversified high-threat and volatile environment—and always under ambiguous, uncertain, and rapidly changing circumstances, situations, and conditions. With the concurrence and support of the CEO, the security organization serves as the nucleus of corporate strategic security planning. In this decisive leadership role, the security director establishes broad security strategies; sets basic policy, protocols, and best practices; oversees security management from the position of stakeholders and the CEO; and engages in decision making. Security managers and supervisors are responsible for the overall execution of security policies, plans, protocols, and security activities and also provide feedback and insight to the director on all matters relating to security, including policy and best practices. The director is the single point of coordination for all security matters within the corporation and between federal, state, and local governments for all law enforcement and homeland security matters. Given the dynamic nature of the threat environment, the director continuously monitors corporate security programs and develops a strong business case for security investment, and investigation when the occasion arises.

Security goals and objectives that complement corporate business strategies are achieved through the exercise of management principles; security best practices; collaboration with C-suite executives, other company managers, and division chiefs; with the approval of the chief executive. Under the leadership of the director, functional responsibilities assigned to a security organization are varied and diversified; they could include one or more of the following:

- Offer strategic advice to the CEO, other C-suite executives, and division managers in implementing policy, processes, and practices, including emergency planning responsibilities.
- Assist division chiefs in promoting security strategies and security awareness, and in developing and implementing business unit security guidance consistent with the policies and practices stipulated within the corporate security plan.

- Promulgate security policies, plans, and protocols, and enforce security practices designed to reduce business risk exposure.
- Sponsor programs and measures that contribute to the objectives of diversified security programs, and maintain the currency of the security plan and related protocols.
- Organize, direct, and coordinate physical, electronic, cyber, information, and personnel security programs for a wide range of assets that are owned, operated, maintained, or leased by the company.
- Apply unified criteria for determining criticality and prioritizing security investments.
- Direct staff who are engaged in security and emergency preparedness planning activities to eliminate or mitigate business risk exposure.
- Develop security restoration and recovery plans for implementation in the aftermath of an attack, industrial accident, or natural disaster.
- Coordinate security emergency activities throughout the company to promote effective event-driven response and recovery procedures that support business unit operations, as well as business unit response and recovery activities.
- Maintain liaison with city, state, and federal law enforcement agencies and the state-level Department of Homeland Security.
- Participate in information sharing analysis centers, InfraGuard meetings, joint task forces, commissions, and groups involving antiterrorism strategies, threat advisories, and joint planning operations.
- Represent the security interests of the company at external security meetings and conferences.
- Present briefings to executive management and governing authorities.
- Develop and maintain current the corporate threat estimate profile (or Threat Forecast) using a uniform methodology for prioritizing critical assets, threats, hazards, and consequences.
- Gather and analyze threat intelligence information and threat advisory notices.
- Set priorities for strategic security planning to reduce business risk exposure.
- Approve security and security-related training programs for company employees and specialized security seminars for senior managers, designated staff members and security supervisors.
- Evaluate the effectiveness of security emergency preparedness planning activities to respond to and recover from emergencies and disasters; and make midcourse corrections to reduce or remove identified program deficiencies and weaknesses.
- Approve security design criteria and system performance standards; play a key leadership role in the strategy acquisition of physical and electronic security, cyber and information technology hardware and software, personnel security and related products, and management consultant services; influence the development of statements of work and bid specifications; and judge proposals and cost estimates for security projects.
- Establish action plans, milestone schedules, and outcome measurements to achieve security goals and objectives.
- Work with outside consultants as appropriate for independent security services.
- Analyze security requirements, establish and develop performance standards, and measure program effectiveness consistent with value and industry best practices.
- Review corporate emergency preparedness and business continuity plans for consistency and interoperability, and to ensure that security emergency response and recovery actions directly support business-critical emergency operations. Provide crisis management support to the corporate crisis management center.
- Participate in the exercise and testing of the emergency preparedness plans and, in particular, security operational capabilities.

- Prepare contract guard requirements, participate in contract negotiations, measure , evaluate performance, and continuously monitor service enhancements, improvements, and contract management and leadership.
- Collaborate with the corporate public affairs division in performing liaison duties with the media and other public relations functions.

A Reliable Organization and Management Assessment Model That Resonates with CEOs

Fig. 14.1, A Proven Organization and Management Assessment Model, graphically displays the critical elements of investigating organization, management, and leadership characteristics.

Purpose of Measuring Organization and Management Competency

The model offers an independent judgment of the unit's capability to perform its mission against established criteria, to comply with regulations, or to ease anxieties among executive management or the board. Security appraisals can be operational, management, performance, or compliance reviews, or any combination of these, depending on the client's desire for productivity output. The process may lead to the redesign of the organization, staffing adjustments, or change management.

Operational and management reviews enhance the entity's effectiveness, efficiency, and productivity by identifying what does and does not work, and by identifying candidate areas for improvement. Performance (or competency) and compliance reviews ensure that programs and specific projects accomplish their intended purpose and contribute to a better understanding of costs and benefits.

The model helps to:

- examine the human side of the enterprise to determine individual and group characteristics, interpersonal communications, working relationships, social behavior patterns, work and social interactions, attitudes, perceptions, and expectations; roles, responsibilities, and authority; mission awareness; the effectiveness, efficiency, and economy of managing the security workforce; performance proficiencies, qualifications, experience, expertise, and capabilities; and leadership and management traits and attributes
- review the organization's design, makeup, structure, and governance to determine the strengths and weaknesses of the organization and identify what areas require continual improvement to make important business-related decisions on where to use scarce resources and funds
- formulate or modify the organization design and strategic planning framework that integrates governance and management performance improvement, identifies unworkable measures, and provides enterprise-wide solutions to enhance organization productivity, including change and people strategy, and change management, when appropriate
- uncover root causes of ineffectiveness, inefficiencies, and excessive costs; inadequate internal controls; unworkable measures, practices, and norms; weak accountability; and the mismanagement of operations, programs, or resources

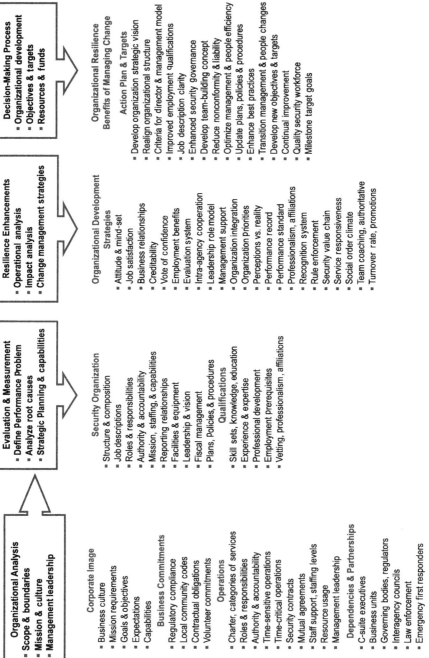

Figure 14.1 A proven organization and management assessment model (Sullivant, 2007, pp. 55–84).

- evaluate how the security organization operates today and its capability to meet the needs of the company tomorrow, and to provide decision makers with an understanding of how best to manage the security organization and those areas needing special attention
- accelerate performance by integrating and aligning security processes, protocols, people, and information systems with enterprise business strategy, goals, and objectives; to implement a system of management improvements, internal controls, and performance parameters to overcome unit deficiencies, weaknesses, and inadequacies

Unresolved problems can create dysfunctional relationships in the workplace. Ultimately, they become impediments to flexibility and in dealing with strategic change in an open-ended and creative way. Intervention offers the promise of continually improving security activities by mending dysfunctional units; bringing them into line with regulatory compliance standards or expected performance and best practices; rebuilding organizations to improve performance and regain confidence and trust; and in getting startup organizations up and running to their full potential at the earliest possible time.

Measuring Security Management and Leadership Competencies

For the purposes of this chapter, let us agree that security management is the art of overseeing the efforts of people, and it comprises planning, organizing, coordinating, controlling, and directing activity to accomplish security goals.

- Planning involves deciding what needs to happen in the future and generating policy, plans, and protocols for action.
- Organizing is the process of making sure human and technology resources and logistical support are put into place.
- Coordinating involves creating a structure through which goals can be accomplished.
- Controlling is the monitoring of activity and progress against plans, protocols, goals, and objectives, including milestones.
- Directing determines what must be done in a situation and getting people to do it right the first time.

Security directors, managers, and other security professionals in responsible positions have the authority and responsibility to make decisions to carry out the security mission, and they are accountable for that. As previously discussed in Chapter A User-Friendly Security Assessment Model, performance effectiveness metrics resonate with chief executives because they focus on topics of most interest to them. Fig. 14.2, Management and Leadership Performance Effectiveness (P_E) Metric and Calculation Criteria, follows suit with this concept. The metric may be used for both the "before" evaluation (existing performance effectiveness, P_{E1}) and "after" mitigation implementation (effectiveness of proposed risk treatments, P_{E2}), as discussed in Chapter A User-Friendly Security Assessment Model.

Appendix A, "Case Histories: Management and Leadership," illustrates some examples of management and leadership incompetency that directly influence individual and group productivity.

Examples of Performance Effectiveness Competency Areas Important to Executive Management	P_E Level	P_{E1} Measurement Rating		
		Numerical	Narrative	
Management Skill-Sets				
Planning				
Organizing				
Coordinating				
Controlling				
Directing				
Leadership Traits & Attributes				
Strategic vision				
Crafting strategies				
Executing strategies				
Ethical practices				
Fostering team-building				
Independency & objectivity				
Trustworthiness				
Problem solving skills				
Oral & written communication skills				
Executive management exposure/experience				
Operations management exposure/experience				
Technical/program management exposure/experience				
Financial management exposure/experience				
Quality assurance exposure/experience				
Total quality management exposure/experience				
Candor, integrity, loyalty & credibility				
Provide advance information				
Seek other leaders input				
Stay engaged				
Implement change				
Rapport, trust & confidence				

Figure 14.2 Management and leadership performance effectiveness (P_E) metric and calculation criteria.

Legend:

P_E Levels	Likelihood Measurement		Performance Measurement
	Numerical	**Narrative**	
High	0.90	H_E	*Evidence of specific capabilities and performance effectiveness clearly exists.* Operational, regulatory, and compliance requirements have been fully met. Positive evidence of specific capabilities to address areas examined exists in concept, planning, and execution. Areas given this rating represent a high degree of performance effectiveness. When such actions are integrated with similar activity, high performance effectiveness is anticipated to occur.
Moderate	0.50	M_E	*Evidence of general but not specific capabilities or performance effectiveness exists.* General evidence of performance effectiveness with limited capabilities provides reasonable security measures when used in conjunction with other related activity. The area is a valid candidate for increased performance of deficient capabilities and for continual monitoring and improvement.
Low	0.10	L_E	*Little or no evidence of capability or performance expectation.* Ineffective or no evidence of satisfactory capability exists, or activities are not compliant with regulatory and statutory requirements, fail to meet obligations and commitments, and/or fail to contribute effectively to other related security programs. Function requires greater attention from management to prevent further slippage. Area is a valid candidate for mid-course corrective action. Management should flag this activity as a matter of special interest, requiring immediate attention to correct deficiencies, weaknesses and inadequacies on a priority bases. Area qualifies for direct intervention from management, constant monitoring and continual improvement. With respect to other operations, it is below acceptable performance standards.
Uncertainty	0.01	U_E	*Area not measured.* The status of this activity is in the embryo state or has not sufficiently progressed to a mature development state to determine its overall value to the corporation or security organization.

Figure 14.2 Continued.

Benefits of an Operational and Management Audit

Realized benefits can include:

- transforming low-performance or dysfunctional organizations to new heights
- introducing best practices specific to organizational needs
- transferring knowledge that is needed to smoothly implement customized strategies and solutions
- determining what improvements are needed to make important business-related decisions on where to invest scarce resources and funds
- accelerating performance by aligning security organizational processes, people, and information systems with enterprise strategy
- implementing a system of management improvements, internal controls, and performance parameters to overcome the root causes of ineffectiveness, inefficiency, excess costs, and the mismanagement of operations and programs

Conclusions

CEOs dictate the direction and tone of the security organization and set the climate for security performance and accomplishment. The key role of any CEO is to take prudent and reasonable action to prevent harm to human resources and damage or destruction to assets that support critical business operations. These actions, though simple, are not always cheap. But let us not confuse "cheap" and "expensive" with "cost-effective." Within the realm of business survivability, deterrence, delay, prevention, protection, detection, assessment, response and recovery from both a corporate and security organization level are considered cost when the cost to implement and maintain a security program is significantly less than the expected cost of losing corporate image, brand and reputation and/or assets, resources, productivity, and revenues, including downtime, restoration, recovery, training, and start-up costs.

The model promotes accountability of strategies, processes, and practices. It evaluates performance, management efficiency, and compliance; examines qualifications, experience, and the expertise of the security workforce; assesses capabilities to achieve goals, objects, and targets; and looks at social behavior and working relationships internally and with external organizations.

The challenge, then, is to commit to obtaining the body of knowledge, skill sets, and expertise to pursue the saving of lives and the protection of assets from those who wish to do them harm, as well as from hazards and weather-related calamities, and translate these elements into profound outcomes that create opportunities to deal effectively with ambiguous security challenges. CEOs must view the safety and security of their people as a nonnegotiable requirement. CEOs must also assert genuine leadership, communicate to employees what needs to be done, and make pragmatic policy decisions to empower others to make responsible security-related and business decisions, take appropriate action, and be responsible and accountable for their behavior. It will require courage, shared sacrifice, and a willingness to compromise and make the tough choices that are essential to setting a new course for the security organization.

Appendix A: Case Histories – Management and Leadership

Background Information

This information is a review of relevant case histories. The information is shared for a better understanding of the scope of problems security directors face on a daily basis, and for further research for the interested reader. **Source:** The Information represents eyewitness accounts and personal observations I noted and reported in the course of performing security assessments, audits, and inspections, and during one-on-one interview sessions with numerous CEOs, chief operating officers, and other corporate senior officials, directors of security, their respective staff members, and other company employees.

Overview of Selected Case Histories

At sites where executive management showed little or no interest in security planning, there was noticeable frustration among the general staff and the security organization with the pace of implementing security enhancements (*poor management and leadership skills, poor planning and strategic vision*).

One CEO acknowledged during the exit briefing that, in retrospect, having realistic priorities would have been beneficial in achieving security goals (*executive leadership to correct the program was absent*).

Another CEO at a different company told me that strategic security priorities generally were not met because there were too many, all had equal importance, and there were no funding or resources allocated to implement the plan (*leadership inexperienced in managing and overseeing programs*).

A few officials acknowledged that most problems stemmed from turf battles between executive management and their direct reports over delegated authority to run operations free of executive interference versus expert belief they had the experience and judgment to exercise their duties and responsibilities. Here, improved coordination and shared responsibility would have prevented most, if not all, of the problems at this location (*lack of leadership confidence in staff performance, authoritative management style, and no team-building skills*).

Several security organizations were found to be severely stressed because of workload, extended work periods, shortage of personnel, high turnover, and other factors that affect morale and motivation. Poor leadership skills—including not caring for people—precipitated failed performance. The mood of these organizations often switched from frustration and disillusionment to open self-loathing (*weak management and leadership attributes, poor communication skills, not caring*).

At several enterprises, many business units were hostile toward the security organization and working at cross-purposes for several years without executive management intervening. Relationships between the security organization and other departments were to the point where loathing among the staff had drained talent, time, and money from the enterprise's business operations (*poor executive leadership, communication skills, and interpersonal relationships; total absence of professionalism*).

In several instances I found upper management guilty of lax oversight of employees and ethical lapses in running the company. Management also failed to heed clear warning signs and take reasonable and prudent actions to resolve ineffective and inefficient operations across a wide spectrum of security activity (*arrogance and mismanagement*).

At many locations, a clear trend of ineffectiveness, inefficiency, and lack of strategic vision to implement the complexities of a comprehensive security program were found (*poor security management, leadership, and vision*).

At many locations, security planning, coordination, development, and implementation were weak or lacking across a wide spectrum of security activity (*weak security management and leadership, inexperience*).

At several security organizations there was a lack of focus, vision, leadership, structure, and discipline. Officers neglected to properly investigate complaints or incidents, or to write reports. Although security management did an excellent job maximizing the talents and skill sets of selected officers by assigning them to special projects, management failed to share with the general security workforce the scope and purpose of these special projects and their results, or to identify the officers working on these projects. This created tension and resentment among the security workforce and the perception that the security director was engaging in favoritism (*poor management, bad work habits*).

At one location the security organization had strayed so far from the path of responsible management that the concept of leadership had no meaning for the security force. At this same site there was squabbling between various supervisors and the security manager in the presence of security officers and contract guards, including myself as an invited security consultant to help resolve their management and leadership problems. The security manager, although a certified protection professional (CPP)—did not exhibit the skills necessary to bring all elements of a corporate-wide security program to bear (*inexperience, inability to effectively communicate, very poor "people skills"*).

At several locations, the lack of strategic threat analysis, asset vulnerability, and loss of consequences undermined the organization's ability to effectively provide security to assets that needed it most (*inexperience, lack of understanding the importance of strategic threat analysis*). This entity will continue to face difficulties in trying to implement security programs that have undefined unified parameters and risk-based metrics to measure and evaluate progress, performance, and productivity. At this location, the lack of professional security leadership experience and expertise serves to underscore the immaturity of and weakness of the single corporate security strategy developed (*lack of strategic vision, inexperience*).

Building Competencies That Count: A Training Model

Training, a motivated and disciplined workforce and exercising leadership competencies is the only way to achieve corporate security goals and objectives—anything else is a waste of time, effort and money.

John Sullivant

Top Takeaways

- importance of building competencies
- perform a training needs analysis
- reliable research data to validate training requirements
- use selective effective learning techniques to get your point across
- evaluate and measure training outcomes
- planning and practicing scenarios to respond to incidents

Overview

Over the years, security awareness training programs have produced little in terms of motivating the workforce, enhancing security, safeguarding classified information, or defending against cyber crimes, cyber terrorism, and cyber warfare. For the most part, these programs have been underfunded, conducted by overzealous or inexperienced trainers, and often do not appeal to the values and ethics of most employees who receive such training. A major weakness of these programs is they are given only upon the initial hiring, for which about 15 min of a 3-day program are allocated to the general topic of security with little or no specificity. Moreover, recurring security awareness training is seldom provided. Specialized security training for the security force fairs somewhat better than employee security awareness training but requires much improvement to meet the demands of today's challenges. Although security training is slowly gaining attention in the boardroom, it does not reflect a genuine management priority in all instances.

On the bright side, organizations are doing a much better job of collecting and analyzing risk-based performance data, and are keeping management better informed of the wellness of employee security education, as well as the security organization's performance effectiveness, efficiency, and productivity standing. Because much of the enhancement effort depends on changing beliefs, attitudes, and the behavior of individuals and groups, it follows that embedding policies, protocols, practices, and training is a good idea in helping organizations understand the best way to work with people to achieve corporate security goals and objectives.

Why Security Training Is Important

Five reasons stand out regarding why security training is important. *First*, many executives view training as a "nonproductive" activity, meaning that training takes people away from their jobs, and that costs money. At the highest end of the spectrum, it goes against the grain for some executives to pay personnel for nonproductivity, unless there is a visible, tangible return on investment. To overcome this setback, one needs to build a case for training that focuses on reducing turnovers, increasing organizational resilience, attracting quality people, saving time and money, and creating opportunities for higher profit margins, which will—within a realizable time frame—return the investment through increased productivity, less absenteeism, and fewer accidents and losses.

Second, security training is important because it establishes a continuing attitude that can motivate an individual to report otherwise unnoticeable actions of others and report security vulnerabilities that could, if allowed to hibernate within the bowels of the organization, cause injury or loss of life, or damage and destruction to critical assets, as well as damage to the company's brand, image, and reputation.

Third, competency training is very important; it is designed to yield specific behavioral learning outcomes that support successful job performance, productivity, and safety. I define "competency" as a group of related individual skills and attributes that influence a major job function, indicate successful performance and proficiency, are measurable against standards, and are subject to continual improvement through training and experience.

Fourth, training enables organizations to create benchmarks by assessing the current level of competency in comparison to preset performance expectations. Exposure to competency training offers every person in the organization something of value. Most leaders know workers on the front lines are the people who are most likely to have occasion to notice something out of the ordinary that may flag a vulnerability or threat to the entity. Therefore, a major theme of all security and security-related training programs should be to motivate individuals to bring potential issues to the attention of management in a timely manner without retribution, so problems can be fixed while they are still manageable. This approach helps reduce vulnerability creep-in

Last, and most important, training increases the ability to reappraise stressful situations, decrease rumination, and increase emotional intelligence and mindfulness. According to the New Hampshire Technical Institute Business Training Center in Concord, New Hampshire employees become less judgmental after quality training, and others perceive them as more personable and approachable. Increased mindfulness has been shown to help people sustain attention, increase working memory, improve immune system function, reduce stress and anxiety, reduce depression, and increase focus, clearer thinking, and judgment.

Because security training affects and influences various operations in different ways, its orientation must take on a different meaning for each corporation, business unit, manager, and employee.

Goals and Value Are Drivers of Effective Training

Security careers span diverse industries in every sector of the global economy, ranging from positions with small and medium-sized businesses to leadership roles that are essential to protecting every aspect of an enterprise. The security industry is changing swiftly and growing rapidly, relying more than ever on workforce innovation, productivity, training, education, and professional development and growth to be successful. You should capitalize on these emerging trends to benefit your organization and the development of your people.

- Training focuses on the job that an individual currently holds.
- Education focuses on the new skill sets that an individual may require in a future position, learned through formal accredited courses of instruction.
- Professional development focuses on the activities that an individual may participate in (in the future) through professional courses or seminars.

A Reliable Training Model Resonates With Chief Executive Officers

Fig. 15.1 Meaningful and Useful Training Development Model, resonates with executives because it highlights a practical systematic process to identify job performance standards and competency demands, and to develop course objectives, outlines, and instruction that can withstand the test of both professional scrutiny and academic certification.

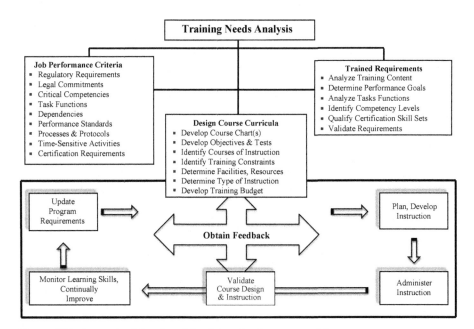

Figure 15.1 A meaningful and useful training development model.

The model has meaning and value to executives because it is sufficiently flexible to fit any security organization, large or small, public or private. It can be used to review existing courses or develop new acceptable training programs (Sullivant, 2007, pp. 185). This model has proven its value because is has shifted the compass of educational psychology from the traditional approach, which uses multiple types of questions to measure learning, to a balanced nexus of knowledge and performance-based measurement. Past and present innovative course designers, including myself, have continually advocated this approach for years, only to be set back by limited budgets or rebuked by superiors who lack an understanding of the full benefits and return on investment such a training approach can deliver.

Independent Research and Credence of the Model

Today, new evidence vindicates those who have demonstrated this vision. Many industry leaders are now benefiting from adopting this form of analytical analysis in training development. Two recent events can be credited with changing the learning landscape.

First, several recent security surveys report that most security violations, cyber breaches, theft, and noncompliance incidents occur because of ineptness, carelessness, resentfulness, non compliance, ignorance, and other employee motivational factors that contribute to low levels of proficiency and poor-quality work. These surveys show that:

- 62% of those surveyed say their behavior and performance had a low to moderate affect on security.[1] 48% of the employees surveyed claim that security policies did not apply to their job function.[2] 49% of the employees surveyed thought security was not their personal responsibility.[3]
- 58% of employees say they receive inadequate or poor training on the job.[4] 52% of the companies surveyed say they did not provide cyber security education to their employees.[5]
- A separate survey reported that 55% of government officials identify carless and untrained employees as the greatest source of security threat and low productivity at their agencies.[6]
- 53% of chief executive officers surveyed say the main risk to corporate America is human error, carelessness, ignorance, poor training of employees, and weak supervision.[7] The same number of chief executive officers also say accidents, security violations, and compliance issues result from undisciplined employees.[8]

---

[1] SolarWinds Federal Cyberfsecurity Survey Summary Report, March 26, 2014, Chantilly, VA 20151: http://docplayer.net/2500018-Solarwinds-federal-cybersecurity-survey-summary-report.html
[2] SolarWinds Federal Cybersecurity Survey Summary Report 2015, Chantilly, VA 20151: http-//www. solarwinds.com/resources/surveys/solarwinds-federal-cybersecurity-survey-summary-report-2015.aspx.webloc
[3] Ibid
[4] http://www.businesswire.com/news/home/20150420006379/en/LogRhythm-Survey-Finds-Employees-Place-Organizations-Risk
[5] Ponemon Institute surveyed more than 160,000 security professionals in 15 countries. Retrieved from: http://nsi.org/SecurityNewsWatch/NewsWatch/7.23.14.html/. Ibid
[6] SolarWinds Federal Cybersecurity Survey Summary Report 2015, Chantilly, VA 20151: http-//www. solarwinds.com/resources/surveys/solarwinds-federal-cybersecurity-survey-summary-report-2015.aspx.webloc
[7] IT Governance's Boardroom Cyber Watch Survey https://virtualizationandstorage.files.wordpress.com/2013/02/cyber-watch-survey-report-final.pdf
[8] SolarWinds Federal Cybersecurity Survey Summary Report 2015, Chantilly, VA 20151: http-//www. solarwinds.com/resources/surveys/solarwinds-federal-cybersecurity-survey-summary-report-2015.aspx.webloc

Second, an independent security industry survey of risks and professional competencies performed by the ASIS Foundation, in conjunction with its parent organization, ASIS International, and the University of Phoenix (2014), profoundly compliments the reliability of many of the case histories I report throughout the pages of this book, as well as my training needs analysis model. Survey results add further credence to the concept of "vulnerability creep-in" presented in Chapter The Many Faces of Vulnerability Creep-in.

When the ASIS Foundation invited 483 members of ASIS International who hold executive or senior-level positions to participate in a survey to identify security risks, challenges, and professional competencies, they performed a great service to the security profession. The ASIS Foundations partner, the University of Phoenix, provided an even greater service when the university system validated the survey findings with quantitative data, thus helping to verify and prioritize the identified security risks, challenges, and critical competencies.

Challenges identified by the University of Phoenix include, but are not limited to, the following:

- Aging workforce and loss of management knowledge base
- Managing issues and limited budgets
- Managing scarce resources
- Use of security technology or information technology

The purposes of this book, critical competencies are those skill sets needed by security professionals—particularly senior officials—who are placed in a position of trust to:

- advance corporate goals and objectives
- provide advice to executive management and the senior staff
- exhibit leadership traits in all settings
- train others to the proficiency levels demanded by the mission, regulatory guidance, and other obligations

With respect to senior security professionals, the University of Phoenix analysis validated and prioritized 22 critical security competencies. I summarize these leadership competencies and their management categories, as reported by the University of Phoenix, in Fig. 15.2. Security Competencies

Based on survey results documented by those individuals surveyed, the University of Phoenix then ranked the competencies and divided them into the three categories shown in Fig. 15.2: most critical, medium critical, and least critical. The listing does not represent my order preference. I contend that the particular industry sector and the affected security organization would determine the meaningful value and criticality of each competency when measured against the importance of its particular mission goals and objectives. For instance, I suggest that:

- "Technological excellence," although rated least critical, would certainly carry significant weight in a national research, development, evaluation, and test environment, placing it in the most critical category. I served more than ten years in a national and international Research, Development, Test and Evaluation (RDT&E) arena working with the National Nuclear Security Agency under the START Treaty and at the Air Force Test & Evaluation Center having an active security management responsibility for the Space Shuttle Program.

Competencies By Critical Rank Order	Management Category
Most Critical Competencies	
Decision making	Organizational leadership
Oral communication	Communicating with others
Critical thinking	Organizational leadership
Maximizing performance of others	Focusing on people
Persuasive influencing	Communicating with others
Medium Critical Competencies	
Collaboration	Focusing on people
Anticipatory thinking	Organizational leadership
Organizational compliance	Organizational leadership
Self-regulation	Organizational leadership
Balancing priorities	Organizational leadership
Aligning organizational objectives	Organizational leadership
Security-related literacy	Industry & technological knowledge
Message development	Communicating with others
Business and financial literacy	Industry & technological knowledge
Enterprise risk assessment	Organizational leadership
Enterprise risk management	Organizational leadership
Succession planning	Focusing on people
Least Critical Competencies	
Global awareness	Industry & technological knowledge
Public speaking	Communicating with others
Technological excellence	Industry & technological knowledge
Multicultural versatility	Focusing on people
International & multicultural competence	Focusing on people

Aligning organizational objectives identifies and implements security-related goals that align with overall corporate goals and comply with regulatory standards.

Anticipatory thinking proactively seeks to identify potential security industry risks, and develop and implement strategic plans to address long- and short-term goals to ensure organizational preparedness to mitigate and respond to risks.

Balancing priorities takes actions that demonstrate a balance between security needs and individual rights.

Business and financial literacy exhibits sufficient business, financial, and legal understanding to speak the language of company executives, make the case for the return on investment of the security functions, develop meaningful business recommendations, and successfully deploy security strategies that align with corporate goals.

Collaboration accomplishes security-related work activities and goals by effectively working with a diverse group of people in a team environment and engaging others in best practices.

Critical thinking gathers and analyzes data, using logic and reasoning, to make sound short- and long-term security-related business decisions.

Decision making makes sound, fact-based, and timely security-related decisions, even when under pressure, that reflect the long- and short-term security interests of the organization.

Enterprise risk assessment proactively uses knowledge or risk assessment theories and crisis indicators to effectively recognize crises or potential disasters.

Enterprise risk management takes a holistic approach to risk management, working to breakdown silos between physical and technological security and provide comprehensive risk management solutions.

Figure 15.2 Security competencies.
Source: University of Phoenix, Security Industry Survey of Risks and Professional Competencies, ASIS Foundation (2014).

Global awareness is the understanding of global security issues and how the organization will compete to successfully achieve security-related business objectives worldwide.

International and multicultural competence seeks understanding of perspectives, traditions, values, and practices of culturally diverse individuals and applies understanding to perform security-related tasks effectively.

Maximizing performance of others supports, encourages, and helps other security professionals achieve their full potential, and coaches and provides effective learning resources and experiences to help other security professionals maintain security systems and follow protocols.

Message development develops and delivers messages that need to be communicated to audiences.

Multicultural versatility adapts one's own behavior to demonstrate proper and culturally appropriate behavior when dealing with others from different cultures and countries on security-related issues.

Oral communication expresses thoughts verbally in a clear, succinct, logical, and organized manner.

Organizational compliance develops, follows, and enforces standard security operations procedures and crisis/emergency protocols.

Persuasive influencing uses compelling communication to persuade others to listen and commit to, and act on, security-related issues.

Security-related literacy stays abreast of security industry trends and best practices and maintains access to current industry data to inform organizational decision-making and operations.

Self-regulation remains in control and calm when under pressure to identify resources and lead others when responding to and recovering from emergencies.

Succession planning anticipates long-range security staffing needs and develops the internal talent necessary to support the organization's strategy.

Technological excellence proactively seeks to maintain and expand hard science, technology, engineering and math knowledge needed to perform tasks involving security-related technologies and understand emerging information technology security solutions and system integration processes.

Figure 15.2   Continued.

- "Business financial literacy," rated medium critical, would command a most critical rating for those associated with the banking and financial industry or involved in investigating financial fraud, waste, and embezzlement. My experience in banking and financial security projects has taught me that the business lexicon is an essential communications tool, not only in the banking and financial industry but in every industry. I emphasize communicating with executive management in chapter Effectively Communicating with Executives and Boards.
- Last, in a high-risk, highly visible international security arena, "multicultural versatility" and "international multicultural competence" would play an important role in sensitive multicultural business and government environments, being noteworthy of a most critical rating in most international settings. While serving on the United States Air Forces Command Staff along side my NATO staff peers, I worked closely with representatives of all NATO countries in highly visible and uncertain environments and situations. I also was involved in several private enterprise projects in South Korea, Zambia, Greece and Turkey. The exercise of diplomacy and discretion in dealing with cultural diversity, including respective national customs, traditions and norms coupled with uncertainty and highly visible political exposure

in all international assignments was crucial. I am convinced that one cannot perform well in this type of environment without understanding and being sensitive to culture diversity when leading and working with ethically diverse teams, including high government officials.

Criticality of competencies can also take on a very different meaning and value when analyzed in light of a security organization's critical operational competencies, such as deterrence, delay, prevention, protection, assessment, responding to, and recovering from a terrorist act, criminal activity, industrial mishap, manmade or natural disaster, or weather-related calamities. These activities call for leadership traits necessary to direct security forces and other company employees in times of crisis, saving lives and further preventing damage or destruction to assets.

These competencies are discussed later in the chapter. For now, it is important to know that in navigating through the model, the experienced analyst needs to have advanced knowledge of the risks that might cause harm or loss to the enterprise, the challenges that might impede security's development, cohesiveness and effectiveness in responding to risks, and the political-social sensitivity of the work environment.

A good means for determining training needs for senior security professionals is to review the research accomplished by the University of Phoenix[9] and other fine research institutions with your own independent research, and adopt the results to fit your needs. While there never is a single solution for all expectations, survey findings do perform a very important function. Survey results can act as a benchmark to measure the existing performance of senior security professionals by identifying gaps in their performance effectiveness. Corporations can fare well by developing industry-aligned academic and training programs that adequately prepare security professionals, security workforce members, and enterprise employees for security risks, challenges, and competencies.

To date, however, there exists no agreed-upon, complete set of competencies used across all roles and levels of the security force. Nor do binding, uniform educational guidelines for organizations exist to develop these competencies. This training model, tailored to fit your needs, can address these deficits by subscribing to guidelines that meet your day-to-day requirements as well as emergency needs. Whenever your thinking and planning are in doubt, applying the duty to care principle (discussed in Chapter The Many Faces of Vulnerability Creep-in) may offer you a reasonable and prudent solution to a practical problem.

Performing a training needs analysis as the first step in the training developmental process. This involves four tasks: identify job performance criteria, identify trained personnel requirements, analyze existing training programs, and design the curricula.

Identify Job Performance Criteria

This involves researching the sources that create the job activity. Sources can be regulatory requirements, legal commitments, company policy that addresses the specific aspects of job activity (eg, why, when, where, how), job descriptions, and results

---

[9] Security Industry Survey of Risks & Professional Competencies, University of Phoenix, 2014.

of independent studies and case histories embedded through this book, including the competency study by the University of Phoenix. This research and analysis results in baseline training requirements that are subject to identifying trained personnel requirements and training limitations and constraints.

Identify Trained Personnel Requirements

This involves researching how the regulatory, legal, or policy requirements for the job activity directly affect specific performance needs at the job level. Not all aspects of a particular job require formal training, and those tasks need to be filtered out of the course curricula. In many instances filtered tasks are better suited for on-the-job training rather than a formal academic setting. (More on this topic in a moment.)

Analyze Current Training Programs

The purpose of evaluating security training is to:

- identify deficiencies and gaps in the proficiency of the security workforce
- determine the adequacy and usability of instruction given
- identify training needs against requirements to determine what modifications or new training programs are necessary to provide skill sets and knowledge base to meet the demands of the job
- assess emerging training needs to develop on-target, "just-in-time" training programs that meet the needs of the security organization
- function as a platform for developing and validating new training needs

Design the Curricula

The architecture of a sound training program comprise curricula course charts, course outlines, student populations, facility requirements, and training materials. The best training approach is one that provides student-centered instruction that presents the knowledge and skills that are essential to perform the current job or proficiency training oriented toward preparing individuals for a future promotion or job. Regardless of the training goal, training programs should focus on building a culture of security to act securely and responsibly.

An effective means for accomplishing these goals is to:

- conduct a training analysis to identify job performance criteria against trained personnel requirements
- design and deliver training facilities and training aids and materials to support training objectives
- design and validate the course and conduct instruction
- continually evaluate the effectiveness, efficiency, and productivity of training and make mid-course adjustments to enhance and improve training to keep current with the business environment, including new processes and practices

Types of Security Awareness Training Programs

Building security awareness means creating a corporate-wide appreciation for how security is fundamentally integrated into day-to-day business operations. A focused security awareness program reduces risk exposure and enhances personal protection. Corporate security awareness programs may consist of, but are not necessarily limited to, the following topics.

The Employee Security Awareness and Emergency Response Training Program

Employees want to feel safe and secure in the workplace. Employee security awareness training should be given to all new and transferring employees. To have meaning and value, training should be directed toward security policies, procedures, and requirements that are particular to the general workforce. At a minimum, everyone should have a general knowledge of:

- threats facing the corporation
- the threat alert notification system
- assigned emergency response responsibilities
- how to report security incidents or unusual occurrences
- what to do in the event of emergency

Persons granted unescorted entry into restricted or controlled areas should:

- receive orientation training on entry control procedures
- understand methods to verify someones right and need to be in the area
- understand the responsibilities and duties of an escort official
- understand methods used to gain unauthorized entry to such areas

Specialized Security Training for Designated Enterprise Employees

Selected middle managers, first-line supervisors, and other persons should receive training designed to maintain proficiency and keep this group apprised of threats, security practices, protocols, and mission changes that affect corporate business security goals. First responders should receive additional comprehensive training to effectively carry out their assigned responsibilities with assurance that their personal security will not be jeopardized. The sections below describe some sample courses.

Emergency Operations Center Responder Training

This training prepares employees assigned to the corporate crisis management center to perform assigned duties.

Emergency Preparedness Training

This training provides to corporate first responders training to respond to varying threat scenarios, such as a bomb threat, active shooter fire, explosion, environmental contamination medical emergency, and building evacuation.

Cyber Security Training

This training provides designated employees training to safeguard the information technology network and telecommunications systems.

Security Alert Status and Security Reporting Protocols

This training provides managers and operators of command centers and control rooms the interrelationship of critical time-sensitive and time-dependent security reporting requirements and actions to take that are associated with the threat alert notification system.

Contamination Detection and Surveillance

This training provides designated engineers, scientists, laboratory technicians, and field personnel with the training necessary to use and test environmental monitoring devices, analyze and interpret results, and take appropriate emergency response actions, as needed.

Executive Management Security Awareness Seminars

This training is for corporate officers and other decision makers who must be aware of the security programs from a business perspective. Security awareness training for this group focuses on strategic issues. For them to fulfill their responsibilities, it is essential that they have a clear, concise, and unambiguous understanding of the threat, its consequences, security planning strategies, and security operations. Security training courses for the senior management staff could include, but are limited to, the following:

Crisis Management Training for Staff Members

This training provides orientation training to decision makers with respect to assigned crisis management roles and responsibilities.

Security Strategies and Security Planning Seminar

This training provides to decision makers a clear, concise, and unambiguous understanding of relevant and effective security strategies that will foster public confidence. It can include security emergency and business continuity planning to sustain business operations, and the application of integrated security, security-related, and safety principles.

Executive Protection Seminars

This training provides to executive management an overview of protective requirements against kidnapping, hostage taking, personal assault, and mobility vulnerabilities. It may also include preventive and protective measures for the protection of self and family members, within the residence as well as in other locations.

Specialized Security Staff Training Program

Formal training and certification requirements for the security staff are vital in building a stable security force culture and operational capability. The purpose of this training is to develop specific skills and capabilities that the person being trained will regularly use on the job. Here are some samples.

Security Officer Training

This training, performed when an employee is initially hired, provides security officers with administrative orientation and training to qualify for basic security duties and responsibilities.

Flight, Seas Coast, or River Observer Training

Where corporate aviation and water security assets and resources are used to support security operations, this training provides selected security officers with the necessary skill sets to conduct security air and water surveillance operations to determine the status of ground conditions, the ability to direct responding ground forces to the location requiring a specific security response, and to call in additional responders as required.

Workplace Violence Training

This training provides security officers with an understanding of basic tactics and methods to use when responding to workplace violence incidents on corporate property or when assisting the human resources office in processing disgruntled or hostile terminated, or other potentially dangerous employees.

Emergency Security Response Procedure Training

This training provides security officers and security supervisors with proficiency-level certification training for responding to varying event-driven scenarios. This training may include intelligence gathering, analyzing the scene, field tactics, fields of fire, self-defense techniques, and communications.

Security System Operation, Maintenance, and Testing

This training provides proficiency (certification) training to security force members who are responsible for operating, maintaining, and testing integrated security systems. Training include how to override selected system parameters, temporarily block individuals enrolled in the system from gaining access to restricted areas, generating security management information reports, and performing critical system functions necessary to protect the integrity of the system or safety of personnel.

Security System Enrollment Training

This training provides designated security members with proficiency (certification) skills to prepare and issue identification credentials, to enroll personnel in the system with approved access levels, and, when necessary, to remove individuals from the system when given the proper authorization to do so.

Special Security Event Training

This training provides designated security members with training required to support special corporate activities such as open houses, social events, or other gatherings, usually on a one-time or infrequent basis.

Security Management Training

This training provides security supervisors with the means to distinguish the severity of a threat, apply deductive analysis, and effectively determine the appropriate tactics and methods to use when responding to a threat scenario.

Security System Administration Training

This training provides designated security staff members with proficiency (certification) skills to adjust system parameters and perform detailed diagnostic testing.

Course Design Brings Instruction to Life

Designing a course in collaboration with the corporate human resources division ensures the continuity of learning concepts, operations, requirement, practices, responses to security incidents, and security alert conditions and actions, as well as the uniformity of quality instruction. Training new employees—particularly security officers—can be a scheduling challenge. Obstacles such as availability, work priorities, and overtime pay can directly affect the quality of training and learning. You must plan, develop, and implement training needs in a manner that is cost-effective to your organization. The following instructional techniques and methods are beneficial management tools to use for course planning and design consideration.

Classroom Instruction

The lecture method is a common method for sharing information and facts, particularly for large groups. This approach is mostly used to address basic general training topics.

Instruction, coupled with other learning techniques, can be effective when the instructor, students, education tools, and the learning environment are closely integrated with the use of audiovisual aids such as charts, graphs, slides, videos, chalk boards, and models. Instruction may be conducted during any shift or at other times such as a scheduled training day. This training includes:

- theory and application of principles
- new protocols, processes, and practices
- problem-solving exercises

Computerized and Programmed Instruction

This instruction can be modular and self-paced, and can be scheduled at any time based on work priorities, availability of resources, and just-in-time training objectives. Both computerized and programmed instruction are effective one-on-one learning tools.

Through the use of a computerized self-paced design, learning materials can be repeated as often as necessary so the student can master the material at his or her own pace. This method of instruction can take place on the job, during all shifts, 24/7. The approach is cost-effective because no special training day for an individual or group is required, only a time frame, such as 30 days, to complete the lesson. Using a corporate-provided network, trainees can access information for any subject matter, any time. Tests can easily be administered at the end of the learning presentation, with the trainee instantly knowing how well he or she did. Should the results of the learning effort be unsatisfactory, the system provides instructions on what to expect next. Results are recorded instantaneously in the trainee's personnel file, with a summary printout provided to the trainee's immediate supervisor.

Programmed instruction is presented in written form. This instruction follows the same path as computerized instruction but is completed more slowly because it requires more reading time to cover the course material. The material is presented in a series of carefully planned and interdependent learning modules. The trainee controls the process and moves ahead only after learning and understanding each previous step. Programmed instruction, as with computerized instruction, does not present a scheduling problem. It can be accomplished independently and on the job. The supervisor or training manager provides immediate feedback and offers tutorial assistance for any problem area that may be encountered by the trainee, and records the results of training in the trainee's file.

Correspondence Study/Training Bulletins

This method of instruction consists of passing on information during guard mounts and posting information on bulletin boards or at specific post assignments that are affected by the material. Personnel are empowered to read the training bulletins during the work shift, as time permits. It is a quick and effective way to distribute a new process or procedure that significantly affects security operations. This method is time sensitive, and its implementation requires immediate execution. To ensure the protocol is understood, supervisors, under this training concept, make regular (but unscheduled) visits to each post and:

- ask specific questions about the new protocol
- observe the security officer in an actual situation involving protocol application
- set up a hypothetical situation requiring the security officer to demonstrate his or her working knowledge of the protocol

Seminars

This learning technique is effective for small groups and combines presentation, visual aids, materials, and participation across a broad spectrum of learning objectives. It offers the opportunity to enhance team-building skills, professionalism, social behavior, and decision-making competencies. Materials are often distributed to attendees before the start of the seminar so they can be prepared to participate in the session based on the review of the material. Discussion involves theories, concepts, and their effective application through demonstrative planning problem-solving skills.

On-the-Job Training

On-the-job training (OJT) is performed on the job. OJT involves learning by doing, watching and listening while actually working the job in the actual work environment under actual work conditions. It also involves a trainer or the supervisor observing and monitoring the physical skill-sets learned and the degree of associated knowledge gleamed from performing the job. Such training increases a security officer's skills and knowledge, measures his or her understanding and application of both existing and new practices and processes, tests new skills and knowledge, and permits the supervisor to make immediate midcourse adjustments to correct noted weaknesses and deficiencies in understanding or in applying skill sets. One-on-one or group OTJ occurs when the supervisor observes the ongoing performance of the security officer and provides immediate feedback in response to situations that were not correct or where the security officer hesitates or appears unsure or confused.

Field Training (or Drills and Exercises)

This approach is used to demonstrate motor skills, critical thinking, and team-building skill sets during a crisis. It may include such competencies as:

- assault line
- AWAT or combat tactics

- building and area search techniques
- command, control, and communications
- coordination with internal and external agencies
- fields of fire and suppression fire
- force protection   .
- ground intelligence
- leadership
- map and compass reading
- patrolling and blocking forces
- perimeter control
- preservation and control of the affected area
- response techniques
- retrograde maneuvering and withdrawal techniques
- tactical deployment techniques
- terrain association

Practical exercises demonstrate the application of theories and concepts through appropriate event-driven actions. Realistic exercises serve several purposes. They allow management to:

- assess plans and procedures to determine their feasibility under actual conditions
- assess whether personnel understand their emergency response functions and duties
- identify areas for continual improvement
- enhance coordination, communication, and proficiency among the participants
- enhance the ability of management and the staff to respond to crisis
- use results of exercises as lessons learned

Field training exercises are used to present employees with situations that might actually be experienced on the job but cannot readily taught or performed by any other learning technique. Attendees are expected to take actions that would actually be executed during an actual encounter with an adversary or hostile force under real-time conditions. The advantage of such training is that time can be compressed and long periods of delay can be telescoped into the amount of time allocated for the exercise. Participants learn from simulation and imitation experience without paying the price of making wrong decisions or taking incorrect actions in an actual encounter with a hostile individual or group. Experience gained and errors committed during field training exercises offer valuable insights to the planning process and build strong individual and group bonds and levels of confidence. Drills and exercises also serve to enhance the public image of the corporation and increase the confidence level of employees, management, and the community.

Objectives and Scope of Security Field Training and Exercises

Drills and exercises are an integral part of the overall corporate emergency planning effort. To the extent feasible and practical, security exercises should always be incorporated within corporate-wide exercises. The security director, however, usually conducts field-training exercises independent of other corporate business units. Security exercises provide the opportunity to test skills and knowledge in order to identify strengths and weaknesses; learn new skills; practice decision-making, techniques, and communications; and determine gaps in existing plans, procedures, and practices. Four types of learning can be achieved by performing training exercises:

* learning by doing
* learning through imitation
* learning through observation and feedback
* learning through repeated trials
* learning through video replay of actions and direct critique

Planning Security Field Training and Exercises

Planning considerations include:

* individual and group safety, including equipment safety
* use of equipment and communications used on the job
* participation in the actual work environment and under simulated threat conditions
* the ability to control the environment to bring about conditions that will obtain desired responses from participants
* immediate direct feedback to a decision a participant might make

The security director works with other staff members and local community authorities to determine the type of field training and exercises to be performed, the scope of involvement, and exercise limitations. Exercises are structured and organized in a manner in which results can measure performance in the following areas:

* capability to implement extended work schedule
* crisis management organization and leadership
* evaluation of response time
* inspection of equipment and demonstrated knowledge of its care and usage
* interaction and coordination within defined groups
* dependency groups internal and external to the security organization and the corporation
* mobilization of personnel and equipment in response to an emergency
* response tactics and decision making
* safety and force protection
* supportability of other divisions' emergency response actions
* timeline to provide expanded security coverage and duration of coverage

Developing Security Field Training and Exercise Scenarios

Developing security exercise scenarios requires an extensive knowledge of adversaries' modes of attack, their capabilities, and previous activities. It involves a great deal of research, planning, and coordination; strict controls; and approval from all levels of management. Serious effort is made to combine the appearance of reality with training controls so that the transfer of learning to the job is optimized. The security director, supported by other members of the security and corporate staff, develops realistic preplanned drills, condition simulations, field problems, and scenarios.

The goal of planning field exercises is threefold. *First*, and most important, a key ingredient of planning, developing, and implementing security drills and exercises is to prevent placing exercise personnel and those who are on duty but not involved in the exercise at risk of injury. Any and all scenarios must refrain from carrying out any action that confronts on-duty security officers, contract guards, members of a support force, or other employees with deceptions, which can:

- interfere with actual security operations in progress
- distract them from performing their assigned security mission
- be interpreted as a hostile act
- jeopardize the safety of individuals or the security of assets
- induce the use of deadly force
- instill in employees performing routine duties a sense of fear or uncertainty that a real attack may be occurring

Forcible breaches of a boundary barrier, failure to heed a security challenge, and similar overt actions are examples of prohibited deceptions.

Second, scenarios must be designed to demonstrate how well the security organization can perform its critical operational mission to deter, detect, delay, assess, respond to, and recover from a variety of threatening security or security-related events, while concurrently supporting corporate business goals.

Third, scenarios must capture how security leaders demonstrate critical competencies such as decision making, oral communications, critical thinking, maximizing the performance of others, persuasive influencing, and other important competencies under stressful conditions.

Inherent in exercising these competencies is the effectiveness of command, control, and communications among all participants. Equally important is the public relations department announcing company-wide exercises within the community in advance to alert the public (and government) of the training exercise. Fig. 15.3 graphically illustrates a suggested approach to measuring security performance during field training or drills and exercises. Since the threat situation is not a static entity, neither should its measurement metric. In Fig. 15.3, Scenario 1 offers security management the flexibility to add to the metric any of the threats previously discussed in earlier chapters, or to accommodate any unique threat area(s) of meaningful value to the executive management team. This simple tailoring process allows you to measure the results of any threat scenario that may be important to you at a particular time.

Scenario 1 - Critical Operational Competencies by Selected Threat Venues & Modes of Attack Metric

Selected Threat Venues Modes of Attack	Critical Security Operational Competencies					
	Deter	Delay	Detect	Assess	Respond to	Recover from
Bomb threat						
Penetration attack						
Destruction of critical asset						
Air contamination						
Frontal attack						
Impersonation scheme						
Kidnapping						
Shooter incident						
Train/tanker accident						

Legend:

Effectiveness	Numerical Rating	ID Rating	Performance Measurements
High	0.90	H_E	Positive evidence of competency to address threat
Moderate	0.50	M_E	General evidence of competency to address threat
Low	0.10	L_E	Little, ineffective, or no evidence of competency to address threat

Figure 15.3 Critical operational capabilities and competency under stressful engagement with adversary.

In Fig. 15.3, Scenario 2 equally is not a static activity. This metric addresses a large-scale event that calls into play several independent yet inseparable critical competencies that could determine the outcome of a given security event beyond the execution of actual tactical movements, deployment techniques, or other battle formations and engagement activities.

Conducting Exercises

Typically, three types of exercises are used by the industry: tabletop, limited, and full-scale. Tabletop exercises involve the review of plans, maps, charts, diagrams, drawings, protocols, checklists, and processes to ensure clarity and purpose of execution. These reviews should be performed using the guidelines offered in Chapter A User-Friendly Protocol Development Model. The review also includes emergency response plans and event-driven response and recovery procedures. A good idea is to walk through the various scenarios with key participants to determine their understanding and knowledge of the subject matter, as well as their rationale for selecting a course of action in response to a particular threat scenario and to give personnel the opportunity to ask questions. Tabletop exercises help to build confidence in both the management staff and in those individuals who are expected to respond to crisis.

Scenario 2 - Critical Competencies Under Stressful Engagement with a Hostile Force

Critical Competencies	High	Moderate	Low
Command, control, & communications			
Contain/neutralize adversary			
Coordination/collaboration			
Critical thinking*			
Decision making & leadership*			
Deployment techniques			
Fields of fire & suppression fire			
Force protection			
Inspection of personal gear & equipment			
Maximizing performance of others*			
Oral communication & message delivery*			
Personal hygine & safe use of equipment			
Persuasive influencing*			
Preserve evidence & control access to area			
Secure/control affected area			
Take custody of adversaries			
Retrograde movement & recover			
Withdrawal			
Team building & succession planning*			

Legend:

Effectiveness	Numerical Rating	ID Rating	Competency Measurement
High	0.90	H_E	Positive evidence of competency to perform task
Moderate	0.50	M_E	General evidence of competency to perform task
Low	0.10	L_E	Little, ineffective, or no evidence of competency to perform task

* Denote items that are critical competencies listed by the University of Phoenix in its security survey analysis.

Figure 15.3 Continued.

Limited security exercises are activities internal to the security organization. They serve as training sessions and planning for corporate full-scale exercises scheduled in the future. These exercises allow the security organization to run practice drills during security operations with available on-duty security personnel.

Full-scale security exercises are conducted in concert with corporate-wide drills and exercises. It is highly recommended that a full-scale corporate exercise involving a bomb explosion or a chemical, biological, and radiological attack, or any incident that requires the evacuation of a building or major complex, the establishment of an emergency safety area, or the participation by community first responders, be conducted at least annually.

Lessons Learned

It is important that security organizations evaluate their vulnerability posture after each major security incident, disaster, industrial mishap, and field-training exercise to help improve practices, confidence, and response capabilities. In addition, the lessons learned process should be used to identify new security priorities and investment, take advantage of emerging approaches and new technologies, and perpetuate a proactive security culture throughout the corporation.

Professional Development Is Key for Security Planners

For all practical purposes, except for attending an accredited university security management program—such as that at the University of Phoenix or other equally fine universities—this training may only be able to be applied through self-imposed research, reading, correspondence courses, observation of other leaders, and learning to excel in using the critical competences discussed in this chapter.

Benefits Management Enjoys by Adopting the Model

The benefits of training help to improve security organizational performance and individual and group proficiency, while increasing security awareness; unit effectiveness, efficiency, and productivity; and security resilience. This model leads to the solid development of training programs that encompass just-in-time training involving individuals, groups, and agencies that personnel work with in real incidents in the actual work environment.

Conclusions

To create an overall effective security organization, including a useful and meaningful training program, it is important to create first a security culture that is curious about error, or unsatisfactory performance, rather than one that has a "shoot the messenger" mentality where retribution and punishment are expected, and thus reporting is avoided.

Curiosity is a sign of willingness to learn why things are not as they seem and is a starting point for change. Training widens the understanding of human performance and social behavior, and the workplace environment, and reinforces practical skills and important reminders, such as lessons learned from previous exercises and drills.

It is important to note that the complexity of the subject matter being taught largely guides the method of instruction. Other course design considerations include class size and student background; learning objectives and level of proficiency to be obtained; quality and expertise of the faculty; adequacy of facilities, equipment, and training aids; and available training time.

When carried out according to its intensions, training strengthens organizational values and attitudes; improves individual and group proficiency; and builds confidence in the workforce, security management, executive management, boards, and, where appropriate, regulators and other governing bodies. Training therefore serves as a platform to implement change solutions to operational and behavioral problems.

How to Communicate with Executives and Governing Bodies

The only thing more difficult than talking is listening, and most of us rarely are good at doing either, particularly when the topics are security, safety or the budget. Always say things that matter and speak in a language management understands.

John Sullivant

Top Takeaways

- objectivity and perception in the security world
- formulate a proactive relationship with executive management
- fact-finding and effectively communicating ideas
- think and speak in a language executives understand
- communicate with the C-suite and gain their buy-in
- CEOs need value information from you
- deliver powerful persuasive presentations
- build and defend a business case before executive management
- deliver meaningful options and alternatives the CEO can use
- listening and responding to questions

Overview

Chief executive officers (CEOs) reveal the corporate vision and then encourage, cheerlead, direct, and organize the company to work toward goals and objectives. Successful CEOs focus on things that matter, communicate constantly, have limited objectives, finish projects or stop those that need to be stopped, and support people. To achieve these goals, CEOs expect their senior security professional to focus on tomorrow rather than on yesterday by providing substantive updates, realizing that not all news is good news, always saying things that matter and that executives and governing bodies do not already know, and speaking to them in the language they understand, care about, and can act on.

Why Would a CEO Ever Ask You for Help?

Executives need advice from people who see the world from their perspective. They have a great need for a trusted source of unbiased information, to hear hard truths quickly, and should not be the last to know what is happening. As an executive's senior security professional, your perspective matters if problem solving is about tomorrow, even if the topic is about yesterday's mistake; you need to use time wisely and say things that matter in a brief, candid, and powerful way.

To be of value to your CEO you must have at your fingertips important security-related business knowledge that helps the business run. This calls for the ability to extract wisdom and useful conclusions from unrelated information and facts at a moment's notice. It calls for developing expertise beyond your security responsibilities and to understanding the broader issues the company faces. This includes providing advance warning plus options for solving (or at least managing) trouble or opportunity, and the unintended consequences both bring to the table. This also means helping with the dynamics of dealing with the board of directors with respect and preserving the corporation from realistic threats. You must also understand the pattern of events and issues that matter to the business so you can plan for them. How can you do this? The answer is simple: know what executives are trying to accomplish, what motivates them, what matters to them, the problems they face, how they think and make decisions, and how they achieve success. Do these things and you will gain management's attention, trust, confidence, and loyalty.

CEOs also expect you to respond through real-time, face-to-face communications between C-suite executives, the board of directors, managers, and subordinates. However, face time with the CEO matters only when the advice you give matters, and only if such advice can help the CEO run the company better, thereby making tomorrow better. For example, show how security initiatives contribute to the corporation keeping money, making money, and saving money. If you can do these things well, you will gain the respect and trust of C-suite executives and others.

Why Should a Chief Executive Listen to You?

Right from the start, first impressions tell the story of your upbringing, education, demeanor, dependability, and reliability. Taint any one of these personal attributes and your image, brand, and reputation can begin to falter. CEOs look for these attributes in their senior security professional because they are fundamentally important to effective decision making based on uncertainty, oral communications, critical thinking, structured brain storming, conceptual analysis, maximizing other's performance, and persuasive influencing.

CEOs communicate verbally and talk in the future tense about tomorrow and beyond, and often about territory no one yet owns or occupies. It is up to the staff to digest and translate the CEOs vision into a narrative that can be shared by the board of directors and those tasked with implementing that vision. That is the purpose of having a trusted staff. As security director, you fill a major trusted advisory role on this staff.

As a security professional in a key leadership role, you wear two hats in which you must be equally competent. You are an operational line manager as well as a trusted senior advisor to executive management. In the former position you manage and direct security operations. In this role you oversee activities that range from enforcing security practices to offering related services such as patrolling, crime prevention, site and facility protection to responding to and investigating incidents. In the latter position—which is still in its infancy in many organizations—you fulfill a corporate staff management role with great potential for becoming an influential voice in executive management's ear. In this role you focus on the strategic vision, planning, developing, and implementing policies and best practices, and cohesively integrating the various security programs that enhance and improve corporate security resilience. Some organizations have recognized the value and benefit of this capability and have propelled the security director into a " trusted consulting role" providing advice directly to the CEO, other C-suite executives, and the board of directors. Other corporations are holding back in making this change.

By default, you are the point person for all security matters, with the awesome responsibility to brief and update the CEO, senior staff, and the board of directors. And you must use the language they understand, care about, and can act on. You will gain the attention of the CEO as long as:

• you think, act, and talk security strategy from a business perspective
• the CEO trusts your advice
• the CEO believes you have a sense of what it takes to achieve success

As you move up in responsibility, authority, and accountability, this trust becomes increasingly crucial. Here are some tips that can help you be successful:

• Speak the language executives understand, care about, and can act on.
• Impressions count: focus on the future and develop a management perception.
• Be a verbal visionary. Be that window for tomorrow.
• Be trustworthy, candid, and professional. Give advice constructively.
• Build a solid business case. Know when to pull your parachute cord.

Let me briefly summarize each of these tips.

Speak the Language Executives and Board Members Understand, Care About, and Can Act On

You must learn to blend security terminology sparingly with management's language to get your message across in a clear and simple manner. If you can master management's language and apply its usage to your organization, you will receive a very positive reception when dealing with the executive team.

Communicating With Executives and Board Members Is a Work in Progress

Communications is not a one-time adventure. It is a continuous journey with no end. Every time you write a memo, every time you talk on the phone or speak one-on-one or to a group—it is a continuous saga. To be successful in your communications with executives and board members, you must never bother this group with detail or trivia, Always keep your message, simple, short and to the point, and logically organized.

When you offer too much information, or overly complicate the goal you are trying to achieve, or exhibit poor organization skills-sets, your message becomes confusing and distorted, making it hard to relate your topic to wider business strategies that do not relevant to executive and board decision making.

Use Terms Management Understands and Can Act on

So, how do you speak to management in ways that are valuable and useful or strategic? *First,* seek to learn before speaking. *Second,* when you do speak, speak the language management uses because that is what they understand. While they may be familiar with some general security terms, they may not understand most professional and technical terms you customarily use when communicating with other security professionals. Saturating your message with security language when communicating with executives will not get that message across. Below is a short list of terms that resonate with executive management.

• Alternatives	• Perspective
• Asset protection	• Process strategy
• Best practices	• Productivity
• Business strategic vision	• Profitable deployments
• Capital investment	• Profit margin
• Competitive intelligence	• Quality assurance
• Cost-effective	• Quality controls
• Crisis consulting	• Return on investment
• Crisis management	• Risk avoidance
• Customer loyalty management	• Risk reduction
• Customer reengineering	• Risk exposure
• Downstream impact analysis	• Risk management
• Exposure management	• Risk transfer
• Financial exposure and protection	• Staff development
• Image, brand, and reputation	• Stay the Course
• Internal/external dependencies	• Strategic planning
• Link analysis	• Supply chain impact
• Management development	• Team building
• Mid-stream adjustments	• Total quality management
• Motivation strategy	• Troubleshooting
• Operating capital	• Trusted agent
• Operationally focused	• Unintended consequence
• Operational review and analysis	• Upstream impact analysis
• Options	• Validation
• Partnering	

For some, learning to communicate with executives using a nonsecurity vocabulary may be a new experience, but if you want management to listen to and understand your message, you must step up to the challenge by learning management's lexicon. A good source for finding business terms relevant to your corporation and industry is the language used throughout corporate plans, policies, directives, general correspondence, financial and marketing literature and formal conversations.

To be useful, for example, security information must have value and meaning to the CEO and be presented in a business context: What is the risk exposure? What do we do if? Where do we stand on security performance? productivity? What about our profit margin? One way to get your message across to management is to demonstrate how security values complement business values: express these relationships in business context, and explain how security activities contribute to making money, keeping money, saving money, and protecting the corporation's investments.

Impressions Count

Getting your message across to management involves not only substance but also appearance and demeanor; style and body and facial language; speech and voice; and image, brand, and reputation creditability. Lets take a moment to review each of these attributes.

Appearance and Demeanor

First impressions are lasting impressions. Clothes and personal appearance send powerful messages before you even say a word. Clothing and accessories indicate who you think you are and what others think of you. Clothes help you fit in as well as stand out. Dress according to your company's dress code and what is customary for the occasion. The better you appear the better impression you will make.

Style and Body and Facial Language

Style, facial expressions, eye contact, smiles, and gestures add a distinct personality to your message and inspire understanding and confidence. Posture and gestures reveal what you think of yourself and your audience. Rigidness communicates anxiety and insecurity. Be alert but not tense. Be relaxed but not too relaxed. Be self-aware. Use gestures to convey a feeling or to emphasize a point.

Speech and Voice

Choose words that create a favorable impression with the listener. Eye contact and a quality voice pitch make for enthusiasm, informality, humor, and sincerity. Good volume, tone, and pitch add variety to your message. A monotone will bore your listeners. Speaking too slowly or too quickly may make your listeners uncomfortable. To emphasize an important sentence, for example, say the first part in a normal voice, then pause and whisper the last two words, and pause again before speaking. A pause gives you time to think. It gives the listener an opportunity to absorb and retain what you said.

Image, Brand, Reputation Credibility

Your audience wants to know who you are—your image, brand, and reputation—and why they should listen to you: because of your experience, expertise, and authority in the field. If the audience does not know you, establish your credibility at the very start of your presentation. Tell a brief but exciting story about a profound experience you had.

Tips That Will Help You Get Your Message Across

Executives are creatures of habit and social norms. They expect you to be persuasive and acceptable in presenting your case. This section describes tips that can help you resonate.

Preparing Your Message for Delivery

Use the experience and knowledge of your "number 2" and staff members to help you gather the information you need to make your point. Update metrics. Always remember your goal: to get your message across using clear, distinct, and powerful language your CEO understands, cares about, and can act on. A good "A-team" can do that for you. Always bring your number 2 and (if seating permits) at least two subject matter experts in the area you will be talking about to any management presentation you give. The prime responsibility of your subject matter experts is to take key notes that require follow-up action, to observe the body language of those in attendance while you are speaking, to help with visual aids and distribute handouts, and to participate in the question-and-answer period (only if you call on them for support). Having your number 2 help to prepare the message and be present provides him or her with useful insight into the senior management decision-making process and experience to give future presentations in your absence.

Practice your approach in front of your staff and seek their candid advice to improve and refine the presentation. At the onset, it will be natural to use your notes or script to practice, but do not get too dependent on these. You must put them aside when the curtain goes up.

Giving strategic advice to executives has as much to do with image, trust, and confidence as it does with words, knowledge, and expertise. Nothing will tarnish your image, stain your trust, or lower your confidence level among your audience than if you memorize or read your message.

Memorizing Is a No-No

You cannot be effective in a memorization mode. What happens if you are interrupted with a question from the audience or distracted by some nearby activity that causes you to mentally loose your place or forget the last words you spoke? When you memorize, the material controls you. Instead, you need control of the material.

A good policy is to practice your message using your notes until you master the material and are able to speak with authority on the issues without hesitation. Practicing your lines is similar to what actors do. They rehearse scenes over and over again until the director is satisfied he or she has captured their best performance with the camera lenses. The main difference between you and actors is that when you are on center stage, it is a live performance. I often rehearse presentations a dozen times or more. I do not stop until I am comfortable with what I have to say. I consistently make adjustments and refine the content of my message before the presentation. Often, I even change it while speaking.

Reading Too Is a No-No

When you read, your notebook and podium stand between you and the audience. You lose any opportunity for naturally using eye contact, gestures, facial expressions, and tone of voice to attract and keep the attention of the audience. In fact, reading your message can cause you to lose your audience. It is your job to keep their interest in what you say. On a personal note, another reason I do not like reading is that I have to wear glasses to read the script or have it typed at a 20- to 24-point font size. Then I have to remove my glasses so I can make eye contact with the audience. All that movement becomes a distraction to the listener.

One last thought on memorizing or reading your message. Once you begin to speak, everything human falls away. Remember, you are not there to give a speech or lecture, or to explain complex or technical information. You are there to establish trust, confidence, and rapport; to demonstrate character and integrity; to showcase your knowledge of the topic you are talking about; and to persuade your listeners to give you want you want. It is difficult—if not impossible—to achieve these objectives by burying your nose in a notebook. That works for ostriches, not serious-minded persons. The audience is not in your notebook; they are in front of you, and they want you to be personable. They want to see the whites of your eyes and sense that you acknowledge their presence. You must reach out and touch their sensitivity so they can relate to you and your value system.

Think Strategically

Always focus on the future whether you speak, write or even think about what you want to do. Don't waste time and energy dwelling on the past. Always look forward into the future.

Strategic Thinking

The most fundamental task for a CEO and board of directors is to set the right goals so the organization can establish strategic objectives and processes that lead to success. Strategic thinking helps you understand how executives approach problems. Strategic thinking is the vision of the future, but too often we are bogged down in what happened yesterday, last week, or last month. We spend far too much time and energy figuring out how we got to where we are and who is to blame for getting us here. We should instead focus on how to move forward in an organized and judicious fashion and how to learn from our experiences. Know where you have to go. Show your audience how you are going to get there. Be constructive: give insightful and perceptive analysis and advice. Focus on the future.

Process Thinking

Most CEOs prefer to use process thinking. Process thinking is a problem-solving approach that divides issues into symmetrical local, sequential segments so problem solvers can proceed to work and think in an orderly, logical, and incremental fashion. Process thinking incorporates an integrated systematic approach to problem solving that offers a range of recommended options plus the assumptions and rationale that support them. It focuses on executive goals, perceptions, and vision, providing substantive intensity (Sullivant, 2007, pp. 213–216). All the strategy models presented in this book embed the process thinking approach.

Risk-Based Metrics Resonate with Executives

Metrics have no value unless they are tied to, aligned with, or part of the larger organizational risk process and a continuous improvement program. Metrics that are tied directly to the organization's security strategies—the corporate business plan, security plan, security emergency plan, crisis management plan, and associated security protocols—can have a direct relationship with compliance or nonconformance to those guidelines, as well as performance effectiveness, efficiency, and productivity; they can also warn of worsening security risk situations. All areas matter to executive management.

Develop a Management Perspective

People in staff functions tend to believe that their recommendations and big ideas will save the day for management. But CEOs give more credence to recommendations and ideas that come from operating managers. This distinction is so important it bears repeating. In Chapter Introduction I talked about why most CEOs prefer not to be briefed by staffers. Earlier in this chapter I talked about you wearing two hats. As an advisor, it is crucial that you talk and write about your staff's functional responsibilities in operational management terms rather than just in the terms of staff security expertise. Always write in language that is meaningful and useful to management. Express solutions in management language, rather than in staff language. The failure to align activities and solutions with management goals and objectives is often the reason most staffers are considered less important than the operations team. Get your message across as an operating manager, not a staffer.

Think in Terms of Business Operations and Business Risk Exposure

You should always see things from the CEO's point of view. Credibility requires that you speak to risk exposure in both your oral and written communications, providing advance warning plus options for solutions and managing trouble or opportunity, and unintended consequences and risk reduction, in a business and financial context. Be curious: investigate and master new and less-well-understood information. Question all assumptions and validate or seek alternative viewpoints. Develop a business management mind-set, behavior pattern, and attitude that attracts management's attention to give you standing and a pathway to occasional visits to the CEO's inner circle of advisors other than giving formal presentations (Lukaszewski, 2008, pp. 40).

Carve Out Recommendations in a Business Context

Let me put things into perspective: management's job is to run the business; your job is to help management do theirs. This is why it is important you know what the business is about. To truly act in the best interests of the business, you must bring in important and useful security-related business knowledge—beyond that already known by the CEO—to run the business. Management generally looks for these types of feedback:

- Strategies, mistakes, and successes: Where does security stand on performance effectiveness, efficiency, and productivity? Where does it stand on best practices?
- Emotional intelligence about the temperament of the workforce: What should executives know? Do employees feel they have a safe and secure workplace?
- Threats and exposure, unplanned visibility, and organizational forecasting: What should executives worry about today, tonight, and tomorrow morning? What can be deferred?

Offer Constructive Options

Be a force for prompt, positive, and forward thinking. Be reflective, but take only useful, positive lessons from the past. Seek out relevant patterns and experiences to formulate new insights for the future. Solving security problems using a systematic/process approach and developing mitigation actions from a business and management perspective is a step in the right direction. Always focus on team success and leadership to achieve useful, important, and positive outcomes.

Be Trustworthy, Candid, and Professional

Do Others Perceive You as Trustworthy?

Executives must trust you before they will act on your advice. You must gain their confidence in your judgment, integrity, and reputation or they will turn to others for security advice. You must be unconditionally honest from the start and demonstrate your value system in all words and deeds. Your standing as a trusted agent only counts when combined with kept promises, careful talk, self-control, truthfulness, and confidentiality.

The stakes are always high in the relationship dynamics between a trusted security director and the C-suite executives who relay on that security director for results. Trust is one of the important reasons people are promoted. Losing trust is also a primary reason people are ignored, demoted, or even fired. Having the boss trust you gives you access to information, meetings, and the influence over others (provided that they trust you as well). Trust requires truth; truth requires understanding and recognition of the viewer's point of reference as he or she sees it (Lukaszewski, 2008, pp. 59). Lukaszewski advocates that trust involves five critical ingredients:

- **Candor** is truth with an attitude, insight, and honest perspective. A candid person interprets and clarifies information in ways that are obviously helpful and avoids being self-serving.
- **Credibility** is the acceptance by others of your behavior, record of accomplishment, and delivering what you promise.
- **Integrity** is the inclination to do the right or most appropriate thing at the first opportunity or whenever there is a choice to be made. A person with integrity is someone you can count on to steer you in the right direction or help you make the normally correct decision, often on the spot, every time.
- **Loyalty** is a genuine affection for an individual or circumstance. It is willingness to go anywhere, do most anything, follow the lead given, and spontaneously speak up for an individual or circumstance.
- **Competence** is the ability to apply special knowledge, experience, and insight to resolve issues, questions, and problems, putting the power of your intellect and expertise to work.

According to Lukaszewski (2008, pp. 60, 61), six elements are needed to establish and maintain trust.

- **Provide advance information whenever you can**. Providing advance information is important because its absence can have a negative impact on a trust relationship. Executives expect to be warned of danger, damning decisions, or threats and disloyalty.
- **Seek the leader's input**. Asking for input is the second most powerful element of trust. It gets others involved, lets them know where you are coming from and where you want to go, and demonstrates your team-building and leadership skills. Taking action without asking for or seeking input is considered arrogant and not empathetic.
- **Listen carefully**. Learn to listen before you speak. Trust depends on careful listening from every side.
- **Implement change based on what you hear**. Changing announced actions, behaviors, and outcomes is a reflection of what is heard.
- **Stay engaged**. This requires you to take the first step to initiate, maintain, or keep moving the relationship.
- **Engage others**. The most powerful gesture you can make to build trust is to invite those affected by your decisions and authority into the decision-making process.

Lukaszewski (2008, pp. 61–63) also contends that trust is not everlasting. He has a top-ten list of the most frequent and most easily avoided trustbusters.

- **Arrogance** presumes you have permission to make unilateral decisions without input from others.
- **Broken promises** means you are not able to meet or do not want to keep commitments.

- **Chest beating** is a self-validating and condescending behavior that puts distance between those who want to trust and those who need to be trusted.
- **Creating fear** usually occurs when one party damages or threatens to damage another, creating feelings of dread, helplessness, even betrayal of the relationship.
- **Deception** is intentionally misleading through acts of omission, commission, negligence, or incompetence, which can create feelings of separation, distance, and disappointment.
- **Denial** is failing or refusing to come forward and acknowledge mistakes and errors in judgment or blame shifting.
- **Disparagement** is shifting blame to others or faulting conditions, circumstances, and outcomes.
- **Disrespect** is trivializing or degenerating the reputation of an individual, product, or organization.
- **Holding back** is deliberately withholding information, support, administration, cooperation, or collaboration.
- **Underestimating events or danger** fails to accurately identify faulty thinking that can lead to mistakes, errors, and bad behaviors.

For the security professional, this is a list of warning signs that could indicate that the trusted relationship between you and executive management may be on the path toward demise.

Do Others Perceive You as Being Candid in Your Dealings With Them?

Executives expect you to offer unvarnished and candid advice.

- Be straightforward about risk and uncertainties.
- State your position clearly and persuasively.
- Disclose setbacks and other bad news early and openly to avoid or preempt worsening problems. Act in real time to solve problems before they become unmanageable.
- Resist the temptation to "protect the boss" by withholding important information and facts, or by under reporting or over reporting, as this practice erodes trust.
- Obtain and report the facts within the context of their discovery and the investigation of the facts.

Lose any self-imposed false impression you may have that the more time you spend with the boss, the more likely he or she will call on you for future advice. Never lose site of the fact that time with executives is always limited, focused, and operationally oriented. Anything else is unproductive and could be disastrous for your career.

Always Project a Positive Image in Your Business Affairs?

Executives expect you to be professional and transparent in all your business affairs. Some desirable qualities that can project a positive image and brand include, but are not necessarily limited to, the following (listed in alphabetical order):

- Act in real time to address real problems. Always have honest introspection.
- Actions should be unchallengeable and explainable. Exhibit a sense of reality.

- Anticipate and identify problem areas early, while they are still manageable.
- Apply critical thinking skills and act decisively. Focus on the ultimate outcome.
- Attract other leaders. Provide strategic, insightful advice. Nourish team building.
- Provide clear and decisive judgment in making critical decisions in the face of uncertainty.
- Empower subordinates to give you candid advice. Listen to those around you.
- Exercise strong leadership, even under uncertain and visible circumstances.
- Preserve and uphold the highest standards of ethics and professionalism.
- Relentlessly clarify the record, correct mistakes, and issue an apology for wrongdoing.
- See critical issues as executive management sees them.
- Translate strategies into meaningful measurable activity and workable solutions.
- Cultivate trust relationships and build confidence with executives.
- Demonstrate consistency, confidence, and competency.
- Launch aggressive drives against ineffectiveness and inefficiency, and slash unproductiveness.
- Stimulate team problem-solving initiatives to their full potential.
- Regard differing views as opportunities for understanding and personal growth.
- Address every concern or question and avoid judging the questioner.
- Always be open, accessible, and willing to help management tackle issues.
- Avoid whining, bickering, and arguing. Leave your ego at the nearest exit.
- Develop followers, even in the face of aggressive negativity, anger, or arrogance.
- Dump any cynicism you might have about management and others.

Be a Verbal Visionary

CEOs drive and lead organizations by what they say. You must be prepared to engage in fast-paced discussions in real time, which requires strong verbal skills, and to do so in the territory of the executive, which is the future toward which the boss is steering the organization. Your greatest responsibility of leadership is to identify the vision for the security organization and get others to contribute willingly to achieving that goal. Your second-greatest responsibility is to get the resources and funding needed to move ideas forward.

Use Risk-Based Metrics to Develop a Telling Story and Tailor It to the Audience

Risk-based metrics ensure that you have a measurable means of communicating risk to executives. Using a metric provides objectivity that helps you and decision makers resolve conflicts about the process or procedure rather than personality.

- Put your ideas together in a logical way, and practice being concise and vivid.
- Speak like someone you would like to listen to.
- Say important things. Say things that matter.
- Speak to the facts, not speculation or opinion.
- Ground your vision in a reality that attracts your audience.
- Use your strong sense of identity to share your goals, objectives, and sense of destiny.
- Remain one step ahead of everyone—anticipate problems, and opportunities, and have a plan.

Find a way to tell a persuasive story or give compelling examples of your experiences and personal history that tend to blunt people's feelings or emotions, and about realistic risk and what you did to reduce it, so they let you continue talking and so they listen.

- Talk specifically about business and security objectives.
- Make the story compelling by naming actual business resources threatened, the value of those resources, and the consequences of loss should an event occur.
- Use positive, direct, and powerful language to get the audience's attention and keep it.

Comparisons help people see the right and wrong side of a situation, and the right question at the right time can open minds to help people recall ideas well after your presentation is over.

Tell the story in plain, positive language. Ensure the story has a moral, a lesson, or a reason for being told that the listener can immediately relate to. Say things that you know people will remember and will want to pass on to others. A good story can have a great influence on listeners. Speak in simple terms to keep people better focused on what you are saying. It forces them (sometimes against their will) to take notes. People who take notes usually come back to ask questions and to open a dialog with you, and that is what you want them to do.

Operational Metrics Fail to Resonate With Executives

In telling your story, refrain from using operational metrics—metrics for example that simply identify the number of attempt criminal acts, traffic accidents, traffic violations, or other non-risk activities. These metrics tend to be based on invalid and unreliable data because they rely on voluntary reporting of activity. One cannot draw accurate risk-related conclusions from this information. Such data do not resonate well in the boardroom because they are not linked to, aligned with, or part of a larger risk process. Executives fail to understand their meaning in a business risk context. Use operational metrics only for your own background information and within the security organization, or to develop a case history to support security- and risk-related metrics or the productivity of processes or practices.

Be That Window for Tomorrow

Measuring Tomorrow's Results

Problems are always about tomorrow, even though you may be fixing yesterday's mistakes. CEOs need help getting tomorrow right, so focus your advice there. Learn from your own experiences and those of others, then translate outcomes into lessons learned that executives need to hear. Focusing on the future will help you build these strengths:

- Gain experience and important knowledge of the business that can make you more effective and efficient.

- A knowledge of patterns can tell you which strategies to use to avoid problems. Focus on the ultimate outcome and use the right patterns to make your comments and writing more memorable.
- Understand strategic patterns so you can be an intelligence forecaster of circumstances, conditions, and reactions.

Information about the past can be useful if you can analyze and learn from patterns, then apply their meaning to tomorrow. These insights can help you understand better the situations your CEO confronts.

Measuring and Communicating Risk-Based Metric Results Over Time

This allows comparisons that can be a useful vehicle for communicating risk-based metric values and results. Metrics that show progress toward meeting specific strategic goals can tell a compelling story through the unfolding of events over time. Distinguishing metrics that are time-sensitive from those that provide value over time can also enhance the overall value of your presentation.

Give Constructive Advice

Always offer clear, constructive, and accurate strategic and tactical advice that is practical, pragmatic, purposeful, and focused, on the spot, 24/7.

Always Be Professional and Display a Positive Image

Always be positive in your approach, mannerisms, and comments. Never criticize anyone or make a negative comment about any failure or shortcoming you are presenting. Never exhibit arrogance or a condescending attitude. Bickering, arguing, and failing to listen may lead to explosive confrontations followed by bitter relationships. Never burn a bridge behind you. Because most of us remember the negative sting of criticism, the CEO may shut you down on the spot and reject you as an advisor. Should this happen, your ability and opportunity to contribute to the corporation may end. Instead, make constructive suggestions so that you are heard, and put your energy to positive use enhancing and improving the situation.

Select a Beneficial Approach That Resonates with Your Audience

There are many approaches to delivering a message, and many corporations and agencies have developed their own style and format for briefing executives. These tailored-made templates serve these corporations well in terms of information flow and sequence, and you should have no problem tailoring your briefing to this format. Few, however, emphasize time constraints and attention span. Personally, I favor the approaches created by two different men: Milo O. Frank and James E. Lukaszewski.

Frank and Lukaszewski both address time and attention span. Both approaches resonate with audiences and could help you develop powerful presentations. Both concepts are simple and direct. Both have powerful attention-getter elements.

Frank (1986, pp. 9–119) designed an attention-getter approach, which he coined "30 s or less." The approach emphasizes presenting a business case in segments of 30 s or less. The bases for Frank's 30-s rule rest on two compelling reasons why 30 s is the ideal length of time to get your point across: time constraints and attention span. People tend to loose interest in a topic after 30 s, and their minds start to wonder to other things.

Lukaszewski (2008, pp. 25–84) designed a similar approach referred to as the "3-min drill." His concept organizes a business case into segments of 30, 60, or 150 words to address topics in 3-min intervals, as well as to gain listener attention and retention. Lukaszewski's approach calls for a word count to be eventually translated into a measured unit of time.

I prefer Frank's approach (modified slightly) over Lukaszewski's approach because, for me, it is easier to manage the topic and control my time by restricting my comments to 30-s segments rather than counting words. The editing process then is simplified. Another reason I like Frank's concept is that each bullet point can be a separate and distinct 30-s message. This keeps the visual aid neat and clean, and me on track and moving forward. I am convinced that the best way to keep the interest and attention of an audience is to do and say something new and interesting every 30 s.

I encourage you to review and practice each concept, then select the approach you feel at ease with. You may prefer to pick and choose the best aspect from each approach to further develop your own particular comfort level, as I have.

Staying within Time Constraints Helps Win the Battle

CEOs are tough. They do not have time to wait for you to get your point across; they will not listen to you for long. Neither will the senior staff, board of directors, or community governing bodies. Use time wisely. The operative rule is to say less but make it more important, and to write less but make it more powerful. One powerful element of communications is to be concise and to the point. Say what you have to say once, and end your message quickly—in 10 min or less.

The first few words you speak form a positive or negative image in the minds of those in the audience. Your closing must also resonate with your audience. It determines whether you get what you asked for. Everything between your opening remarks and closing statements must be one powerful attention-getter after another, each in less than 30 s.

Capturing the Attention Span of Your Audience Helps Win the War

Attention span and attention-getting bullet points go hand in hand. At the onset— even before you start developing the content, sequence, and organization of your message—you must recognize that the attention span of an average individual is only about 30 s. That's how long people will pay attention to what you have to say without drifting off to think about what they are going to do after the meeting, where they plan to go tonight, or what they plan to wear tomorrow. The movie and TV industries and the media all have mastered the 30-s rule; you know it as the 30-s commercial, which attracts interest, keeps attention, and sells millions of product lines. With practice, you can sell your idea to executive management in 30 s or less.

Build a Solid Business Case

Most colleagues agree that less is more. So do I. Always be brief, clear, and to the point. This is worth repeating. Talk less but make it more important; write less but make it more powerful. Keep your presentation to 10 min. Here is a six-point approach that can help you deliver your message:

- Report the facts.
- Set a course for the future.
- Identify business impact.
- Introduce pathways to achieving your goal.
- Pick a preferred path.
- Close out.

Point 1: Report the Facts

Describe the nature of your business, problem, or situation in 30 s or less.

- Be careful not to under- or over report. Both can have harmful affects.
- Introduce a clear objective that captures the interest of your audience.
- Know your topic and present it as concisely and memorably as possible.
- Present bullet points that include only top-level information.
- Stay on track toward achieving your objective.
- Present important data and facts, but always recognize that they are debatable.
- Tell a story or personal experience that will keep the audience on the edge of their seats.
- Personalize your story so it has meaning to your listeners.

Put to work strategic tools such as meaningful graphics to express your ideas clearly and memorably in 30 s or less.

- Use risk-based metrics in a clear and concise manner that energizes the CEO.
- Create a simple dashboard slide that attracts the attention of management.[1]
- Risk charts (but not too many) resonate with senior management.
- Simple graphics and powerful words make your message memorable.
- Use clear, simple language that your listener will understand.
- Show the probability and severity of potential events.
- Allow executive management to make the decision you want them to make.

[1] A dashboard containing multiple charts and graphs may be useful internally within the security organization for briefing other groups but for presentation to senior management, a single graphic with powerful data on one side of one sheet of paper can be worth at least a notebook full of words and tabs.

Point 2: Set a Course for the Future

Tell executive management what you want and where you want to go in 30 s or less.

- Offer unvarnished and candid advice. Keep executives firmly grounded.
- Be straightforward about risk and uncertainties. Be reasonably free of bias or manipulation that can distort the facts you report.
- CEOs do not like to be given ultimatums. Too many security professionals unknowingly do this. Be alert to this pitfall and stay clear of it. Offer a limited range of constructive options in a preferred sequence that the CEO can act on.

Point 3: Introduce a Pathway to Achieving Your Goal

Always credit management with knowing more than you do, even if you think they do not. Believe me when I say they need to know far less than you think they do to make a decision. Keeping your message free of confusing details helps management better understand your objective. And, because management knows there are many ways to achieve a goal or objective, they expect a short, concise menu of decision options to consider. The goal is to have several ideas to choose from rather than being stuck on one option.

- Always propose three options—one of which is to do nothing.
- Introduce the do nothing option first and highlight its business impact in 30 s or less. Doing nothing is a provocative strategy and often the most appealing for many executives because it gives them time to reflect by postponing a decision. To be noticed, mention doing nothing first—before the boss, other executives, or lawyers mention it.
- Present the remaining two options (in order of preference) and why they are acceptable in 30 s or less. To keep your image, brand, and reputation, as well as your trustworthiness and creditability, intact, never present an idea that you cannot do or do not want to carry out. Setting these priorities establishes a sense of urgency for the CEO. Do not distract him or her from focusing on your priorities.

Point 4: Pick Your Path

Suggest the option you believe to be the best and state its benefits in 30 s or less.

Point 5: Identify Business Impact

Put yourself in the boss's shoes and explain how your idea may threaten the company, why it matters, and available opportunities to strengthen business operations. Do all this in 30 s or less. Identify positive and negative consequences that could arise, including collateral damage related to your choice, if applicable, and why mitigation actions reduce risk while improving and enhancing security resilience—and do this in 30 s or less. Shy away from such conclusions as speculative fear, the "only solution syndrome," and an easy "cookie-cutter solution" in your presentation. They never work.

A good CEO has the ability to accept, absorb, and apply the advice you are giving. To ensure you do your part in helping the boss be a better decision maker, allow your presentation to enable him or her to do just that.

Point 6: Close Out

When you tell the CEO what you want and why, that is your cue to get off the stage.

- Conclude your briefing by summarizing your risk mitigation strategy in 30s or less.
- Provide a cost estimate summary and a milestone schedule showing major activity in 30s or less.
- Anticipate issues that your listeners might raise and answer any questions in 30s or less. Offer positive answers on the spot or promise to give an answer as soon as possible after the meeting.[2]

Be prepared to answer constructive as well as confrontational questions. Managerially relevant questions foster productive discussion and the exploration of ideas. These questions and your answers to them give the boss a more critically essential understanding. Confrontational questions presented by the staff may be perceived to demean, malign, or murder your ideas and advice. Those in the room, particularly the CEO, always remember this type of questioning and who in particular among the staff is pursuing this type of questioning. For whatever reason, these staffers persist and resurface at the worst possible times. Answer these questions with the same objectivity and professionalism you used when answering relevant management questions.

At the end of the question-and-answer period, thank everyone for their interest and the time taken away from their busy day. Now you can really relax—you're done, until the next time. Wait to be excused or for the CEO to adjourn the meeting.

Know When to Pull Your Parachute Cord

Even the best of professional athletes do not win every time, but they always return to try to win the next game. Even with all the hard work and diligence you put into your proposal, be prepared for the possibility of your idea being rejected by the senior staff and disapproved by the boss. Some reasons for this decision may stem from:

- the idea not being part of management's strategic interest or focus. You should have known this before hand, in which case you should have never given the briefing.
- the idea being developed without input from the boss or someone the boss trusts, not being staffed properly or sufficiently coordinated with all divisions, or usurping the legitimate territory of others. Rework the presentation, do your homework, and return to the table later.
- management not supporting or participating in the effort. Timing is off, resources and funding are not available, or the message was not convincing enough. Come back again better prepared.

---

[2] If formal minutes of the meeting are taken, it is an acceptable protocol to provide a memo to the secretary of the meeting answering or clarifying any issues that were brought out during the question and answer discussion. Typically, the contents of the memo can be inserted into the minutes or added to the minutes as an addendum. The contents of such a memo explaining or answering a particular question can then be reviews by all present when the minutes are distributed. Objectives can be immediately responded to. In some instances the topic may even be brought up again for discussion at the next regular meeting. Most CEOs, however, prefer the parties to get together before the minutes are final and the next meeting is scheduled.

- the idea falling short of adequately addressing the business side of the enterprise. Go back to the drawing board and come back later.
- the idea being too advanced for the time and not really understood by the staff. More research is needed before introducing the idea again in the future.

Disappointments such as these happen often, and you must be able to recover from such defeat. In the case histories mentioned above, your trust and confidence may have been tarnished; people may question your management and leadership skills, or perhaps your ability to work hand in hand with the staff on critical issues needs to be refined. Regardless of the reason for failing, pick yourself up, dust yourself off, heal any wounds with the staff that may exist, and discuss the shortfalls of the presentation with your number 2 and your security staff. Listen to what they have to say and heed their advice. Have them review the contents of the briefing, handouts, and notes. Ask your number 2 to comment on your approach and demeanor. Ask the staff for candid advice on what you could have done better. Learn from your mistakes and move on.

Present Program Results Regularly

Present selected metrics monthly, quarterly, semiannually, or annually to various audiences and at different intervals. Tailor the content of each briefing to fit the particular audience and their area (s) of interest.

Keep in mind that data age over time and can become historical and less actionable, and thus potentially less valuable. For example, some threats and hazards are seasonal or even situational. You can blend in the appropriate topic at selected briefing intervals if the information is relevant and current. Distinguishing metrics that are time-sensitive from those that provide value over time enhances the overall value of your recurring presentation. Here are some tips for tailoring your briefings to specific audiences:

- C-suite executives, the senior management staff, boards, and community governing bodies are interested in only top-level metrics about significant corporate-wide problems affecting image, brand, and reputation; security performance strengths and weaknesses; threats, vulnerabilities, and anticipated improvements; costs to facilitate executive decision making; investments; and profit margin.
- Maintenance and operations staffs focus on the detailed aspects of their particular areas of expertise and responsibility. They want to know how good or bad things are, and what it takes to improve their areas of responsibility or to fix mechanical problems as soon as possible.
- Regulators, consultants, inspectors, and auditors are interested in the root causes of ineffectiveness, inefficiency, and lack of productivity within the scope of their review charter. They look to correcting management, leadership, ad logistics issues that affect compliance performance and productivity.

Multilevel tailored metrics—each geared toward the particular audience—best serve the interest of the security organization as well as the corporation. You can layer slides and metrics to organize your thoughts, establish relationships, and set priorities for each audience you address.

Conclusions

Work Hard to Establish and Maintain Trust and Respect

If you can put yourself in the boss's shoes and look at things from a business perspective; talk the language management understands, cares about, and can act on; think and make recommendations using management's process approaches; and then apply what you know, you will be respected and have influence with the CEO and other executives.

Collaborate to Narrow the Communication Gap

Staff functions exist and are funded by executives to address challenges and to help executives do their jobs. But this desire to fix things can become a difficult task if the right team is not in place. When executive management, the staff, or security leadership creates circumstances, conditions, and behavior patterns that lead to problem situations, the complexity of problem solving can create greater challenges and sometimes tough working relationships between executive management and the security organization.

In earlier chapters, I mentioned that the greatest majority of security problems stem from:

- inappropriate, weak, or poor security measures
- inadequate security policies, processes, and practices
- poor security awareness and ineffective security training programs
- human fallacies and technology deficiencies and breakdowns
- barriers and obstacles that contribute to ineffective and inefficient security performance
- weak or poor management and leadership practices, and poor decision-making

These issues deserve executive management's attention, or they will never be resolved. It is crucial that the communication gap between the CEO and the security organization be closed. The effort calls for trust, confidence, maturity, professionalism, strong working relationships and leadership, and a strategic vision that focuses on the best interests of the corporation. There is no doubt that such a drastic change in a single organization can create chaos and bring about resistance and turf maneuvering, but these challenges must be met and hurdles overcome. A corporation that embraces the concept of total quality management and team building (Schmidt and Finnigan, 1994, pp. 10–29) can overcome many of the barriers and obstacles that exist.

Last, the security profession has been partially successful at recognizing systemic security deficiencies, weaknesses, and inadequacies, but less successful in acknowledging, identifying, and addressing the root causes of these systemic problems. Properly designed risk-based metrics offer a focused analysis of why conditions repeatedly arise and of opportunities to explore strategies to address root causes. One of the greatest challenges CEOs face is the commitment to acknowledge the route causes of such problems and to fix them quickly.

Focus on the Ultimate Outcome

Achieving success and obtaining goals only happens in the future, never in the past. Stay focused on the future and what you know you can accomplish based on where you have to go.

Making a Business Case

In 30 s you can deliver a powerful and memorable message. In 30 s you can communicate effectively, persuasively, and concisely, and you can capture your audience's attention, keep its interest, tell a wonderful story, and ask for (and get) what you want. The right message enables you to get your point across and keep it where it belongs: in the mind of your listeners. If you wish to keep the interest and attention of your audience, say something important every 30 s. I suggest you do it in 10 min or less.

How Will You Know if You Are Successful?

The best way to get a CEO to accept your ideas is to offer advice that is simple, sensible, positive, and practical. Use your competency to become an important and influential resource to your CEO 24/7. Work to make this relationship effective. You will know you have succeeded when:

- people continue to tell your stories
- you are quoted in other meetings and seminars, or even when you are in the room
- meetings are held up until you arrive
- the boss and others routinely suggest that ideas, concepts, plans, and policies be run by you early in and at the end of the process
- others have respect for you and hold you and your ideas in high regard
- leaders tell you and others how you've helped them, and your insights become evident in their decisions, actions, beliefs, and strategies

Success does not require you to have a seat at the executive table, only an invitation to visit the corner office and the boardroom when needed. To get there you have to be sought out by the boss or someone the boss totally trusts. If you offer value, and if the boss knows of that value and has respect for your critical thinking, you will be noticed. Once accepted, you will be expected to contribute something positive, useful, and of value, from the boss's perspective.

Much Work Remains to Improve Communication with Executives

During the past decade, the security profession has made great advances in connecting with chief executives. As the importance of security and the significance of diversified threats expand, so must your ability to communicate effectively with executive management. One of the greatest challenges you will face is not how to reduce risk, but how to convey the benefits of risk reduction in language executive leaders understand and care about. Much work remains to improve communication skills in this regard.

A Brighter Tomorrow: My Thoughts

Where trust is high, and ideas flow freely, much work can be accomplished. Finger pointing on the other hand stifles creativity and is a leadership fallacy best left at the doorstep.

John Sullivant

Top Takeways

- embrace a brighter tomorrow
- apply strategic visionary thoughts
- preserve the corporate image, brand, and reputation
- strategic planning is everything
- leadership traits for the next generation

Overview

The deficiencies, weaknesses, and inadequacies unveiled throughout the pages of this book have been reoccurring for a very, very long time. I and many of my colleagues have been witnessing and reporting on these conditions for over five decades. With hindsight, my view is that this phenomenon has always existed but has seldom been noticed because previous evaluation practices have focused on security hardware and software performance. Only within the last two decades have consultants been asked to investigate the "human side" of the enterprise and report the status of adequacy of training and policies, social behaviors, work habits, attitudes, interrelationships, or the mind-set and security knowledge-base of both executive and security management.

It is time to plan for the future by reflecting on the past and the present and to recognize our successes and failures, accounting for the areas we must grow in: better communications with C-suite executives, better synergy with the senior staff, forward-looking leadership skills, and the development of advanced competencies for the emerging generation of security leaders.

A Perspective for the Future

The mere existence of conditions, circumstances, and situations that help to create a vacuum for potential deficiencies, weaknesses, and inadequacies is unacceptable and certainly should not to be condoned by any responsible leader. This is a pervasive problem, and I believe its mere presence needs to be eradicated by both executive and security management wherever it crops up.

But changing a cultural mind-set can be a bit more complicated than changing engrained policies and behavioral patterns. This calls for an enlightening experience in new concepts, ideas, approaches, and technologies, followed by a continuing internship in planning, coordinating, developing, and executing first-class security operations and programs. No doubt this is work in progress, and all of us have a tremendous amount of hard work ahead of us.

As early as chapter Introduction, I was unflinching in stating that some decision makers—security professionals among them—do not fully understand or grasp the essential principles of security or the criticality of their interconnectivity. Many have difficulty recognizing the holistic benefits of embracing security programs and system integration means and techniques, including the importance of the criticality to deter, delay, prevent, protect, detect, assess, respond to, and recover from security events in a timely manner. I make no apology for these eyewitness accounts and my subsequent analysis of my observations. My only regret is not being able to share with you all my findings, timing and expense to address all the issues being prohibited. My representative introduction of five decades of experience is sufficient to grasp the tapestry of my work.

I am not yet suggesting the security industry is doomed, only that it is approaching a pivotal point in our history that will soon challenge us to renew our business relationships and practices, and embrace new technologies that are shifting from proprietary databases and hardware to open wireless architecture with published specifications and new management and leadership characteristics yet to be developed or recognized. It is time for a major change in our thinking of uncertainty and unwillingness, and in our priorities to push for professional and technical development to meet a brighter tomorrow.

And let us not lose sight of the opportunities that executives have and the challenges inherent in today's business and threat environments by exercising the necessary leadership to prevent the usual delays and bottlenecks associated with building security resilience. Understanding the magnitude of this crisis is both urgent and important.

The time has come to reflect on the past and the present and look to the future. It is time to account for your successes and failures, and that in turn focuses your energy on those areas in which you can nurture and grow. An easy first step is to share this book with your boss and chief executive and have a real dialogue about the tough security issues executives have been hesitant to talk about. Perhaps it may be time to ask your chief executive the toughest question of your career: How can I help you be a better security decision maker? A second easy step is to share the contents of this book with your staff and members of your security organization. The next step is somewhat harder - its getting a concensus from your peers and others that the theme of this book has value and is on target, and mobilizing resources to make behavioral changes suitable to your enterprise in general and in particular to your organization, and the security industry, to deliver a better tomorrow. Some tips that will help make a better tomorrow are the focus of this closing chapter.

The Evolving Business and Threat Landscape

Business Environment

Until corporate culture changes, security organizations will continue to face difficulties in trying to carry out programs that have undefined parameters and standards of performance, as well as measurement and evaluation criteria that are not meaningful or useful to executives. Having a clear understanding of how to relate security goals and objectives to business goals and objectives remains a significant challenge for most security organizations. Many have an inclination that things are not what they should be, but have no idea where or how to start addressing potential problems. Such organizations could benefit greatly from the knowledge and expertise of an independent security consultant. A clear understanding and use of the basic principles of a security risk management framework and its measurement and evaluation platform are essential to program success. Get aboard and embrace these principles as part of your daily routine.

Threat Environment

New threats are escalating in probability, breadth, and severity. By recognizing these emerging patterns, you will be able to develop preparedness measures in the early stages of security planning. But identifying and understanding new threat conditions is only half the equation. Prioritizing threats, vulnerabilities, and assets; developing mitigation strategies and solutions; formulating action plans; and monitoring the effectiveness of approved actions are the second part of the equation that requires strategic thinking and steadfast determination.

Many companies believe they know what their security problems are and have the solutions ready to be implemented. But experience has proven that such conclusions are mostly based on incomplete and inadequate information, and sometimes speculation leading to poor decision making and often to a false sense of security. Many of these same companies and others are not fully aware of, nor do they understand the significance of, the threat landscape. This is because most companies see little value in developing a threat profile to use to identify and prioritize threats, vulnerabilities, and the protection of assets. My work has shown that threat analysis is a useful tool in establishing priorities, but none of the strategies I reviewed over the years seemed to be preceded or guided by such threat analyses. This is a void of great consequence and we must have the fortitude to change the mind-set of executives who resist meaningful and useful intelligence that would help them make the right security choices in saving lives, protecting property, and sustaining company brand, image and reputation.

Corporate governance also has enormous concerns about protecting intellectual property, yet it does little to safeguard its information, processes, and secrets, or punish employees who violate protocols and norms and ignore security practices. At the 25th Annual Global Fraud Conference, Held in San Antonio, Texas, in June 2014, keynote speaker and former FBI Director Louis Freeh urged 3,000 people in attendance to use tougher security measures to protect their intellectual property. During his presentation he emphasized financial. Institutions in particular are more vulnerable and are hacked more often than any other business sector. Financial institutions soon may be required to beef up their internal protection of intellectual property[1] through the application of new federal regulations. Other regulated industries such as utilities, energy, telecommunications, transportation, and public health will soon face new security standards as well.

With the constant threat of disasters, both natural and manmade, security professionals must be proactive, incorporating plans as a fundamental part of any security operation. Preparedness begins with understanding the business's goals and objectives, followed by knowing corporate commitments, obligations, regulatory requirements, management knowledge base, and the corporate culture.

The ability to keep up with evolving threats, coupled with the operational and performance demands imposed on security organizations and the rapid pace of regulatory changes, is a major challenge for many security directors. The increasing number of security concerns has forced many organizations to place company survivability and security resilience on par with each other, including placement on the agendas of corporate chief executive officers (CEOs) and their boards.

Corporate Image, Brand, and Reputation Hang in the Balance

Companies spend billions of dollars investing in their corporate image through trade, brand name identification, and image to establish and maintain their reputation at almost any cost. The value of this ongoing campaign possibly represents a corporation's largest inventory (Broder, 2006, pp. 233). It is no wonder good corporate leadership does not look kindly upon any business unit—particularly safety, security, and compliance groups—that place its image, brand, or reputation in jeopardy. Moreover, an organizational culture that applauds innovation and flexibility rather than suppressing it, gives security directors and other managers the freedom to take risks, and praises people for recognizing and owning problems, rather than chastising them for reporting problems, is the leader of the pack.

The Challenge of Exposing Vulnerability Creep-in

Vulnerability creep-in is a malignant product that has to stop being used as an excuse for not moving forward. It has to be cleaned up, swept away, and never allowed to return. An independent objective security assessment or audit can determine the range of security enhancements that may be used to remove or minimize the root causes of ineffectiveness and inefficiency created by vulnerability creep-in. This examination process breaks down each site, facility, system, and function into the smallest segments possible to make the investigative process manageable. The profile proceeds to identify weaknesses in the corporation's ability and capability to deter, prevent, protect, detect, delay, assess, respond to, and recover from specified threat conditions.

---

[1] http://www.fraudnewsamerica.com/fraud-news-now/louis-freeh-speaks-acfe-conference/.

Security's Weakest Link: Human Fallacies

It is common knowledge across the security industry that human weakness, not processes, protocols, practices, or technology, put organizations most at risk. Apparently, however, this is not common knowledge throughout the executive management sphere of influence. Or, perhaps they know but fail to acknowledge it.

A recent survey[2] by Secure World in June 2014 found that 56% of workers have not received any security awareness training. Another study[3] found 95% of the breaches traceable to human error. Despite this fact, security awareness training is still ignored by many organizations. If there is a common thread that all security experts agree on, it's that poor training and unaware employees lie at the root of most of all, cyber security breaches.

In the past, disgruntled staff lacked the tools to easily steal secrets or cause serious harm. Now, virus toolkits are available to provide inside attackers with a cheap and easy way to cost companies millions of dollars and ruin organizations' reputations. What, then, can be done to protect corporate interests?

- Have a systematic approach to monitoring employees' access to the computer network and, in particular, what they are downloading.
- Monitor people who ignore or bypass procedures to ensure that they are not acting illegally.
- Deny computer access when a person goes on vacation or is notified of his or her termination.
- Ensure that the person being let go does not exit with sensitive documents or have access to computer systems.
- Provide sufficient budgets for cyber security countermeasures designed to protect systems from attacks initiated from inside or outside the company.

The first (and best) line of defense is employee and management awareness. The more people understand and care about how their behavior affects the company's security posture, the better off the company and employees will be.

Cyber Incident Response Capabilities

Overall, organizations are not ready to handle their mandated incident response requirements. Having a plan in place to address incidents enables organizations to counter issues and breaches when they do arise. But only 43% of all U.S. companies have formalized incident response plans, while 53% do not have formal incident response teams.[4] Both of these situations lead to a disjointed approach to managing and remediating incidents, resulting in delayed or incorrect responses.

10% of U.S. companies have effective incident response capabilities. Only 26% of the companies report dissatisfaction with their incident response capabilities, citing lack of time and resources to review and practice procedures (62%) and lack of budget (60%) as key impediments to effective response.[5]

---

[2] https://www.secureworldexpo.com/56-workers-may-not-receive-any-security-awareness-training.
[3] https://www.duosecurity.com/blog/human-error-accounts-for-over-95-percent-of-security-incidents-reports-ibm.
[4] https://www.sans.org/press/sans-institute-releases-results-of-survey-incident-response-how-to-fight-back.php.
[5] Ibid.

Cyber Security Threat Gains Executive Management's Attention

The increasing frequency, sophistication, and business impact of many cyber attacks have pushed cyber security planning and protection from an operational concern of corporate security and information technology (IT) departments to the agenda of boards and CEOs at many organizations across America.[6]

Senior executives face an information gap that makes it difficult for them to align investments in risk protection with the true strategic value of an organization's digital assets. Every organization that has suffered a recent security breach also has already had some form of cyber security in place. Beyond that, too many organizations fail to align IT security capabilities with larger corporate security goals and overall risk appetite.

Measuring and Evaluating Performance and Productivity

Most security programs lack risk-based metrics to measure and evaluate their effectiveness.

Prioritizing

One of the biggest challenges organizations have is prioritizing, understanding, and addressing vulnerabilities in a business context, including placing a monetary value on the worth of an asset, as well as on the loss of the asset if it is damaged or destroyed. Some CEOs, staff, and employees, and even some security organizations, underestimate the threat and do not understand the implications or consequences of losing critical infrastructure and assets. A major goal for a security director must be to clearly communicate security dangers and mitigate risk exposure in language that is meaningful to executives but without making "fearful" statements that may lead to workforce panic or unrest.

My past work in reviewing various strategies and mitigation solutions has revealed the importance of identifying and prioritizing issues that require immediate attention. While many organizations have developed strategies that identify some top priorities, an equal number of strategies contain more priorities of seemingly equal importance that cannot be realistically achieved. The development of a threat estimate profile is the vehicle to use to accomplish this priority goal.

Protocols and Practices

Security policies have their place, but they are of little value if they fall short on results and employees do not understand the rational behind the rules. Many employees fail to adhere to security policies because of a lack of understanding and poor communications from their security department, or they do not always follow their company's security policies.[7]

Many security contracts and agreements are written poorly. Most contract guard forces lack tactical response and search-and-rescue expertise, as well as adequate

---

[6] http://www.reuters.com/article/ny-bain-company-idUSnBw055053a+100+BSW20140305.
[7] https://www.nsi.org/Security_NewsWatch/NewsWatch/7.9.15.html.

training to meet the demands of the security mission. In many instances I have observed "response" to be the purview of local law enforcement, while site contract guards stand by and watch, contributing nothing to the response—not even checking the area to make sure it is secure.

Many security protocols are poorly written and have been successfully challenged under litigation. Protocols must be crafted to pass the test of legal review and must be clear, distinct, and brief. But brevity does not equate to losing site of a publications' meaning and purpose for the sake of reducing the page count. Protocols must outline authority, responsibility, and accountability for implementation and identify the fundamental aspects of a process.

Security Design Performance and Program Integration

Understanding the security design process is critical for every stakeholder responsible for security resilience. Before you begin talking about security solutions, you have to understand the process and key players involved. Security experts will define the steps in a proven process: from establishing the need for security, through asset and risk assessment, to the development of functional requirements and mitigation solutions.

Years ago, little (if any) thought was given to building security into the design of a facility. The experts of those days considered such an idea unnecessary because if security were needed in the future they would simply add it. Then came along some bright developers and enlightened owners and entrepreneurs who recognized that building security into the facility design process was more cost-effective than adding it onto a project as an afterthought (Broder, 2006, pp. 252).

As a consultant to the US. Army Corps of Engineers in the early 1980s, my team introduced this engineering concept to the Department of Defense. It eventually became Department of Defense policy for all new military construction projects, and over the years it has saved U.S. taxpayers billions of dollars in design, engineering, and construction costs (Sullivant, 2007, pp. 57–61).

The moral of this story is that the security director—not engineers, designers, accounts, or even CEOs—set the ultimate criteria for security design quality and security system performance. There is no room in this business for an engineer, designer, or some other individual to exhibit a "take it or leave it" attitude. This person is not helping you solve your security problem: he is the security problem, and a major contributor to vulnerability creep-in. Stay clear of accepting or signing off on a security design that falls short of specification expectations under the guise that it will be modified and upgraded later. This seldom happens, if ever. This rationale, often presented to you by the design and engineering group and supported by the accountant, is typical of how vulnerability creep-in sets in.

System Reliability, Dependability, and Availability

In today's business world, corporations that have management information systems, control systems, security systems, and other systems that are unavailable and people who are unproductive for hours, days, or longer can be disastrous. Companies cannot afford to be without the technology and information necessary to conduct their business affairs. It is not just manmade threats, such as criminal activity and acts of terrorism, or weather-related calamities and industrial accidents that have upper management's interest. It is common events such as system failures, equipment malfunctions, and lack of system protection features. Redundancy and backup systems can increase system reliability and dependability. Newer self-healing systems can also increase system survivability parameters.

Technology and Other Protective Measures Avoid Paying in the Courtroom

Violent incidents continue to occur at businesses where cameras and other security technologies are used but not functioning and where there are no logs, incident reports, or security personnel records. It is not a coincidence that criminals select these soft targets and repeatedly target these businesses and prey on their customers and employees. Businesses that ignore security system maintenance and fail to keep performance standards end up paying for such negligent security management. Businesses with cost-effective security programs and the use of state-of-the-art proactive measures to minimize exposure have successfully defended themselves in liability litigation alleging security inadequacies.

Integrating Physical and IT Security, Business Continuity, Crisis Management, and Emergency Planning

During the past decade, much discussion and some action have taken place to converge physical security and IT security. What has been overlooked and is now gaining attention from senior management is the convergence of crisis management, business continuity, emergency planning, and organizational (and security) resilience. The integration of these separate but related disciplines is crucial to the synergy of emergency response and business recovery. Eliminating the duplication of effort, reducing ineffective use of resources, and narrowing the gap of inefficiency and productivity are key benefits to placing these activities under a single leadership umbrella—preferably that of the corporate security director.

Training Programs Need a Major Uplift

People are the weak link in any organization. Because people are a major capital investment and the most important asset of any corporation or agency, it would greatly benefit management to properly train employees to become more proficient and productive. Realistic training increases the motivation of the workforce. It provides for greater unity among the workforce and frees supervisors to provide quality oversight of their teams' performance. For all these reasons and many more, training programs—particularly security awareness training—need to mature as the evolving threat becomes more intense and complex and consumes more resources and funding not readily available.

In Chapter Building Competencies That Count: A Training Model, I mentioned typical security awareness programs in the public and private sectors are weak, half-hearted, and ineffective. In most cases, new employees receive some security awareness training when they join a company, but typically that training is not reinforced on a regular basis. As a result, employees ignore and even undermine security programs. Even excellent security awareness programs associated with highly sensitive and compartmentalized information do not seem to deter those who have crossed the line to do others and their country harm. The Snowden's and Manning's of this country are examples.

While billions of dollars each year are spent on security hardware and software, most data breaches and information losses are based on the weak link in the security chain: people. Yet very little time and money are spent giving effective security awareness training to employees whose primary responsibility is to protect information. People can either make or break information and cyber security programs—and the entire corporation. Employees are the weakest link in the security chain because they are vulnerable, vindictive, often misguided, and greedy. Only a few are adequately trained to be security-conscious. Most people receive little or no training that would help prevent many of the losses companies sustain.

Too many enterprises plan and develop training programs from a tabula rasa instead of using experience, history, and common sense as a starting point. This is the reason so many security awareness and security orientation training programs, although designed with the best of intensions, fall flat on their proverbial faces. All to often the result is a complete "epic fail" because course designers and course-approving officials forget, ignore, or simply do not know what most security experts know does not work. Because of the emerging threats that we face today, the design and content of security awareness and security orientation programs should be tailored to help attendees perform their jobs today and for the near future.

Security Emergency Plans and Response/Recovery Procedures

Of all the deficiencies noted, poor security emergency planning and lack of organizational readiness capability and ability are rampant throughout most of the industry, but some enterprises, such as nuclear power plants and chemical facilities, have excellent programs that meet or exceed regulatory performance expectations.

Communicating with Executives and Governing Bodies

Accepting Responsibility

A new trend is emerging: security is no longer a cause of embarrassment. It is a matter of management accountability. The CEO has always been responsible for the overall growth, safety, and security of his or her corporation. But the dynamics of the diversified threat, and in particular the cyber threat, now make security a fundamental bottom-line issue that can no longer be ignored or swept under the rug by executives. There is no argument that the cost of investing in adequate security is significantly lower than the cost of responding to and recovering from a major security event, disaster, or major cyber breach.

Communicating and Interacting with Executives and Governing Authorities

Many security directors and IT security professionals continue to struggle with expressing their ideas to executive management and the board. The greatest challenge they face is not how to reduce risks but how to convey to leadership the benefits of security risk management. Their situation gets even tougher when they are in a state of continuous conflict between the business wanting to drive innovation and the security team needing to rein in risk. Executive decision makers want to know the business is adequately protected against risk but need to weigh the risks of yesterday and today against the opportunities of tomorrow.

Join the many security directors who have taken the lead and are driving the security dialogue with the CEO and the board, changing the conversation so that security and risk can be considered alongside other risks that boards oversee. Security strategy and security risk can now fit comfortably with other strategies and risks the board addresses.

Reporting the State of Security Readiness

It is a god idea to report the "state of security readiness" to CEOs, their staff, boards, and other governing bodies or community groups on a regular basis. I recommend using this schedule as a guide:

- CEOs and senior staff: monthly or quarterly
- Boards: semi-annually, annually, or as circumstances and conditions warrant
- External governing bodies or community groups: annually or as deemed necessary

Such presentations may be beneficial whenever special circumstances arise, such as an increase in the threat condition by the local government, after there occurs a major security event or incident that could dangerously affect public health and safety, or whenever business goals, objectives, or operations significantly affect existing security capabilities and abilities to support corporate initiatives.

Security Leadership Needs a Touch Up

Executive Management in the Shadows

Too many chief executives are on the dark side of the planet when it comes to protecting resources, assets, facilities, functions, and processes. Ignoring a problem with the hope that a security event or incident may never occur is wrong (Broder, 2006, pp. 250). It is making a life and death decision that no CEO has the legal or moral authority to assume. Everyone makes mistakes. The issue is not necessarily that mistakes happen, but rather why they happen, how we plan for them happening, and, when they do occur, how we recover from their impact. Once a strategy is put into motion, CEOs need to know whether the strategy is doing what it is supposed to do. If not, immediate midcourse corrective action must be introduced to address the discovered issues. A quality performance measurement and evaluation program that focuses on continual improvement would allow the organization to keep up with business changes, new security practices, and technology advancements.

Security Management Is Holding on

The future of security management is shifting away from individual facility security toward enterprise security management. This involves the integration of environmental controls, information systems, and security systems to operate more efficiently and, in some environments, merge into a new technology platform. Once developed and fielded, these capabilities can translate into effective, efficient, and productive gains.

A wise and experienced security director can demonstrate how security, when properly planned, coordinated, developed, and executed, and with proper oversight, can hold down costs across the broad and show a reasonable return on investment. Effective security and safety practices also foster leadership accountability.

Slippage of Leadership, Foresight, and Execution of Responsibilities

The security professional has more challenges to face than he or she may be capable of handling. This means that the consequences of failure can be more devastating than ever before, particularly when dealing with the establishment if it consumes a large portion of your time on a reoccurring basis. Security professionals are great at identifying deficiencies, weaknesses, and inadequacies and fixing the symptoms. What they struggle with is recognizing and addressing the root causes behind recurring activity. The security director's job, then, is to keep substance from forming into a basis for a crisis and, if such a crisis should occur, to contain its effects. This puts the security director in a very difficult position if the basis for a crisis turns out to be the workings of executive management (Tarlow, 2002, pp. 58). However, professionalism demands that you always be prepared for such an exchange of the highest order (Sullivant, 2007, pp. (56–109).

Management Is Losing Ground on Oversight Responsibility

When an organization identifies a weakness in security, it is standard industry practice (when mandated by regulators) for management to record the problem, find a way to fix it, and assign a deadline for completion. As management makes progress and the weakness is eventually remedied, corporate records are then updated. Organizations then provide progress reports to the governing bodies that are responsible for overseeing security matters. Without this basic evaluation system in place, it is impossible for the organization to tell whether problem areas or compliance matters are being addressed.

While such a corrective action program does not exist for unregulated industries, many corporations have adapted this approach. It makes good business sense to adopt a comprehensive performance measurement and evaluation program. Yet just about every aspect of this essential measurement and evaluation process is either missing or had broken down at several organizations I visited: problems were identified but never fixed, fixes were scheduled but not completed, and fixes were recorded as complete when they were not. These breakdowns were reported during previous visits, yet monitoring the progress of corrective efforts relative to known weaknesses was not effective, and nothing had changed to bring most of the organizations around to good business practices. An accurate measure of security program effectiveness will never be achieved at these locations unless the corporate culture changes its management practices.

The challenge CEOs face is to commit to obtaining the body of knowledge, skill sets, and expertise to save lives and protect assets from those who wish to do them harm, as well as from environmental hazards and weather-related calamities, and to translate these into profound outcomes that create unparalleled opportunities to deal effectively with ambiguous security challenges. CEOs must view the safety and security of their people as a nonnegotiable requirement. CEOs must also assert genuine leadership, communicate to employees what needs to be done, and make pragmatic policy decisions to empower employees to make responsible decisions, take appropriate action, and be accountable for their behavior. This requires courage, shared sacrifice, and a willingness to compromise and make the tough choices essential to setting a new course for the organization.

Management is Either Ignoring Issues, Covering Them Up, or Has No Clue What's Going on

Another disturbing issue deals with the perception some CEOs have about security performance. Some executives see their organization's security program as far more mature than do those at the managerial level and below. Experience tells us that these perception gaps stem from poor communication and collaboration among the different roles involved in planning, developing, and implementing security operations. Weak or no performance measurement and program evaluation criteria, and a combination of incomplete or inadequate reporting, add to the dilemma.

The challenge for CEOs is to assert genuine leadership in cultivating communications among the senior staff, the security organization, and employees, with the goal of raising awareness about the importance of listening to reasonable and prudent arguments for accepting cost-effective strategies. Equally important is the crucial need to establish and maintain a solid business relationship between the security director and CEO that fosters candid decision, mutual respect, and trust in enterprise security matters. CEOs must have candid and factual information if they are expected to make sound security policy decisions.

Management Social Behavior and Ethics Need Polishing

An equally important challenge to building security resilience is removing sheer arrogance, complacency, indifference, apathy, ignorance, and fear, followed by fallible decision making, near-reckless planning, and negligent management. We also face another challenge: management putting its head in the sand over many issues that should receive their attention and failing to act in a responsible manner. Also, let us not forget that management's ignorance or failure to act in a reasonable and prudent manner often is responsible for liability injuries caused by third-party crime. A wise leader will do everything within his or her power to prevent such an embarrassment to the company's image, brand, and reputation, yet litigation cases are on the rise across the nation. If allowed to flourish, these factors can directly and indirectly contribute to the weakening of security resilience in many ways. Work conditions can affect your well-being and livelihood. Circumstances can influence your status and judgments, and situations often temper your objectivity.

The challenges for CEOs, then, are to:

- establish and maintain a proactive security mentality
- identify and remove obstacles that stifle and impair modernizing the security program
- continue individual and group development to build self-confidence
- research and explore new possibilities to bring home new ideas
- seek outside consultation and strategic advice from qualified independent consultants
- expand their knowledge base through lessons learned reporting
- meet with security management and review the "state of security" on a regular basis

Through your influential leadership, you must make CEOs recognize the benefits of a corporate commitment to advancing security in the throngs of a rapidly and dynamically changing business world, advancing technology, and a shifting threat environment. You must be the pillar that stands between management and the wholesale scuttling of the integrity of security.

Change Management in the Wind

CEOs, staff members, employees, and the security organization must be on the same team and work together to achieve common business and security goals and objectives. When this relationship breaks down, governing boards may impel corporations to call for new leadership.

Corporate Boards Are Pressuring C-Suite Executives to Demonstrate Leadership

Chief executives who hinder the buildup of security resilience will either take the initiative to improve their company's security program or can expect shareholders to demand their removal. Security experts agree that companies of all sizes are imperiled by diversified threats, and executive leadership must institute a culture change that values security as a foundation of doing business.[8]

[8] Talking points offered by the Armed Forces Communications and Electronics Association (AFCEA) International Symposium, held June 24–25, 2014, in Baltimore, MD. http://www.afcea.org/cyber/.

Security Directors and Managers Are Under the Gun to Produce

Security directors and managers may also lose their jobs if a major security event or cyber incident takes place without well-crafted security response plans and realistic event-driven response procedures.[9] Security professionals who want to keep their jobs must develop clear and distinct security policies, emergency security response plans, and event-driven response procedures, including comprehensive cyber security incident response procedures, as well as explicit security training programs that focus on preparing employees to do their jobs. There is no excuse for not training and, where appropriate, certifying personnel to perform their duties and responsibilities. This includes general security awareness training for all employees; information and cyber security awareness training for employees who have access to sensitive and classified information and use computer systems; general and specialized training for the security force; and educating executive managers, senior staff, board members, and governing bodies on the company's state of security readiness and other security matters.

Chief Information Security Officers Are Corporate Scapegoats

Chief information security officers (CISOs) are not faring well with executives. According to a recent report issued by Threat Track Security, in August 2014, many CEOs view them as scapegoats.[10] This report highlights that:

- 75% of C-suite executives do not view CISOs as part of the business's leadership team.
- 66% of CEOs say CISOs do not have a broad awareness of organizational goals and business needs outside of data security.
- 44% of CEOs say they would blame CISOs for any data leaks.
- 25% of CEOs would blame their cyber security decisions for hurting the financial strength of the company.

CEOs and CISOs remain far apart on how to best address cyber threat issues. The problem is further exacerbated by the lack of communication between the offices of the CEO and CISO.[11] 36% of CEOs say that the CISO never reports to them on the state of IT infrastructure security, as opposed to 27% of CEOs who say they receive updates on a somewhat regular basis.

CISOs are pointing the finger directly at the workforce as the primary concern, citing that a lack of employee education and diligence represents the greatest threat to the security of the corporate IT infrastructure. CEOs disagree, believing that external phishing attacks represent the largest threat to the organization, and that companies have sufficient time and resources to adequately train and educate their employees to effectively mitigate threats. This division between CEOs and CISOs should be a wake-up call for every organization to demand better alignment between the executives

---

[9] http://www.fierceenterprisecommunications.com/story/poorly-handled-data-breach-could-cost-ciso-his-or-her-job-warns-gartner/2013-06-12.

[10] http://www.threattracksecurity.com/resources/white-papers/chief-information-security-officers-misunderstood.aspx.

[11] http://www.coresecurity.com/content/CEOs-Lack-Visibility-Into-Origin-and-Seriousness-of-Security-Threats.

charged with protecting their most vital assets. The gap between how these encampments view threats to IT infrastructure security needs to be resolved quickly before it becomes detrimental to the nation's economic security and national security interests.

What Does Work May Surprise You

Successful Security Programs Integrate People, Processes, Best Practices, Technology, Strategic Vision, and Strong Leadership

Successful security programs require the right mix of people, processes, best practices, and technology at a quintessential level of integration with strategic vision, strong security leadership, and insight.

Integrated Security Risk Management

Security assessments for critical infrastructure have traditionally followed four paths: a distinct separation from IT security, physical security, business continuity, and emergency management. The gap between all paths is slowly closing under the umbrella of a single integrated security resilience assessment model, such as the one presented in Chapter A User-Friendly Security Assessment Model.

A thorough security assessment should be a top priority for a corporation's management team. A security assessment should be conducted at least every 18–24 months; whenever a major change in mission occurs; when business operations are relocated; when facilities are retrofitted or modified, or when new facilities are planned; and after each major emergency. Security assessments, including penetration testing by trusted third-party security consultants, are now just as important as marketing new business and delivering quality products and services (Sullivant, 2007, pp. 55–84).

Mitigating Risks to a Company's Image, Brand, and Reputation

Risk to a company's image, brand, and reputation is a relevant component of any security risk management program. Should any of these risks occur, it could rapidly cascade throughout the enterprise and produce adverse affects on value, supply chain relationships, market position, revenue, employee moral, and stakeholder confidence. Mitigating the risks to company image, brand, and reputation is a responsibility shared by the entire business.

Developing Relationships of Openness and Trust is a Key Condition for Success

Where trust is high, ideas and communications flow easily. Where trust is low, everything becomes foggy. People hesitate to point out problems, suggest new ideas, approve ideas, or take responsibility for their mistakes or actions. They go to great lengths to create a paper trail to protect their position just in case things go wrong. Many corporations have learned the hard way about wasted energy that goes into unproductive memos, superfluous copies, and defensive conversations (Schmidt and Finnigan, 1994, pp. 9). Whenever one-on-one talks with upper management or governing bodies take place, a better business relationship may come out of it, but past experiences suggest that nothing substantial will change until individuals start being held accountable for their actions.

Making a Business Case for Security Investment

One of the greatest challenges facing security directors is rationalizing funding for security investments. A focus on "how to get the money" is starting in the wrong place. Understanding how security aligns with the company's goals and how it fits into the corporate-wide risk management picture is essential. That starts with asking pertinent questions (Sullivant, 2007, pp. 199–218): What is security's role in protecting corporate image, brand, and reputation? What are we protecting and why? How is security relevant to protecting those assets? What are the true measurements of success?

While many in the upper echelon are paying more attention to security, they are still not spending enough to protect the organization against diversified threats, hazards, mishaps, and major business disruptions. While 60% Cyber Information Security Officers plan to increase the security budget. The Threat Track Security survey also cited 65% of the CEOs as saying insufficient funds was their number 1 challenge to operating at the security level expected by their company.[12]

Security Transparency

Security abilities, capabilities, and policies should be transparent to all business units and upper management. This approach enables business units to be more clear and distinct in communicating their security requirements and unique differences to the security organization, as well as helping business units to support security practices. There exists an urgent need to show and demonstrate accountability, transparency, and uniformity of security performance standards.

Characteristics of Future Security Leaders

Security leaders are increasingly being called upon to address broad security concerns, and as a result are becoming a strategic voice within their organizations. The constantly evolving threat landscape, emerging technologies, and budgetary constraints are requiring security leaders to play a more active role in communicating with C-suite executives and with their boards, as the increase in security incidents affect corporate brand, image, and reputation and customers' trust in them.

Tomorrow's security leaders have a tremendous vault of historical information and experience to pioneer new security horizons. You must build your career through informed experience, success at each stage of development, and continual advancements

---

[12] http://www.networkworld.com/article/2224389/cisco-subnet/cisco-sees-big-plans-for-big-data.html.

in education. To be successful, you must progress in your career not by chance, but through deliberate planning and creating opportunities. As a member of this select group of security leaders, you will experience a transition from a seasoned profession to a new generation of leaders who will not only be security executives but business leaders as well. This transition actually began more than two decades ago, but it has been slow in catching on across the entire security industry. I predict it will take another decade to really gain a foothold throughout the industry. It is this generation that I believe will gain the greatest benefit from using this book. By understanding the past and utilizing the strategies for building security resilience outlined in it, you will be able to lead the next generation of cultured security professionals to new heights of competency and excellence.

In climbing the ladder of success, decision making, oral communications, critical thinking, maximizing other's performance, and persuasive influencing are among the core competencies I believe you will be required to successfully perform. You must also acquire:

- a strong business vision, strategy, and policies with comprehensive risk management, and effective business relations skill sets
- an in-depth understanding of the concerns of C-suite executives. This is critical as more seasoned security leaders meet regularly with their board and C-suite leaders. Today, the top trends they discuss include:
  - identifying and assessing risks (59%)
  - resolving budget issues and requests (49%)
  - deploying new technology (44%)
- building the trust of the C-suite and board in strategic decision making that is of vital interest to the corporation tomorrow, if not today

Beyond internal relationships, developing relationships with law enforcement, industry partners, and legislators is vital in fostering greater public and private communications.

My Parting Thought

The overarching goal of my message throughout the pages of book has been to inform you, the reader, of the numerous security deficiencies, programmatic weaknesses, and human and technology inadequacies I have uncovered so that you may be able to establish a partnership with upper management and tear down the barriers and remove the obstacles that breed vulnerability creep-in and incompetency within your organization. Achieving this goal will contribute significantly to advancing the security profession as well as organizational resilience.

It's up to you to make change happen. I know you can do it. Now go do it, and God speed.

My warmest regards to every one of you.
—John Sullivant.

References

Broder, J.F., 2007. Risk Analysis and the Security Survey, fourth ed. Butterworth-Heinemann, MA.

Clark, R.M., 2004. Intelligence Analysis: A Target-centric Approach. CQ Press, Washington, DC.

Coolsaet, R., 2011. Jihad Terrorism & the Radicalization Challenge; European & American Experiences, second ed. Ashgate Publishing Co, VT.

Erickson, P.A., 2006. Emergency Response Planning for Corporate & Municipal Managers, second ed. Butterworth-Heinemann, MA.

Frank, M.O., 1986. How to Get Your Point across in 30 Seconds or Less. Pocket Books, NY.

Hunker, J., 2009. Policy development. In: Voeller, J.G. (Ed.), Wiley Handbook of Science & Technology for Homeland Security. John Wiley & Sons, Inc., NJ.

Lukaszewski, J.E., 2008. Why Should the Boss Listen to You? Jossey-Bass™, An Imprint of Wiley & Sons, NJ.

Rumelt, R.P., 2011. Good Strategy Bad Strategy: The Difference and Why It Matters. Crown Business, Random House, Inc., NY.

Schmidt, W.H., Finnigan, J.P., 1994. TQ Manager: A Practical Guide for Managing in a Total Quality Organization. Jossey-Bass Publishers, CA.

Sullivant, J., 2007. Strategies for Protecting National Critical Infrastructure Assets: A Focus on Problem-Solving. John Wiley & Sons, NJ.

Tarlow, P.E., 2002. Event Risk Management and Safety. John Wiley & Sons, NJ.

Additional Reading Materials

ASIS International and Institute of Finance & Management, 2013. The United States Security Industry: Size and Scope, Insights, Trends and Data. ASIS International, VA.

Azuwa, A.M., Sahib, S., Shamsuddin, S., 2012. Technical security metrics model in compliance with ISO/IEC 27001 standard. International Journal of Cyber Security and Digital Forensics.

Blades, M., 2012. Delivering Meaningful Metrics. Security Magazine. Retrieved from: http://www.securitymagazine.com/afrticles/82934-delivering-meaningful-metricsw.

Blythe, B.T., 2002. Blindsided: A Manager's Guide to Catastrophic Incidents in the Workplace. The Penguin Group, NY.

Brenner, B., 2010. Security Metric Techniques: How to Answer the 'So What?'. CSO Online. Retrieved from: http://www.csoonline.com/article/602901/security-metric-techniques-how-to-answer-the-so-what.

Buckingham, M., Coffman, C., 1999. First, Break All the Rules: What the World's Greatest Managers Do Differently. Simon & Schuster, NY.

Bullock, J.A., Haddow, G.D., 2006. Introduction Emergency Management, second ed. Elsevier Butterworth-Heinemann, MA.

Campbell, G., 2012. Metrics for Success: Security Operations Control Center Metrics. Securityinfowatch. Retrieved from: http://www.securityinfowatch.com/article/10840065/metrics-for-success-security-operations-control-center-metrics.

Cole, R.B., 2003. Measuring Security Performance & Productivity. ASIS International.

Emergency Planning Handbook, second ed. ASIS International, VA.

Hallinan, J., 2009. Why We Make Mistakes: How We Look Without Seeing, Forget Things in Seconds and Are All Pretty Sure We Are Way above Average. Broadway Books, NY.

Homeland Security Presidential Directive 8 (HSPD-8): National Preparedness Guidelines, 2011. U.S. Department of Homeland Security, Washington, DC.

Jones, A., Ashenden, D., 2005. Risk Management for Computer Security: Protecting Your Network and Information Assets. Elsevier Butterworth-Heinemann, MA.

Katzenback, J.R., Smith, D.K., 1993. The Wisdom of Teams: Creating the High-Performance Organization. HarperBusiness, NY.

Kehoe, D., 2007. Communication in Everyday Life, second ed. Pearson Education, Toronto.

Lewis, T.G., 2006. Critical Infrastructure Protection in Homeland Security: Defending a Networked Nation. John Wiley & Sons, NJ.

MaCaulay, T., 2009. Critical Infrastructure: Understanding its Component Parts, Vulnerabilities, Operating Risks and Interdependencies. CRC Press, NY.

Mahdy, G.E., 2001. Disaster Management in Telecommunications, Broadcasting and Computer Systems. John Wiley & Sons, NJ.

Maturity Model for the Phased Implementation of the Organizational Resilience Management System, 2012. ASIS Foundation, ASIS International, Alexandria, VA.

McCourt, M., 2011. Measuring up: How the Best Security Leaders Deliver Business Value. Security Magazine.

Mcllravey, B., Ohlhausen, P., 2012. Metrics and Analysis in Security Management (White Paper) Retrieved from: http://www.camagazine.com/archives/print-edition/2003/april/upfront/news-and-trends/camagazine23257.aspx.

Organization Resilience: Security Preparedness and Continuity Management Systems – Requirements with Guidance for Use, 2009. ASIS Foundation.

Presidential Policy Directive 21 (PPD 21): Critical Infrastructure Security and Resilience, 2013. The Whitehouse, Washington, DC.

Protection of Assets Manual, 2004. ASIS International, VA.

Radvanovsky, R., 2006. Critical Infrastructure: Homeland Security & Emergency Preparedness. CRC Taylor & Francis, FL.

Roper, C.A., 1999. Risk Management for Security Professionals. Butterworth-Heinemann, MA.

Scaglione, B., 2012. Metrics: The Evaluation of Access Control and Identification. Security Magazine. Retrieved from: http://www.securitymagazine.com/articles/83134-metrics–the-evaluation-of-access-control-and-identification.

Schmidt, W.H., Finnigan, J.P., 1994. TQ Manager: A Practical Guide for Managing in a Total Quality Organization. Jossey-Bass Publishers, CA.

Sullivant, J., 2009. Strategies for protecting the telecommunications sector. In: Voeller, J.G. (Ed.), Wiley Handbook of Science & Technology for Homeland Security. Copyright © 2009, John Wiley & Sons, Inc., NJ.

Ting, W., Comings, D., 2010. Information assurance metric for assessing NIST's monitoring step in the risk management framework. Information Security Journal: A Global Perspective 19 (5).

Travis, C., Aronson, E., 2007. Mistakes Were Made (But Not by Me): Why We Justify Foolish Beliefs, Bad Decisions and Hurtful Acts. Harcourt, FL.

Whiteman, M.E., Mattord, H.J., 2013. Information security governance for the non-security business executive. Journal of Executive Education 11 (1) Article 6.

Index

Printed in the United States
By Bookmasters